# Inventing the World:
## The Fiction Writer's Guidebook to Craft and Process

## Jack Smith

Serving
House
Books

Inventing the World: The Fiction Writer's Guidebook
to Craft and Process

ISBN: 978-1-947175-08-2

Cover art: "Abstract Line Wave" by geralt from pixabay.com

Serving House Books logo by Barry Lereng Wilmont

Published by Serving House Books
Copenhagen, Denmark and Florham Park, NJ
www.servinghousebooks.com

Member of The Independent Book Publishers Association

First Serving House Books Edition 2018

A generous collection of essays, interviews, and conversations that does nothing less than throw a light onto the mystery of the creative process, Jack Smith's *Inventing the World* is an indispensable guide for any writer at any stage of his or her career. Highly recommended.

— Anthony Varallo, author of *Everyone Was There*

The proprietors of the Mom and Pop Shop that produced the Muses were the mash-up of Zeus and Mnemosyne, Memory, a hieros gamos, a marriage that makes the singers sing and allegorically suggests that creation is modulated between highly crafted reason and an inarticulate spontaneous gift. Jack Smith surveys and maps, in this omnibus collection of essays, the surface and depth of that literary creation, confounding and co-finding, the nuts and bolts of craft wedded to art. And he does so while displaying, in his own writing, a rewarding elegant articulation of the conventions that can be explained and the secrets that must be approached on the slant, askance and akimbo. *Inventing the World* is an exact atlas to this teeming terra incognito of fiction's textual atolls.

— Michael Martone
Author of *Michael Martone* and *Winesburg, Indiana*

Jack Smith provides excellent, practical advice on all the important elements of writing fiction, including character development, creating vivid setting and authentic dialogue, using research, drawing readers in with compelling openings. Rather than offering a one-size-fits-all approach, in various interviews and articles Smith allows successful and gifted writers to offer their insights into how they create outstanding fiction. In this book, one finds great advice and food for thought on almost any aspect of writing craft.

— Robert Garner McBrearty, author of *Let The Birds Drink in Peace* and *The Western Lonesome Society*

"I do not see the world at all; I invent it."

— Franz Kafka, *The Diaries of Franz Kafka*, 1910 - 1923

# Books by Jack Smith

Co-authored with Eddie J. Girdner, *Killing Me Softly: Toxic Waste, Corporate Profit, and the Struggle for Environmental Justice,* Monthly Review Press, 2002.

*Hog to Hog*, Texas Review Press, 2008.

*Write and Revise for Publication: A 6-Month Plan for Crafting an Exceptional Novel and Other Works of Fiction*, Writer's Digest Books, 2013.

*Icon*, Serving House Books, 2014.

*Being*, Serving House Books, 2016.

*Miss Manners for War Criminals*, Serving House Books, 2017.

# Contents

# Preface

This book is meant to stimulate thought on the various elements of fiction and on the techniques of writing good fiction and avoiding the bad. As you'll see, there are many, diverse points of view on how to handle technique in fiction. I feel I've grown as a fiction writer in doing articles for *Novel & Short Story Writer's Market* for fifteen years and articles and interviews for *The Writer* magazine for over ten. I've come to appreciate much more fully the true complexity of the fictional act.

Most of the articles in this collection are on the various elements of fiction — character, point of view, structure, theme and idea — and how to handle these well. Also included are some articles on different technical challenges a writer is likely to face, including handling dialogue, writing solid prose, creating voice, and avoiding clichés. Beyond these fundamentals, I've also included articles on different lengths of fiction, from the shorter to the longer: flash fiction, the short story, and the novella. As well I've included articles on two genres I've addressed: historical novels and humor.

The book ends with interviews of a number of notable writers, three of them Pulitzer Prize winners, a National Book Award winner, and one a winner of both prestigious awards. Like the articles, these interviews focus on the craft of fiction since that's the purpose of the two publications I write for.

The articles on the craft of fiction take up the writing process to some extent, but two articles in Part I deal directly with it: keeping a journal and doing research. Writers are often encouraged to keep a journal. In "Keeping a Journal: What's It Worth?" I interviewed several authors who regularly kept journals for different reasons, among them to store up story ideas, to work out plots for stories they were currently working on, to plan future stories, and to engage in creative thinking. Some kept a journal in longhand, others on their computers. For these writers, keeping a journal was worth the investment of time — and time, as we know, is very important to writers, and the time it takes to keep a journal is sometimes a reason writers don't keep one.

"Story Study" deals with the need to research not just key areas of a story but less important ones as well to make your fiction believable. As a writer, you must make the world you create one that readers can relate to, making characters, actions, and the settings they inhabit, believable and credible, and oftentimes this means direct experience, or field research, and at other times use of print media. As you'll see, writing about what you "know" sometimes means writing about what you can find out as well.

Part II moves to fictional elements — or, we might say, the craft — that which we must absolutely get down well if we want to be successful writers. "Returning to the Elements," the lead-off article, deals with the basic elements of fiction and stresses the importance of handling these adeptly if you want to write great fiction. For this, I interviewed Kathleen Grissom, author of *The Kitchen House*, a historical novel; Catherine Ryan Hyde, author of the famous *Pay It Forward* as well as a few dozen other novels; Virgil Suárez, author of several novels and story collections; and the acclaimed writer Ishmael Reed, author of ten novels, including *Flight to Canada*, *Mumbo Jumbo*, and *Juice!* Each writer offers tips on handling key or fundamental fictional elements.

Once I've spotlighted these fundamentals, I include articles dealing with specific elements, the first being character. "Know Your Antagonist" deals with creating believable, compelling antagonists, complex versus stock characters, ones capable of surprises, but I also bring in ideas of writers who don't think in terms of protagonists and antagonists at all — which may be a surprise, at least for some writers. A second article, "Not Just Second Class: Writing Secondary Characters in Fiction," reveals that secondary characters function in different ways: to help reveal the character of the protagonist, to spark conflict, and to serve as antagonists. How much space should we give to secondary characters? How complex should they be? What if they are so interesting that they overshadow the protagonist? These are surely questions many writers have faced in their writing.

Two articles deal with point of view — the omniscient and the second-person — both challenging in their own ways. "Playing God" shows that the omniscient point of view may be tempting because it gives writers god-like control over their fictional world, but it comes with a price, and there is a good alternative to it: multiple third-person points of view. "Second Degree" reveals the appeal of a little-used POV, the second-person, certainly a risky choice with some definite downsides if it's not adroitly handled.

I move on to a third fictional element: plot and structure. Think of structure as the organizational logic of your story or novel. "If You Build It" covers several aspects of story structure: the five-stage plot structure, various structural elements and patterns, and multiple points of view as a structuring device. Among others, Pulitzer Prize winner Viet Thanh Nguyen discusses the structure of his work, his prize-winning debut novel *The Sympathizer* — with more comments on this novel to follow in my interview of Nguyen in the last section of the book.

Two other articles take up issues related to plot and structure. "Start to Stop" focuses on openings and endings. How can you develop a strong opening? Which type of opening should you use? And — one of the most problematic aspects of fiction writing — how do you find the right ending to tie up the story's conflicts? What if you write books in a series? Both literary and genre novelists speak out.

A third article, "Foreshadowing & Echoing," deals with two key structural devices that knit a story together and some problems with handling them. For instance, how do you avoid being too obvious? How many foreshadowing instances should you provide? Where should you provide foreshadowing? What's echoing about, and how might it work well?

The final element in Part II is theme. "Deriving Theme from Character and Plot" reveals how different writers arrive at theme and how they avoid contriving thematic ideas in their work, depending instead on strong characters and an engaging plot to *suggest*, not state, any overriding ideas in their work. But a question arises: in terms of the whole work, how important *is* theme?

In Part III, I deal with four basic story challenges: handling dialogue well, handling prose, creating voice, and avoiding clichés. "Writing Authentic Dialogue" takes up the problems of writing language and dialect related to region and culture, ethnicity, social class, historical fiction, and workplace jargon. A second article on dialogue, "He Said, She Said," is concerned, in a more general way, with the process of writing good dialogue, the issue of consistency of tone and character, standard dialogue convention, and typical dialogue problems. The last section, as in a number of the articles in this book, provides tips from the pros.

Three articles in Part III deal with prose. "Putting Words to Work" takes up the various uses of figurative language in fiction, how writers discover such language, its benefits — including poetic beauty and suggestiveness of levels above the literal — but also its possible drawbacks if not handled adeptly. "Developing Your Prose Style" is concerned with several issues: prose style types (dense versus spare); editorial preferences at literary magazines; editorial critiquing; form and function, and developing your own prose style.

The third article on handling prose, "Exploring Exposition & Summary," deals with two prose forms many writers have trouble with: exposition and summary. The first has gotten a bad name, being linked to boring and monotonous telling, with "information dumps." "Show, don't tell" is the mantra that every writer learns early on and knows by heart; it's one mandate, perhaps above all the other mandates, that writers feel compelled to follow. Showing means allowing your reader to *see*, and it also means drama — and fiction, bottom line, must be dramatic. So how do you invigorate exposition with dramatic power? How do you also create strong narration, both scene and summary? The latter is often a second trap, right in there with exposition.

The penultimate article in Part III, "Setting the Tone," deals with the nature of voice, which is perhaps one of the most important elements of good fiction: having a voice that draws the reader in and keeps the reader reading. Voice is notoriously difficult to define. In this article, I take up the challenge of creating an authentic voice, a distinctive one — not only in a given work but possibly from work to work in a writer's emerging canon.

The final story challenge in Part III is "Avoiding Clichés," which deals with clichéd plots, characters, and language — with suggestions from professional writers on how to avoid these.

Part IV is centered on length of fiction: flash fiction, the short story, and the novella. "Jumpin' Jack Flash" deals with today's fertile market for flash fiction and what makes good flash, from the perspective of both writers and editors — at both magazines and presses. A question comes up from two top writers of flash fiction, Michael Martone and Stuart Dybek: should flash be judged as either "good or bad"? What's the purpose of flash anyway? They provide insightful comments on what they see as the true purpose of flash.

A second article, "Beating out the Stiff Competition in Fiction Writing," deals with three top literary magazines in the country, their editorial standards, and what several masters of the short story advise on getting your work published. It focuses on short fiction, but also touches on the novel as well.

The third piece in this section, an article/interview, "Rise of the Novella," takes up the novella form, the limited markets for it, followed by a Q&A bringing in comments from four novella writers, including Jane Smiley, and four publishers of this form, among them *The Alaska Quarterly Review* and Nouvella, a press which specializes in this form.

The penultimate section of this book, Part V, deals with two fictional genres and how to master them. "Writing Historical Novels" shows how to conduct historical research, juggle research with writing, handle historical and biographical facts, and create historical settings. For this article, I interviewed authors of several historical novels, including Edward Rutherfurd, *Paris: The Novel*; Lynn Cullen, *Mrs. Poe*; Stephanie Cowell, *Claude & Camille: A Novel of Monet*; and C.W. Gortner, *The Tudor Conspiracy*.

The second article, "In Good Humor," rounds out this section. It takes up the impulse for humor, various purposes of humor, some key humor techniques, and what makes successful humor in fiction. Among the writers contributing ideas for this article were

Sam Lipsyte, Elizabeth Stuckey-French, Amanda Filipacchi, and Ben Fountain.

The last section of this book, Part VI, includes interviews of Tim O'Brien, Vaddey Ratner, T.C. Boyle, Elizabeth Strout, Christine Sneed, Sandra Cisneros, Viet Thanh Nguyen, Alice Hoffman, Adam Johnson, and Sue Monk Kidd, the latter two in *The Writer's* regular column "How I Write." They speak out on their process of writing as well as their craft. These ten author interviews provide a good lens for reading their work.

And now let's begin with the creative process.

How do you set about creating your fictional world?

# Part I
# The Creative Process

# Keeping a Journal: What's It Worth?

Keeping a journal is a typical writerly thing to do. After all, writers are absorbing the world around them, noting things of interest for their work: odd and intriguing things, funny things, human traits, distinguishing characteristics, mannerisms. These things find their way into stories, maybe a bit later, maybe years hence. And if writers don't record ideas and details as they occur, they'll probably forget them. Valuable material could be lost forever. But saving important stuff for later use is only one purpose of keeping a journal. There are a number of other good reasons, as writers have discovered. And the pay-offs can be substantial.

## Different Journal Types, Different Contents

What writers put in their journals depends on their needs as well as how they conceive of the function of a journal.

Some writers keep a journal mostly as a storehouse of information — for later use.

John Flynn, author of a travel novel, *Heaven is a Place Where Your Language Isn't Spoken,* has kept a journal "at varying times, and at varying intensities." His journals have been all-encompassing in detail, including "thoughts, descriptive passages, lists of books, authors, movies, philosophers, dates in history, quotations, all sorts of information that I may find useful in the future." But in addition to all this he will "scribble little notes" to himself and later organize them for use in poems, stories, or a novel.

Kristen-Paige Madonia, whose debut novel will be published by Simon and Shuster Books for Young Readers in 2012, uses her journal to work out plot and characters for current projects as well as to generate ideas for future ones. She also keeps her journal handy to eavesdrop in public places. "I've mined countless coffee shop conversations for character, dialogue and plot ideas!" Madonia also lists books she wants to read as well as book reviews. She takes notes at writers' conferences and readings, jotting down "inspiring quotes or writing and industry advice."

If writers use their journals to record ideas for both works in progress and future ones, they also find them a good place for storing revision ideas. Ronna Wineberg, author of the prize-winning *Second Language*, states: "I sometimes have an idea for how to revise a piece. I write this in the journal — a quick idea, some dialogue, description, or a whole scene or scenes. Then I go back to it when I have time to work on the story or novel."

A journal can also be a place to think out your thoughts — a kind of private sounding board. Harriet Scott Chessman, author of *Lydia Cassatt Reading the Morning Paper*, among other novels, sees her journal "primarily as a space in which I can be free to 'talk' to myself. I try to spill the ideas out, without worrying about how they look or sound. It's a more fertile, intimate, private space, as close to my mind as I can come in words." Overall, this private space helps prepare Chessman for writing her stories.

Author of several works of fiction, most recently *Heidegger's Glasses*, Thaisa Frank keeps what she calls a "writer's log," which departs from any standard kind of journal — radically, she believes. She explains the difference: "That is — I jot down numerous words, phrases and spontaneous outpourings that come from my voice, rather than from socialized language." Her log is a place of risk versus record-keeping of any kind. "I don't keep a journal in the sense of 'journaling' — i.e. talking about my day, my feelings. This sort of journal is death to my writing, because fiction writing is about what I don't know rather than what I already know." If Frank does write about a real event, she goes "into a reverie and a few concrete images appear (a red coat, a conversation, the way potatoes looked on a blue plate)." These are not images observed in the regular manner. "These images," she says, "have nothing to do with the running narrative of my day, which I know about and can't surprise me. They're what I don't know about my day or don't even want to remember." Above all, her writer's log needs to be "dangerous."

If the use and contents of a journal vary, so does the method of keeping one. Some writers keep several notebooks going at a time

instead of what we might think of as the traditional journal look —
that is, all in one volume. How writers use these notebooks varies,
of course.

Dennis Must, author of two collections of short fiction, enters
"bits and pieces in several small notebooks," which he keeps "depos-
ited" in his most frequented places throughout the house. Says Must:
"The one alongside my bed I write in frequently while awaiting sleep
and pondering the scribbling I'd done earlier that day. Also I always
carry one with me when away from the house." What Must keeps
are the fairly traditional kinds of things to store up for future use —
but in his case, in abbreviated form. "What gets entered are seldom
more than a couple words, a sentence or two that I often work off of
the following day. There might be a story idea, a bit of dialogue I've
overheard, say, in a restaurant, the ending of a story that I've been
worrying over for several days, a snippet of a dream, etc. The entries
function in a manner like pods which when opened or explored often
have the potential to lead to full narratives." Dennis Must thinks of
his short, scattered journal entries as "found objects." When he
enters them they tend to "excite the mind as to what they may fully
reveal later."

Midge Raymond, author of the prize-winning collection *Forgetting English*, is also a devoted keeper of notebooks — as many as a
half dozen notebooks at a time. She keeps morning pages, for which
she thanks Julia Cameron and The Artist's Way, but the notebooks
she values the most are her travel-themed notebooks, which she
carries to "record anything new or unusual," whether she's "going
to another city or another country." In these notebooks she records
useful material for story ideas, including "a description of an unusual
person, a strange sign at the side of the road, or part of a juicy conversation I've overheard."

We should probably think of a journal in very broad terms —
as Harriet Chessman makes clear: "It could be that your best ideas
come to you in emails to friends, or in off-the-cuff rants, or Facebook
messages." Chessman herself keeps a computer file of emails called
"Inspiration." She states: "These can be forms of journals too, if you
can figure out how to collect them for a bit, so that they can inspire

contemplation about your current and future projects." By the same token, Flynn supplements his journal with "select paper ephemera such as brochures, maps and business cards." These materials, says Flynn, "stir memories and re-orient myself back into the past."

## Longhand or Computer?

One might think that in this computer age, most writers would abandon longhand entirely. But just as some writers still draft stories in longhand, they also prefer longhand over the computer when keeping a journal.

Harriet Chessman herself prefers paper. "I often use both a large blank book and separate sheets of good, heavy stock paper. Sometimes I open a file on my computer desktop too, although I like paper best, because of the intimacy and the sense of freedom." She enjoys the tactile experience of turning the pages of the book as she reflects on her ideas. The computer screen, she says, "is largely the place of writing with a capital 'W.'"

Midge Raymond prefers longhand period, both for her notebooks and for her drafts of stories. "I've found that my creative energy can get sapped at the computer, where I also spend a lot of time on the day job, so getting away from it helps." Raymond enjoys writing in longhand more than she once did, and she makes sure she has a notebook with her when she stops at a café or sits in the park.

To Kristen-Paige Madonia "the physical act of scratching notes on paper" feels both "organic and inspiring" when she's in the early stages of a new project. She also finds a notebook convenient to carry with her to record memorable ideas before they're lost. While an idea may seem quite memorable at the time, "it's crucial," says Madonia, "to write it down while it's still vivid and fresh." Writing in longhand in a notebook makes this easy to do.

John Flynn also enjoys keeping a journal in longhand. "Something about the act of writing alone, either on a train, or in a café, especially when I'm traveling, is a comfort." But Flynn also uses a computer. "Even when I am not keeping a journal, I keep a file on my computer which is a repository of story ideas."

Thaisa Frank is geared toward the computer entirely. "I always use my computer, since I work on a laptop that's almost always with me. And this technique works well if I print things out right away so I can look at them from time to time. I find notebooks cumbersome and my handwriting is awful!"

## The Benefits, the Pay-Off

If writers commit time to keeping a journal, in whatever form, and for whatever purpose, what's the pay off? Is it merely busy-work? Does it sidetrack you from your regular writing? Writers report several distinct benefits based on their particular journal uses:

### A Storehouse of Useful Material

Certainly not everything stored up in a journal — all the plot ideas, character ideas, overheard conversations, and details of all kinds — will prove useful to a writer looking to mine it for potential story material. But some of it might. John Flynn credits his journal for the descriptive passages in his novel. He also drew on his journal for "specific tidbits of information, such as street names and hotel names." Kristen-Paige Madonia states: "For me, knowing that I have a notebook full of ideas, character sketches, dialogue, and anecdotes makes returning to the blank screen a lot less scary."

Anthony Varallo, winner of the prestigious Drue Heinz Literature Prize, states: "I can't imagine writing without my journal. Many of my stories have come from some small observation I jotted down, forgot about, and later came back to, using it for a story." Varallo does, however, mention a downside he's noticed: "The journal is instructive in reminding me that a good story doesn't necessarily arise from good notes — in fact the opposite is often true: how many mediocre stories of mine arose from pages and pages of 'notes,' per-haps robbing the actual story of mystery and interest. (Sometimes the notes are better than the story, alas.)" Still, having said this, Varallo does believe that a journal can certainly assist the writer: "If keeping a journal helps you get to the next page, then by all means, please keep a journal. That seems purpose enough."

## A Direction for Your Novel

Getting to the next page is one distinct benefit of a journal for Harriet Chessman. In addition to her private forum, she uses her journal to work out story problems and story structure. "I'm someone who thinks quite visually, so it's helpful to have rows and circles and arrows to conceptualize a story's arc or architecture." For those with novel projects, Chessman believes the journal can be a friend indeed. "I think of these pages as my companion during the writing of a book. A novel is so long, and can ask for so much patience and self-confidence as you go down dead ends and find fresh spots to start. It can be enormously discouraging and daunting, especially in the middle, as you're trying to find your way." For Chessman, the journal contains the various "sign posts" the writer needs — as well as "the encouraging notion that you WILL find your way."

## DNA for a Novel

Thaisa Frank reports a startling success regarding her writer's log: "Most strikingly: 16 pages that I wrote over 16 years ago, printed out and then put away, turned out to be the DNA for my new novel, *Heidegger's Glasses.* I'd ignored those 16 pages because I knew they belonged to a novel and I was sure I'd never write one. But they kept appearing — under tax returns, lists from my child's school — as if on springs." When she wrote her novel, she didn't actually look at those pages, but she did have a "dim memory of them." When she received her galley copy, Frank says, "the 16 pages popped out again. I read them over and realized that they were, in fact, the DNA for this novel." This isn't the only time keeping her writer's log has benefited Frank. She credits it with helping her write successful short stories as well as prose poems.

## An Off-Place from the Real Writing

Besides using his journal to store up potentially useful information, John Flynn also views his journal as a place to take a breather from the hard, committed writing of fiction. "A journal helps me clear the slate, so to speak, during times when I've much on my mind, when there is a lot of upheaval going on in my life and I still wish to keep to my writing regimen." Flynn does offer one caveat about this breathing space: "I don't think a journal should be a substitute for the created work." He sees it as "ancillary" to one's regular work — providing a special function: "It's a good way to keep one's attic organized, so to speak."

Midge Raymond's morning pages serve a similar function of renewal. "These pages are sometimes useful to my writing, often not — but they're always useful for clearing my head and creating the necessary mental space to write." Anjali Banerjee, author of both commercial press literary and YA fiction, appreciates this "warm-up" function of a journal because "it can help you to be honest with yourself without the intrusion of the editorial/critical mind."

## A Place to Explore Your Ideas in Writing

For Chessman, one of the primary benefits of a journal is the rich, "fertile" field it provides for exploring ideas in writing. "I think all writing is experimentation. You try this, you try that — the important thing is, you have to hold yourself open and listen carefully to what you're thinking, how you're conceiving of something. A journal — in any form — can be a lively part of this wonderfully rich experiment called writing." Exploration can mean surprises, as Ronna Wineberg has discovered. As writers write, "surprising things may appear on the page" — things useful for later.

## Starting Your Journal

You might delay starting a journal because you think there's a "right" way to keep a journal, calling for some basic, bottom-line commitment. Some writers, after all, do follow a given routine. For instance, Ronna Wineberg tries to write a little the first thing each morning, "even if it's brief." Wineberg says: "I enjoy writing in a journal and starting the day this way." But she does stress this: "It would be counterproductive to view a journal as a chore to be accomplished every day. This would make keeping a journal oppressive."

Harriet Chessman purposely shuns any form of "organized" approach to keeping her journal — whether it's keeping a daily journal or committing herself to recording specific things in it. To

Chessman, this practice feels "too self-conscious and stilted," and she would rather "travel more lightly." She states: "I'm not a hoarder, but more of a bird making a nest in a certain season; once I have no more need of this particular nest, I'm happy to move on."

Some writers have kept journals their whole lives. Others are less committed. And they may write in their journals only occasionally when they do keep one. Anjali Banerjee writes in her journal, on average, two times a week and writes only a couple pages. At the most, she may write in it 20 minutes a day — when she feels "compelled" to, when the "blank page calls to me."

Keeping a journal is a fluid kind of thing. It's also a private one. As Banerjee says, "it's for your eyes only." And the benefits are many.

# Story Study: Conducting Research in Fiction

When you think of research for fiction, you're probably inclined to think of historical novels. After all, if you're writing contemporary fiction, you live in that world, so how much is there to research? Perhaps not very much if you base your fiction on your own experiences. But if you take on other identities —characters quite different from yourself — you may need to do some research — perhaps a lot.

## Research Needs

Let's say you situate a character in a part of the country you're not familiar with. Can you provide a good establishing shot the way filmmakers do? What are some geographical markers you should capture and describe well? Can you give a believable sense for the culture of this place? This may take some research into print media, especially visual media, but better yet, if you have the opportunity to visit, do so. Nothing beats firsthand experience, which allows you to absorb both sights and sounds. Research enough to effectively put the aura of a place on the page.

Setting isn't the only thing you might need to research. Any number of things come into play when you're writing fiction. How do you perform certain tasks at a given job? What are the job responsibilities of that particular position? What's an ordinary day like? To achieve verisimilitude, you need to get these things right. With fiction, you have some latitude, but still you don't want to be so off that you jerk your reader out of the story. If your protagonist is on the wrong side of the law, say, a burglar —perhaps a safe cracker — find out how to crack a safe. At the other end of the spectrum, if your protagonist is a law-abiding citizen — let's assume she's an electrical engineer — be sure to find out what an electrical engineer does. How might an electrical engineer think? If your protagonist is strongly tuned into the sights, sounds, and rhythms of nature, which animals and their behaviors will your character notice? Can you name and describe numerous varieties of flowers and their seasonal appearances?

Research may help you achieve verisimilitude, but in some cases, it does more than that: it's crucial to the story and its basic themes. In that case, your research serves a key contextual purpose.

## Managing Your Research

Research generally involves three major resources: print media, interviews, and firsthand experience. When you see the need for research, how should you go about it? Should you do it all before writing your story or novel, or should you write and research as you go along, filling in details as you see the opportunity?

If the research is crucial to your story's character, plot, and theme, you may want to do much of it before you begin composing. Imagine the following: Let's say your protagonist is a traveler to France, fascinated by the country's major cultural icons: the Arc de Triomphe, the Eiffel Tower, Versailles. Let's say he is especially captivated by Mont Saint Michel, haunted by its architectural splendor and medieval past. Imagine a story centered on this rocky tidal island. You would need to describe it vividly, its location in Normandy, its imposing beauty. How to do this? Watch YouTube videos, look at Google images, read about it, but you must also go there, take pictures, and spend some time if you wish to capture this place in all its grandeur. You need to be fully immersed in your subject before you begin. Think of it this way: you can't write in a vacuum. You must know your subject well — whatever that subject is — before starting to write. (Of course, you can do further research as you compose.)

If the research isn't crucial to the story as a whole, however, you can do it as you write. For instance, let's say your protagonist flips houses. But your story isn't centered on the work itself, but rather on your protagonist's personal struggles off the worksite. Still, you'll need to give your reader a good sense for what your character does at work. How do you hang drywall and mud it? How do you install insulation? How do you make everything meet code? You can take your time with your research, first focusing on character and plot, and then introduce details about the work site as you get a strong sense for them.

## Selecting Research Details

Your research must be incorporated in the story so that it doesn't call attention to itself. It must feel just right. You may end up accumulating a lot of research material, but even so, it must be carefully selected: just enough, not too much. It has a clear function in the story. This function can naturally vary from story to story, novel to novel.

For mystery writer Elizabeth Spann Craig, author of *Quilt or Innocence*, research aided her in adding "texture to scenes." She spoke with quilters and consulted books and periodicals to accurately portray the hobby. In her use of research, she was careful not to get off track, not to risk "overloading readers with details that didn't further the plot." She explains: "Quilting activities as well as a quilt shop provided opportunities for the amateur sleuth to more naturally interview the mystery's suspects and witnesses."

For Jennifer Tseng, research was important in fleshing out the plot of her debut novel. Her work in an island library, like her protagonist's in *Mayumi and the Sea of Happiness*, helped her pick up plenty of good material from colleagues. "Every shift, I would ask the ladies questions: 'How do people meet people on this island?' 'If two people were going to have a secret affair, where would they rendezvous?' 'If the main character were to sleep with a 17-year-old, would you hold it against her?'" From this informal research, Tseng chose stories that helped her develop both character and plot. Tseng states, "The librarians' answers to my questions changed the course of the book. I learned that more townspeople than I ever could have imagined were committing transgressions on a daily basis; on any given day, the town was absorbing innumerable secrets."

Short story writer Robert Garner McBrearty's many menial jobs helped him develop research materials for workplace stories. As a mental hospital attendant, says McBrearty, "I locked in visions of the smoky dayroom [with] patients gazing at an old non-functioning TV set, observed patients lined up sticking out tongues to receive a cascade of pills, and participated in 'seclusions' when patients were rushed to padded rooms." He used this workplace research in his story "The Acting Class," when lovers meet at the hospital. "A mental hospital," says McBrearty, "is the perfect setting for the doomed lovers, who are trapped in their own delusions." For McBrearty, it was important to select from his many experiences the ones that captured the setting but also related closely to character and plot.

## Final Tips

♦ Check facts carefully, but keep in mind that as long as the world you create has a strong air of reality, you can get away with not being completely real-to-life.

♦ Decide on what needs to be researched and the resources you have. Do your research at the most convenient time. The needs of your story or novel will determine the best approach.

♦ Don't let the research overwhelm the work. Choose what you can use and let the rest go. If something's truly irresistible but doesn't belong in a work, pocket it for other possible stories.

# Part II
# Fictional Elements

# Returning to the Elements

As with any art form, fiction writing is a craft, and to write a strong story or novel, you must handle the craft well. Kathleen Grissom, author of *The Kitchen House*, a novel about slavery in 1790s America, says that prior to writing her novel, she was "ill-equipped to write a book." She had written some short stories and taken a few creative writing classes, but a project of this size was new and daunting. Then, diving into it, researching and writing during a five-year stretch, Grissom honed her fictional craft well enough to produce a highly successful novel, earning a favorable blurb from Alice Walker.

The craft demonstrated in Grissom's novel and in other successful works of fiction comes down to several elements readily familiar to most writers: characterization, plot, point of view, setting, scene and so forth. Familiar in name, yes, but handling these elements well is another matter. If you want to hone your craft well enough to land a successful story or novel, you must be prepared to spend the time it takes. But beyond that minimum requirement is a world of other considerations, say experts in the field.

## Creating Your Protagonist

From story to story, from novel to novel, protagonists vary widely in psychological make-up, goals and dreams, in the types of conflicts they face, and in the way they resolve these conflicts. Among all these differences, compelling characters may have some common qualities as well.

Catherine Ryan Hyde, author of *Pay It Forward* and 24 other novels, believes compelling protagonists share two chief traits. "I think he or she needs to be someone with a strong will to move through adversity, and someone readers can relate to," she says, adding that relatable characters also require vulnerability. "We're all vulnerable on the inside, so our hearts go out to anyone enduring struggles we understand." Authors are often told that readers must be able to root for their characters, yet Hyde believes that protagonists don't necessarily have to be likeable or sympathetic. They do need to be human, or readers won't be able to relate to them. To accomplish that, says Hyde, you have to get inside your character's head, and that's when the "humanity will begin to shine through." The better you do so, the more intriguing your character will be.

Of course, it's one thing to know what makes a compelling protagonist and still another to create one. Should you begin with notes for a fully fleshed-out character, or should you discover your protagonist as you write? Virgil Suárez, author of several novels and short story collections, plans out his protagonist in advance of writing. "I love to create an entire biography and history for a character," he says, "even though only 10 percent of what I imagine about a character actually makes it into the story or chapter."

While Suárez does a lot of initial planning, much of his characterization happens as he writes. Intuitive discovery of character may be key to solid character development. Instead of engineering or controlling characters, let their own voices take action. "I'm on the lookout for a fictional person with a good story to tell me," says Hyde. "After I make that connection, it feels more like a process of sitting back and listening." This act of listening worked well for Grissom, who says her two first-person narrators spoke clearly to her: "I wrote down what they were saying." She had to edit later, but through attentive listening she came to know her characters well.

## Managing Plot

If most fiction readers expect a strong protagonist, they also expect a compelling storyline, a plot that connects the various narrative threads into an overall trajectory, or character arc, for the protagonist — or, in the case of two or more protagonists, one that interweaves multiple arcs.

In character-driven fiction, plot naturally comes from character. In listening closely to her characters, Grissom says, her historical novel practically wrote itself. Each day when she began her writing, she would read what she'd written the day before and then begin again. She had no idea where the story was going. "I just wrote it as it came to me," she says. "Just when I thought I had it figured out or knew what was coming next, something else would show up." She was careful not to contrive a storyline that would make certain things happen in certain ways. In fact, when she was tempted to change things, her characters removed themselves as though to say, "That isn't *our* story — write your own story." She learned that she was not the director. She did cut pages, but the storyline remained the same from early to late drafts.

Grissom's character-driven plotting is much the same for Suárez, who declares, "Character *equals* plot. To say that I simply follow my characters around after I put them in a place and a historical moment is to simplify things too much, but there is quite a bit of that in my work."

In Grissom's debut novel and in Suárez's work in general, plot extends beyond the personal level to encompass a larger canvas, including social, historical and political contexts. "Many of my characters," says Suárez, "begin their lives in Cuba and then move to the United States to embark upon new possibilities. A family goes into exile, things change drastically, people have to find a new way of coping, living, moving towards some sort of reconciliation with what has happened to them."

In some fiction such as satire, dystopian fiction and philosophical novels, plot tends to function less as a trajectory for overall character development and more as a tool to develop overriding themes and ideas. "For my fiction," says Ishmael Reed, "ideas come first. And so I have been accused of a lack of character development in my novels. Critics have therefore accused me of creating 'cartoon characters.' In my last novel, *Juice!*, I studied cartooning at the California Cartoon Museum. My protagonist was a cartoonist. It was a response to my critics. Given the new technology, I suspect that future novels will be graphic. Animated."

Over the years, Reed's idea-driven fiction has taken various shapes and forms. Experimentation is vitally important to him. "When I turned 60," says Reed, "I began studying jazz piano. My storylines are similar to playing a jazz solo. I might begin with chords from a standard but will take liberties from bar to bar." In terms of genre, he has experimented with the mystery novel, the western, and science fiction in a new novel about global warming. In idea-driven fiction such as Reed's, character doesn't equal or generate plot; themes and ideas give rise to plot.

## Handling Point of View

Character and plot are two key features of the craft of fiction. A third is point of view (POV). A few questions arise: Should you use first-, second- or third-person POV? Which point of view, in terms of narrative perspective, will create the most interesting story or novel?

Grissom chose first-person because she wanted her characters to speak directly in their own authentic voices. Through third-person omniscient POV in *Mumbo Jumbo*, Reed gained authorial distance in his satirical treatment of black-white relations in America. "All of my books have been experiments with point of view," says Suárez. "*Latin Jazz* is a study in point of view. From third-person limited to second person to a first-person plural. I've always been attracted to the simplicity of third-person limited, but it gets rather repetitive from book to book. The second person can only be used sparingly, of course, and you must have a very strong reason to use it."

Think of it this way: First person invites us into the heart and mind of a narrator speaking directly to us. Third person invites us to peer into the lives of persons at a slight authorial distance. Second person makes *us* the character. Second person POV is risky, and not as frequently used in novels, but Suárez notes, "I've always thought *Bright Lights, Big City*, by Jay McInerney, was a great attempt at it, and I think it worked."

Beyond the issue of person, POV is also the lens through which the narrative is filtered and addresses two questions: What is the best vantage point, or angle of vision, from which to tell the story? Will the reader find this perspective interesting? Hyde finds that novels with more than two protagonists can become problematic. "Sometimes I get a number of strong voices who want to be heard in the same project," she says. "Then I have to make a conscious decision regarding who should tell the story." For *The Kitchen House*,

Grissom originally intended to take only one narrative perspective, that of a young Irish orphan girl serving an indenture, but when she was shopping an earlier draft of her novel, an agent suggested she needed a slave's perspective. She agreed, and she chose an alternating first-person POV, back and forth, from the orphan girl to the slave girl.

Once you settle the matter of narrative perspective, the next equally important question is, can you handle the language, the culture, the sensibility of this particular character's POV? Your job is to create a believable voice. For her slave girl protagonist, Grissom read a number of slave narratives to get as close to the slave dialect as possible. To make his characters real, Reed has worked over the years to adopt various narrative perspectives. "I've developed the ability to throw my voice," he says, "to do the POVs of people belonging to different races and classes. When I lived [in] the Pacific Northwest, I even began taking the POVs of animals. My latest poem takes the POV of an elephant."

## Developing Setting

Setting provides both a visual picture and a context for character, action and thematic ideas in a story or novel. It calls for description, for visual detail. In creating setting, some writers provide spare, suggestive detail, others fully fleshed-out pictures. "Images, images, images," says Suárez, who draws upon his strong photography background for setting. "I've been an avid photographer most of my life. I like to take pictures which I can use later for reference. Of course, I don't just rely upon my own pictures, but I often begin with a book of photographs about a particular place. Time and place help render the moment for me and make the construction of my characters' lives that much easier to believe." Yet in some cases, setting may not be important enough to describe. Says Hyde, "A writer should never give readers information they don't need. In any given story it's either important or it isn't, and it's my job to feel out the difference."

Setting details were essential to Grissom's *The Kitchen House*. Grissom knew in advance of writing her novel that she would need to render the kitchen house in precise detail. "I would need to know how it looked, how it smelled and where every utensil they might need would be. I would need to know it in the same way I knew my own house," she says. She also needed to furnish enough detail that the reader could easily picture the big house — the height of the ceilings, the number of windows, the flooring, the accent pieces. For setting, she did research at every library within driving distance, sought out useful materials from the Virginia Historical Society and visited Colonial Williamsburg. It was important to her to distinguish between the opulence of the slave-owners and the poverty of the slaves.

## Creating Dialogue

"I love puns. I love wit. I love humor," says Suárez. "I look for the way people express themselves. The way they punctuate what they say with silence and nervous mannerisms. I look, I study, I learn."

Everyday speech is one source for the rhythms and pauses of spoken language, but of course writers also find useful models in other writers. "I'm reading Raymond Chandler right now —a master of the American idiom and a textbook on how to write dialogue," Reed says. But he has also drawn on his many years of playwriting. "My experience as a playwright has enhanced my ability to write dialogue."

"I think dialogue is a little bit like music," says Hyde, "in that some people have a natural ear for it, and others have to work hard to get to the same place. I think good dialogue must define the character and advance the story at the same time. It should have the natural patterns of the way your characters would really speak. And each voice should be distinctive."

Fiction calls for great scenes. To pull your reader in, you must be able to write page-turning dialogue. To write a page-turning story or novel, all the fictional elements must be working seamlessly together. When they are, readers will be captivated enough to forget they're reading fiction. They will experience a strong semblance of real life right on the page.

# Know Your Antagonist

You have a protagonist in mind, but what does this protagonist want? What stands in his or her way? The antagonist serves this function of standing in the way, of blocking the protagonist from achieving a particular goal. But what makes a good antagonist? How can you make antagonists come alive in your fiction? What are some principles you can use to develop strong, compelling, and believable antagonists? Do you even need an antagonist?

## Developing Compelling, Believable Antagonists

For Catherine Brady, award-winning short story writer and author of *Story Logic and the Craft of Fiction*, a compelling antagonist is one who is as "complicated" as the story's protagonist. Just as the protagonist must be a "round" versus a "flat" character, in E.M. Forster's terms, so must the antagonist, says Brady. "If the antagonist is a stock figure, then readers won't be able to believe that he can generate real conflict for the protagonist." More specifically: "If we can size up the heroine's husband as a manipulative, belligerent drunk right from the start of the story, we won't be able to sympathize with her inability to leave him or to understand her conflict over doing so."

Lise Haines, author of three literary novels, including *Small Acts of Sex and Electricity*, also sees the compelling antagonist as one with complexity of character. She suggests that "compelling, believable antagonists have much at stake, clear flaws and contradictions, and act out a complicated relationship with the protagonist." She cites as an example her "dark, apocalyptic satire, *Girl in the Arena*," which "freights an alternate history in which neo-gladiator sport is now as big as the NFL. Uber, my antagonist, is a young fighter pitted against an opponent named Tommy, whom he admires and emulates. When Uber slays Tommy, he is expected to marry Tommy's daughter, Lyn, and of course Lyn, my protagonist, hates Uber for taking Tommy away. Uber is both fighter and clumsy suitor; a man trying to get things right yet aware that as a killer, he creates constant sorrow, as a victor, joy."

Geoffrey Clark, author of several novels and story collections, also stresses that the antagonist should be a round character — a realistic one instead of a "consciously symbolic" one. Thus the writer should be careful not "to make an antagonist totally vile and evil; you don't want him/her to be just a kind of case study in pathology." Instead, says Clark, an antagonist "needs a spark of humanity." Looking back on his third book, *Schooling the Spirit*, a novella and six stories, he believes that his antagonist was a flat character: "a very nasty guy, clearly a villain who has no redeeming qualities: he's simply loutish and brutal." In contrast, in his most recent novel, *Two, Two, Lily-White Boys*, Clark feels he has a much stronger antagonist: a young man by the name of Russell "Curly" Norrys, "14 or 15 or maybe 16 — everything about him is ambiguous." Capable of contradictory behaviors, Curly "can be moved to tears by the end of Chekhov's 'Grief,' then be unspeakably cruel to his companions, even to the point of murder (though even that is ambiguous)." Clark appreciates such ambiguity, and this he discovered through non-rational, intuitive means: "Though Curly may be beyond definition by the reader (as he is by the writer) I think I got him right: I trusted instinct beyond intellect; imagination rather than will."

Finding humanity in his antagonists is also important to DeWitt Henry, author of *The Marriage of Anna Maye Potts,* winner of the Peter Taylor Prize for the Novel. "Antagonists usually embody my own worst characteristics or impulses, while protagonists my best, but then in the process of storytelling, I discover humanizing (if not redeeming) characteristics in the person I first meant to condemn." Henry finds Richard Yates's antagonists more to his liking than the "daemonic antagonists" he finds in the work of William Styron "or even Robert Stone." He seeks a deeper ambivalence in the reader: "By nature, I follow Richard Yates when he says: 'I much prefer the kind of story where the reader is left wondering who's to blame until it begins to dawn on him (the reader) that he himself must bear some of the responsibility because he's human and therefore infinitely fallible.' Think of the insufferable Mrs. Givings in Yates's *Revolutionary Road*, whom Yates said he 'kinda loved.'"

Perhaps Ellen Sussman, author of the novel *French Lessons*, has something similar in mind: "I think the challenge for writers is to love their antagonists." This means complexity — a multi-dimensional character: "We have to find something about this person that is so engaging or compelling," says Sussman, "that we have to get to know them and we love watching them in action. Beginning writers often create villains who are terrible — and that results in a two-dimensional character." In creating her antagonists, Sussman goes for paradox: "I want a villain who is terrible and wonderful! Then you're on your road to creating a believable character and one who will carry the story."

Tim Johnston, author of *Irish Girl: Stories*, winner of the Katherine Anne Porter Prize in Short Fiction, emphasizes another key aspect of Forster's round character: the ability to change. For Johnston, the antagonist must not be a static character, just as the protagonist must not be. This means an element of mystery: "I also happen to believe there should always be some mystery about such characters (mystery about *all* characters, perhaps); that the antagonist should not be a purely antagonistic force in the story, but ought to change shape, by which I mean behavior, the way all good characters change shape in the course of good stories or novels." This change of behavior must be incremental, not sudden, says Johnston. In great works of fiction, "the revelation of what is antagonistic about the antagonist is a gradual one; a slow unveiling of character from Ordinary Citizen of The Story, to Primary Bad Guy."

The element of surprise is another aspect of Forster's round character. Steven Schwartz is Fiction Editor for *Colorado Review* and Professor of Creative Writing at Colorado State University and in the Warren Wilson MFA Program. "Successful antagonists," states Schwartz, "are those who keep you guessing as to their true motivations, their trustworthiness, their capacity for good and ill — and the line between these two behaviors." Kristen-Paige Madonia, author of the young adult novel *Fingerprints of You*, also looks for this element of surprise: "For me, the best antagonists are never predictable, and though we know they are, at their root, working against the successes of the protagonist, an antagonist's behavior should surprise the reader."

Josh Weil is author of *The New Valley*, published by Grove/Atlantic in 2009, and winner of the Sue Kaufman Award for First Fiction from the American Academy of Arts and Letters. Weil makes a distinction between the believable and the compelling antagonist. "An antagonist has to be driven by wounds, wants, and emotions just as organically as any other character. If those wounds are honestly dealt with, and the character's actions are addressing them, then the antagonist will be believable. For an antagonist to be compelling, those wounds, desires, needs have to be in conflict with what the protagonist wants." The antagonist will be compelling if this character acts as "the largest, most threatening obstacle standing in the way of the protagonist's goal."

## Antagonists — from Story to Story

Antagonists include a wide range of types, as Lise Haines points out. "In *Fight Club* we see a man pitted against his unleashed self; in *Virgin Suicides* a chorus of sisters go against the fragile yet hard-coated, Crucifix-bearing mother; in *Madame Bovary* we have the boring country doctor and the rake, but isn't this ultimately a story of Emma fighting the antagonist of wealth, stature and a life filled with beauty; Humbert Humbert confronts the two-headed monster of mother and daughter along with his double, Clare Quilty; and so on."

Given such a wide range of antagonist types, how do you apply a general principle — a complex character with the ability to change and surprise — to varying story dynamics? Do different stories call for different modifications of these principles? For Josh Weil, certain core values won't vary. But the need for an antagonist will: "Some stories — many, in fact — might be better served by not trying to simplify and compress obstacles and thematic elements into one character. So writers working on less traditional narratives might do best to cast a wary eye on the idea of an antagonist." If an antagonist *is* needed, Weil points out a possible exception in the treatment: perhaps "a purposefully cartoonish or flat antagonist played for comic effect"; "though, even then," says Weil, "I think adding depth by grounding the character in core needs and desires will only enrich the antagonist and the story, even the humor."

What will certainly change from story to story, from antagonist to antagonist, is the character arc, states Ellen Sussman. "Does he or she change? Is he or she affected by the plot and transformed in some real way? The deeper the story, the more possibilities there might be for the antagonist to develop as a character." The arc can indeed change, Tim Johnston states, noting an exception to his gradual change idea in Flannery O'Connor's "A Good Man Is Hard to Find." In this story, the Misfit, says Johnston, "arrives on the scene with all his badness already in place, and thereafter is revealed, through O'Connor's extraordinary deftness with character and dialogue, to possess a depth of humanity no other God- and law-abiding character in the story comes close to matching — unless it is the grandmother herself, who undergoes her own astounding transformation in that lovely and grim fable."

Steven Schwartz reminds us that change depends on character. Antagonists change "as much as one character varies from another. Remember that the biggest mistake a beginning writer makes about antagonists is to presume their guilt from the get-go." He cites as provocative examples Becky Sharp in *Vanity Fair*, the Misfit in O'Connor's story, and O'Brien in *1984*. "Each of these antagonists is distinct from the other, perfectly suited to their often opaque ends. Antagonists may be familiar and warm, cold and aloof, peculiar and mystifying, or any other combination of characteristics. But what they all have in common — and this can't be overstated — is to relentlessly enforce their will on those around them."

## Things to Avoid

When you realize what makes a compelling, believable antagonist — what those features are — think oppositely for what to avoid.

One is stereotypes. Stereotypical antagonists present a major problem, says Kristen-Paige Madonia: "A story will fall flat if characters are stereotyped because the reader will lose interest. Of course a reader doesn't have to like every character in a novel or a story — in fact it's much more interesting if they don't. But liking a character is different than believing the character and their actions are authentic and motivated by valid emotions."

Illuminating this point further, Steven Schwartz points out that "stereotypical or contrived creations who speak in blisteringly bad dialogue" make for a definite problem. "When people hear 'antagonists,' they sometimes think 'caricatures.' But antagonists, though they might be villainous, must first be human. As a writer, conceive not of these characters by viewing them from the outside, but from the inside — that is, from one's own being, unpleasant as that may be to recognize."

The good/bad dichotomy, then, needs to be avoided. Catherine Brady puts it this way: "In creating effective antagonists, it's easy to make the mistake of assuming the antagonist must be the 'bad' character, the protagonist the 'good.'" An antagonist, says Brady, "represents a very potent external obstacle for the protagonist, but what the antagonist has to be capable of doing is opposing the protagonist in a way that generates strong internal conflict; his job is to make the hero's choices more difficult." But what if your antagonist *is* absolutely bad — what then? Brady's solution is this: "If your antagonist is genuinely a diabolical creature, then you have to be sure that something else about the dramatic situation generates difficulty for the protagonist: Is the protagonist or the reader seduced by this bad boy? Or does the protagonist mistake what it will cost to defeat him?" For Brady, in most cases, the antagonist should be seen in more complex terms than the simple good/bad category allows. "More often, antagonists are not absolutely evil, only misguided creatures convinced of their own rightness, or creatures whose evil is disturbingly mixed with traits that they share with us — the con artist who always remembers to send flowers to his wife on her birthday." It works well, says Brady, to "grant some credibility" to your antagonist's perspective and "to avoid an ending in which the antagonist is unmasked as unequivocally wrong. You don't want to solve the mystery of this person's moral or spiritual failings for the reader; you want the reader to continue to be troubled by them long after the action ends."

In writing her novel *Towelhead*, Alicia Erian was tempted to create an absolutely evil antagonist. "I really was compelled by my anger toward my abusive father. Having said that, I was also smart enough to know that if I didn't find some way to make the Daddy character multi-faceted, my book would stink. So I grudgingly and resentfully tried to round him out. Even I liked him in the end, which made me angry!" But as she points out: "As a reader, I love being tossed around. I love being forced to ask myself why it is that I'm willing to give credit to a jerk. This is an engaging and interesting way to respond to a story, I think." And this is surely because this ambivalence will cause the reader to be more "troubled," as Brady says, than an "unequivocally wrong" antagonist would.

Avoid melodrama, says DeWitt Henry. He admits that it's "always a temptation, with good opposing evil, hero opposing villain." His novel presented this problem: "The template of *Anna Maye* is probably Cinderella, for instance. But the discipline of fiction demands that the author grow past simple oppositions." Henry's solution was for his two major antagonists, Mary and Louie, to become complex versus one-dimensional melodramatic figures: "In their meanest or most selfish acts, both Mary and Louie rationalize. They think they mean well, mostly."

The problem of the one-dimensional antagonist may result from the antagonist being conceived of as a mere contrivance, or a "tool in the narrative," says Josh Weil. For him, it works this way: "If the character arises naturally from the protagonist's struggles then that's a good sign. If the protagonist isn't struggling enough and the writer feels a need to throw another obstacle in there, the temptation to use a character as a tool that way should send up some red flags."

## Stories without Antagonists

Do some stories *not* need an antagonist — as Josh Weil has suggested? Steven Schwartz places the issue in this context: "In the age of voice-driven and lyrical narratives, contemporary short story writers are as reluctant to use such an old-fashioned term as 'antagonist,' just as they are 'plot.' The fact remains, however, that your main character has to face adversity, which usually comes in the form of an antagonist."

Perspectives on this question do vary. Dennis Vannatta, author of three short story collections, states: "I can't recall ever creating an antagonist in a piece of fiction. I just don't think in those terms." Dennis Must, author of two story collections, makes a similar comment: "When writing a story, I honestly don't think of protagonists or antagonists, finding the definitions too self-limiting. In most of my work where conflict is created between two characters, the denouement often ends up equivocally. The roles of protagonist and antagonist are frequently interchangeable."

Anjali Banerjee, author of several commercial works of fiction, both literary and young adult, doesn't think in terms of protagonist/antagonist either — at least not in the traditional sense. The antagonist becomes a psychic projection of her main character. She states: "Maybe the visible antagonist is a function of the concrete/external plot. In other words, often the protagonist has an internal emotional arc in the story and an external, concrete goal. The antagonist as a concrete character is a way to 'push back' against the concrete goal, but the antagonist also represents the darkest aspect — or weakness — in the hero."

Robert Stewart, Editor of *New Letters*, provocatively shifts the attention not only from the protagonist/antagonist issue — but from story dynamics, and even character: "I have little interest in a protagonist's function in a story, or the story dynamics. I am interested in how the story uses language, which, of course, includes dialogue, which defines the character. The language (including dialogue) of a story needs to reveal an authentic, honest voice, whether abrasive, endearing, or quirky. Anything conventional or generalized is deadly, to me. Just take a look at Ree Dolly in Daniel Woodrell's *Winter's Bone* or Caulfield in *The Catcher in the Rye*, as characters of different cultures. Each character is on a kind of quest, but that, in itself, is not the reason we care about them. Every word they speak defines them as distinct individuals and also as products of their particular worlds. I don't know how that's done, except that it can't be ordered up easily. The writer learns this trick by reading slowly and deeply."

Thaisa Frank, author of the literary novel *Heidegger's Glasses*, thinks in terms of voice, not character. She states, "As a voice-driven writer, rather than a character-driven writer, I'm not good at thinking about characters. My characters show up after I've fooled around with the story. There are two characters in *Heidegger's Glasses* that are antagonists. One is Stumpf and the other is Mueller. They honestly just came to me as a result of being in the setting and the situation."

Her process goes like this: "Especially in a novel I visualize them and feel them kinesthetically — feel how they move in the world. But I start with a title and have a place or a setting. It's almost as though I have to create a setting so they know where to come. I think of them as out-of-work characters in character-land, just like actors who want a part in a play. I don't know quite how they show up. Some of them have bodies and faces I've never seen, and others look remarkably like people I know. Once I get a sense of how a character moves through space — a sense of embodiment, which is always accompanied by a vision of a face and a body — they start to talk and do things for me. Later, of course, I fill them out by giving them more situations to act in — to be more villainous, to be more heroic, or just to speak more naturally. But by the time I do this, the story is fleshed out and they're reacting to the situation. In some of my short stories and my flash fiction, I only have a kinesthetic sense of them. In both short stories and flash fiction it's easier to construct something by following the voice. Sometimes a visualization comes and at other times they're almost allegorical. However it works — I'm always very grateful to them for showing up and wanting work, even when I don't want to work. And when I live with them for a long time — as I did in *Heidegger's Glasses* — they become very real to me."

For Thaisa Frank all of her characters "show up" at some point in the process. She doesn't concern herself with the story dynamics, with character as such — but depends on voice. And so the question of the antagonist's one-dimensionality, or multi-dimensionality, isn't a question she ever takes up. She trusts the process, hears the voice, and follows it.

## Some Final Thoughts

For writers who do focus more on character, and on various story dynamics, the role of both protagonist and antagonist becomes quite important. And they generally agree on one thing: Don't reduce the matter to good and bad. Create levels in both protagonist and antagonist. And complicate, perplex. Alicia Erian offers this intriguing thought: "The best antagonists are the ones who leave the reader saying, 'Am I supposed to like this person? Because I'm not sure that I do. Maybe I do. But I don't think so.'" And a great piece of advice: "Practically speaking, I think that a great exercise is to base a character on someone you truly dislike in real life, because then you will be forced to redeem them in some way, in order to make your story work."

# Not Just Second Class: Writing Secondary Characters in Fiction

When you're writing a short story or novel, you naturally give most of your attention to your protagonist. You focus on your main character's arc, doing everything you can to weed out material that detracts from it. But what about secondary characters? What parts do they play? What parts *should* they play? How developed should they be? As you work and rework your protagonist's trajectory, you need to think about all the characters who interact with your main character and the impact they will have on your protagonist's growth and overall development.

### Discovering the Functions of Secondary Characters

Secondary characters can aid in both characterization and character development. They can function as mirrors in two different ways, says Catherine Ryan Hyde, author of the highly acclaimed *Pay It Forward* and twenty-four other novels. "They can be mirrors in which your protagonist sees things he might not otherwise see. Or they can be mirrors that allow the readers to see things that still aren't getting through to your lead character." This second function is especially valuable, states Hyde. "As authors we're told 'show don't tell,' and that's always sticky and challenging, but especially so when we're supposed to show something about our viewpoint character that he doesn't recognize himself. The author can bounce these things off secondary characters, bringing them into the light."

Anthony Varallo, award-winning author of three short story collections, also emphasizes the characterization function of secondary characters. "Secondary characters are useful in the exact degree that they throw a light upon the primary characters. That is, they are another means of characterization, right up there with physical detail, speech, actions, habits, and the like." Varallo makes adept use of a secondary character as an expository device in "Time Apart Together," from *Think of Me and I'll Know*. Brad, the protagonist, meets with his professor about a college paper he's struggling to finish, largely, says Varallo, because "his thesis statement is abstract and meaningless." In his interchange with the professor, Brad makes an unabashed admission of his scholarly ineptness. Varallo could have revealed this information about Brad directly through first-person exposition, but he chose the dramatic method instead. "In this instance," Varallo says, "I needed a secondary character to draw out that layer of characterization, indirectly, through dialogue." As Hyde points out, secondary characters can provide a valuable dramatic function, an alternative to the protagonist's internal exposition, turning this "into real scenes, scenes readers can see vividly in their heads."

Beyond their function in characterization, secondary characters can also spark conflict. In fact they must do so, says Varallo, "no matter how small, to earn their narrative keep. The best secondary characters make the primary characters feel uneasy, doubtful, or on edge." For Walter Cummins, long-time editor of *The Literary Review* and author of several story collections, "Just about every short story needs at least one secondary character to serve as a source of tension with the protagonist." The secondary character can be an antagonist "in some form of overt competition with the protagonist," says Cummins, or even be "unaware that he or she is an obstacle to the protagonist." A secondary character need not have a physical presence in the story's present time frame, though, says Cummins, "but could enter as a memory in the protagonist's mind."

Character conflict drives action, which drives plot. Cummins distinguishes between two types of secondary characters: functionary and functional. "The functionary," he notes, "serve at tables, collect tickets, etc." They help "reveal the protagonist," but do not drive the plot. The functional type, says Cummins, "play roles that move the plot along and help reveal the main character's dramatic dilemma."

It's the interaction with functional secondary characters that allows your protagonist to "grow, stretch, and change," says Elizabeth Stuckey-French, author of several comic novels. She lays out various possible scenarios: "A secondary character, let's call him Jim, can aid your protagonist, Jenny, or hinder her in her quest. He could even do both. Jim's appearance in the novel should make Jenny's life, and the novel, more complicated. He may have only a walk-on role, or his own subplot, which touches the primary plot, echoing, enriching, and enlarging it along the way. It's best if Jim is connected to Jenny in some important way — for instance, he might be related to her or to someone she loves, he might work with her, be her neighbor, be an old beau reappearing from her past, or perhaps they share a secret. This connection makes him harder for Jenny and the reader to dismiss."

In Stuckey-French's *The Revenge of the Radioactive Lady*, protagonist Vic by chance meets Gigi, whom he knew back in graduate school, at a neighborhood roller skating rink.

From what transpires in this meeting, clearly Gigi is a secondary character who will most likely have an impact on Vic's life. And she does. He comes close to having an affair with her and ruining his marriage.

## Developing Secondary Characters

"Secondary characters receive less page space and, as a result, demand less of the reader's attention," says Varallo. But what's the right amount of space to give them? Where do you draw the line?

To determine how much secondary characters need to be developed, "Initial attention should be given to the role of a secondary character," says Cummins. "Once the writer is clear on that role, the story needs just enough of the character to fulfill his or her purpose." But this doesn't mean secondary characters can't be complex. According to Varallo, "your secondary characters can be as fully imagined and as fully complex as your primary ones. That's actually a lot of fun, to imagine their whole lives." And, for Stuckey-French, it's very important to do so. "I've found that in order to present Jim, my secondary character, in a convincing and engaging manner, I need to know as much about him as I do about Jenny, my protagonist. When drafting a novel I will do a lot of writing and musing in a notebook outside the story, mapping out Jim's life and how it connects to Jenny's, sometimes even keeping a journal or diary in Jim's voice. Not much of it will end up in the novel, but hopefully, as Hemingway's iceberg theory goes, the reader will feel all of Jim's life there under the surface."

Do keep in mind, cautions Hyde, that to achieve depth, you need not go into great detail — which, if you do, can put undue emphasis on the secondary character and his or her role. "A few sentences," says Hyde, "can create a memorable complexity." The lesson here? It's important to humanize not just your protagonist, but your secondary characters as well.

## Overshadowing Protagonists

Perhaps in the process of writing your story or novel, you realize that a secondary character is becoming more interesting than the protagonist. An alarm bell goes off. Is this a fatal flaw?

According to Varallo, "I think you just let that happen and see where it leads you, really. It's sort of like that old driver's ed wisdom about turning in the direction of a skid: You just keep exploring the character and see what you find. You can still tell a story where the secondary characters eclipse the primary ones. Fagin steals every scene from Oliver Twist."

For Cummins, as long as the protagonist is interesting, there's no problem if the secondary character is more interesting. "The protagonist's relation to and interaction with such a character may be what the story is all about. For example, Gatsby is inherently more interesting than Nick Carraway, yet many readers consider the novel to really be about Nick, because Nick is the one who changes because of the relationship." Yet what if, in the process of writing your short story or novel, you see that your secondary character is completely overshadowing your protagonist, stealing his thunder entirely? If this is the case you do need to make a decision, says Cummins. Either you are "getting off-track," or you should assign a "greater role for this character" — perhaps even making the character the protagonist. Or, perhaps, says Stuckey-French, you should go for two protagonists: "If Jim becomes very intriguing to me, then I will write a section of the novel in his point of view, and, depending on how that works out, he might get cast as a major character along with Jenny. It's fun when this happens!"

But let's go back. It *is* possible, of course, for a protagonist to be completely overshadowed by a secondary character who's not only more interesting but also doesn't allow the protagonist much of a role at all. This usually happens, says Cummins, in "first-person stories in which the teller is an observer of others and, as a result, remains indistinct." If the first-person observer is *also* a participant, like Nick Carraway, you've nailed it. But if the observer is *only* an observer, a "peripheral" character, that's a problem, as Janet Burroway suggests in *Writing Fiction: A Guide to Narrative Craft*.

Cummins's story "Kaiser-Frazer," which first appeared in *West Branch*, demonstrates how to avoid the problem of a secondary character totally stealing the show and reducing the first-person narrator to a merely peripheral character. His protagonist is a first-person narrator who is both observer *and* participant. It's a fine balancing act Cummins performs in this story because his secondary character is quite compelling and threatens to overshadow the protagonist, and yet as impressive as he is, he functions instead to help develop the protagonist.

Cummins's protagonist is Bobby, a ten-year-old boy, in the period shortly after the end of World War II. He is sad and alone: his father dead, his mother in the hospital, his older twin sisters working in the city. He wanders his small town until, one day, he happens on a teenager, Tom Maxville, who is staggering down an alley by an abandoned store, "trying to balance a ladder under one arm and carry a bucket of paint and wide brush in his free hand." Tom's excited about a showroom featuring Kaisers and Frazers. Tom, with his clownish appearance, his excited vision of the future, and his unrelenting optimism, could easily overshadow Bobby, making him vacuous in comparison, but by story's end, Bobby fully absorbs Tom's infectious enthusiasm, grows, and becomes a participant in his own psychological recovery. We're not stuck with a mere observer of a vivacious or vibrant secondary character.

## Summing Up

With secondary characters, one thing is certain: You must define the role each character plays in your story or novel and how large that role will be. How much development will you give each character? Whose story is it? Is it basically one story, several, or many? Answering these questions will aid in developing secondary characters that refuse to be considered second-class citizens, that function as mirrors to the protagonist, as sources of conflict, and as fully realized individuals in your fiction.

# Playing God: Handling the Omniscient Point of View in Fiction

Writing good fiction calls for creating both a strong protagonist and a solid plot. If you ignore either of these, your story can be fatally flawed. But there's an aspect related to character that you must also pay close attention to — point of view. POV has to do with vantage point, or *narrative perspective*: whose eyes the story is seen from. Some characters have more at stake than others, more potential for conflict and change. You should gravitate toward these characters to serve as the "lens" for your stories.

A second aspect of POV has to do with choice of person: First and second person lend intimacy, while third person establishes distance. When working in third person, many writers today choose the "third-person limited" point of view, which narrows in on one particular character's mind. If you adopt the "third-person omniscient" POV, however, you have access to more than one character's mind (perhaps several), and you have carte blanche to reveal anything and everything about *anyone* in the story or novel. Some notable omniscient examples from the past include *The Scarlet Letter*, *The Death of Ivan Ilyich*, and *The Grapes of Wrath*. What are the benefits as well as the risks of godlike knowing with the omniscient POV?

## Benefits of Omniscience

Clearly it's beneficial in some works of fiction to get into more than one character's consciousness. Some stories may call for different perspectives played out both dramatically and internally from two or more characters. But the omniscient point of view allows you — or I should say, your author's *persona* — more godlike knowledge than this. In fact, the options are seemingly endless. You may exert your omniscience to describe your characters from the outside: the clothes they're wearing, the look on their faces, the way others tend to see them, the way others have *always* seen them, and, speculatively, the way others will *probably* always see them — this is truly godlike knowing. Indeed, you can do this for your protagonist with the "limited omniscient" POV, but this is more omniscience than most writers wish to exert. Most of the time, they want to avoid the all-seeing, all-knowing authorial view and stick to what the *character* is seeing and experiencing. There are exceptions, of course, such as when the narrator maintains a good distance from the protagonist and calls the character "our hero," or her "our heroine" with playful irony. This demonstrates an external perspective, but the omniscient POV allows much more than this.

You may find it useful, for instance, to describe what several of the local townsfolk are busily engaged in — they're gathering stones for a stoning in Shirley Jackson's classic story "The Lottery." You might, like Richard Bausch, in his opening pages of *Thanksgiving Night*, paint a sweeping portrait of an urban area (Point Royal, Virginia, in this case), creating a cinematic establishing shot before moving into character and story. You might even give the history of a particular place, which might not be feasible to filter through the consciousness of any of your characters because none of your characters knows this history, but you, the all-powerful author, do — and can provide it for the reader. You might, like a 19th-century writer, choose to step back from your characters and philosophize about the nature of people and the world. There's certainly a magic in this kind of omniscience, with the world of your story fully accessible to you as all-knowing author, the god-creator reigning over it.

### Risks of Omniscience

Surely there are risks in exerting very much authorial presence in a story or novel. You risk putting off readers who view this narrative presence as intrusion, the meddling of an unwanted author into the world of the characters. Too much authorial involvement can kill the dramatic power of the work. When the story starts sounding like the author's story, not the characters', you've gone too far. Be careful, then, to exercise judgment on how much you engage in authorial commentary. Award-winning author Anthony Varallo points out that you don't want the "reader sensing too much of the writer's hand in the story," which, he says, "can risk breaking the 'spell' of the story." With the omniscient POV, Varallo recommends finding "the lightest possible touch. I would only use it if I felt I had no other way to tell the story." And Midge Raymond, author of *My Last Continent*, adds, "Omniscience has its rewards but also requires such a fine balance that it can be a challenge to get just right."

## The Multiple Third-person POV

Frankly, authorial presence is mostly a thing of the past. The godlike narrator is gone, supplanted by individual characters who have limited knowledge of the world they inhabit. An alternative to omniscient authorial presence is the *effaced author*. This author may allow access to a number of different characters but make no commentary on them and exclude any material that isn't filtered through a given character's consciousness. This effaced-author approach has become a typical set-up in today's third-person POV fiction. Catherine Ryan Hyde, author of 30 novels, including the famous *Pay It Forward*, doesn't go for the omniscient. She states, "I very often narrate a novel from two points of view. More often than not, in fact. But I do it chapter by chapter, labeling each new chapter with the character name and clearly establishing POV in the first sentence. This gives me all the benefits of being able to tell the story from more than one point of view, but I think it's easier and more comfortable for the reader."

## A Wrap on the Omniscient POV

♦ The third-person omniscient POV allows much more authorial range and commentary than third-person limited.

♦ Use the omniscient POV only when it seems indispensable to character creation and storytelling. Make sure it doesn't damage the dramatic power of the work.

♦ Always consider an effaced narrator instead of authorial commentary.

# Second Degree: The Second-Person POV

Sometimes in fiction, we encounter an authorial narrative perspective that goes something like this: "If you travel this part of the country, you're likely to notice..." This is second-person point of view, and you'll probably find it used quite a bit. But it's not the same as a second-person narration in which "you" become the protagonist. This is a more radical shift, and while this second-person POV has its payoffs, it's also risky. Lise Haines, author of *Girl in the Arena*, cautions beginning writers to be careful. "As we crowd into selfies, photoshop ourselves into landscapes and strap on Oculus, writing students attempt the second-person story with increased frequency, manipulating and reflecting the culture of self," she says. "It can feel like that safe experiment when trying to make a stretch in form, sometimes relying on the list and careful repetitions. But all fine stories require a solid vision regardless of the frame or lens — an awareness that often comes as a humbling workshop takeaway."

## Possible Pluses

Let's say you want to try it out. Why choose the second-person POV? First, consider what's at stake. It's a matter of narrative distance. In a very interesting way, second is related to first. Both provide immediacy. First-person speaks directly to us, involving us in character consciousness — in the character's thoughts, beliefs and feelings. Second-person makes *us* that character — not only externally, but internally as well. The payoff, assuming it works? We gain a special vantage point, a much closer lens than third person, and even closer than first, which is generally considered the gold standard for immediacy. We, as readers, become the "you" of the story or novel. If the POV works, we "dissolve" into this character like an actor or actress in a play. *We're* the ones living the dramatic action of the story or novel —and how as a fiction writer can you involve your reader more than that? How can you grab your reader in a more powerful, existential way? Difficult enough to do well in a short story, second-person is exceedingly difficult to accomplish in a full-length novel. Jay McInerney famously pulls it off in *Bright Lights, Big City*.

## Possible Minuses

But what if, as a reader, I don't want to be this "you" the author requires me to be? With the third person, I can stand aloof at times and share the consciousness of the character to the extent that the writer makes the character sufficiently compelling. With first person, there's that immediacy, especially in the case of a self-absorbed first-person narrator, but still I am distanced by the fact that the character is "I" — and I, as reader, am a different "I." Not the case with second. I am that "you." What if — imagining certain famous characters from literature handled in second — I don't want to *be* Raskolnikov killing that old pawnbroker in *Crime and Punishment*? What if it's just too painful to *be* Paul Sheldon of *Misery* under the tyranny of Annie Wilkes?

With this POV, you face the reader's possible resistance to being placed in this role. Clearly we want to enter fully into a fictional world, but perhaps at some remove. This POV requires that we dissolve in ways no other POV requires. Consider: If as reader, I am "you" making bad choices, rationalizing these choices, blaming others when clearly they're more in the right than "you," this may be difficult or undesirable. What about the case of second person when the humor is at "your" expense? Some readers might resist the voice of the story or novel. And yet — having said all this — when this POV works, it can be quite compelling. It can be haunting, intense, and lyrical. Porochista Khakpour, author of *The Last Illusion*, states: "I sometimes discourage students from going there, but my point is if you are going to do it, you have to do it *really, really, really* well. High stakes, but when done well, as Lorrie Moore and Junot Diaz do, no other POV is more glorious."

## Some Tips

Save second-person POV for times when the dramatic transaction between reader and character needs to be particularly intense

— when you seek absolute fusion between the two. Keep your character sympathetic. How many readers will want to *be* a bigot, a racist, a sexist, an obtuse fool — even a repentant one?

Be sure the voice works. Is it compelling? Does it grab the reader and never let go? It must.

# If You Build It

As a novelist, you must handle certain basic fictional elements — character, plot, and setting — with artistry and polish. Your prose style must be engaging, your scenes energizing, your writing vivid. None of that can work without structure, however. Peter Behrens, author of *Carry Me*, puts it this way: "Be aware that novels tend to be composed of, first, scenes, and, second, summary. The point is to try to find the balance."

Balance must be achieved at all levels of your work, with crucially placed drama points that provide emphasis and effective pacing.

Let's begin with overall structure: the skeletal framework of a novel.

## The Five-stage Story

You might choose the classic five-stage plot structure: exposition, rising action, climax, falling action and resolution. You might also choose the three-act structure — setup, confrontation, resolution — familiar to screenwriters. Both structures can be rigid, although novelistic structure can also be loose as long as it includes some sort of beginning, middle and end. What is drama without these three fundamentals, as Aristotle makes abundantly clear in his *Poetics*? Where is the *story*?

"I suspect that for the most part, I fall into the traditional five-stage plot structure intuitively, and that's likely due to my exposure to the predominant plot structure in the Western literary tradition," says Julie Iromuanya, author of *Mr. and Mrs. Doctor*. Departures from this traditional structure are always risky, she adds. Margaret Verble, author of *Maud's Line*, says that the five-stage story structure remains "the best structure on which to hang a tale." Only seasoned writers, she says, should consider experimenting with "funky structures." Beginning writers should avoid them.

However tried and true the five-stage plot structure, authors find reasons to make slight departures from it. In his debut novel, *The Sympathizer*, Viet Thanh Nguyen deviates in a minimal but important way. "I was aware of the five-stage plot structure, partially through long exposure to it as a student and partially because I wanted my novel to work as genre fiction in addition to being literary fiction," he says. Yet Nguyen deviates from the traditional when a mid-novel interlude veers off the "explicit narrative of a spy caught in history." Here, Nguyen's spy becomes a film consultant on an epic Vietnam War movie shot in the Philippines. "Perhaps this was a digression from the five-stage plot," he says, "but I couldn't help myself. This was my revenge on Hollywood's Vietnam War, and I was going to take it." Although this interlude breaks with the "straightforward action" typical of the five-stage story, it serves to enhance this traditional structure. "The climax and denouement of the section in the Philippines, halfway through the novel, foreshadows the climax and denouement of the entire novel toward the end," says Nguyen. The interlude underscores Nguyen's final authority in the structure department. In the end, the author has to be true to his creativity.

When drafting a novel, Behrens never thinks in structural terms. He doesn't fixate on plot. Instead, he follows characters, sometimes having "a vague sense of the place where the characters end up — their moral, mental, emotional, tactile and sensual surroundings at the end of the story." For him, writing a novel is "trying to learn more about that place and figuring out how [characters] got to that place from where they started." The first draft goes fast. In the revision stage, Behrens turns a critical eye to structure. "When I see the thing as a whole for the first time and know the story," says Behrens, "I go back to the storytelling and try to establish a structure that will keep the story moving at the right pace, engage the reader and get to where I want to go." He learned about story structure from his screenwriting background and in post-production editing. "There are a zillion ways to cut a story up and assemble it," he says. "The movie is made in the editing room." Behrens speculates that the structure of *Carry Me* emerged when he "started scissoring it apart and reassembling it."

Bernice L. McFadden, author of *Sugar* and eight other novels, also doesn't focus on structure in a first draft. For her, it's best to let the story unfold instead of working with a linear approach. Often she writes the ending before the beginning. "If the rising action comes early on," says McFadden, "I write it down and build the exposition around it." When she reads drafts, McFadden is confident that "the structure will unquestionably reveal itself." Usually, it's not the standard five-stage plot — more like "piecing a puzzle together," she says — but it does include a beginning, middle and end.

## Key Structural Elements

Outside of traditional plot structures, character development also affects structure. If you're writing a character-driven versus a plot-driven story, your characters must be "multi-layered, much like an onion," says McFadden, or "round," as E. M. Forster says in *Aspects of the Novel*.

"How and when you choose to peel back a layer to reveal another quality or trait of said character is just as important to the story as rising action, falling action and climax," says McFadden. You mustn't unload a multi-faceted character in one fell swoop. Good character revelation is a matter of judicious timing — and that's structure.

A protagonist's "active goal," says Verble, will serve as a major organizing device for a novel. It is, she says, "the muscle of the story, the conflict between what the character wants, or thinks she wants, and the obstacles, both external and internal, thrown in the way." Verble holds that this crucial structural device should be evident "in clear language" early in the novel. By page three in *Maud's Line*, the reader learns about the main character's situation, what she wants and her need to be free from "meanness and violence." This structural device, says Verble, keeps both writer and reader on track.

The character arc is ultimately generated from the character's active goal, providing a thread from page one to the end. Because of the character's experience, fleshed out in scenes, summary, and expository sections, a protagonist comes to some sort of knowledge, some recognition regarding self and world. This usually means a confrontation with self. "I've always believed that as a writer, it's my job to force my characters to face the very things they fear the most in the space of the narrative," Iromuanya says. "In the best writing, that 'thing' is themselves." In real life, she points out, people may confront their true selves only a few times, but fiction offers other imaginative possibilities. For dramatic tension, says Iromuanya, this encounter with self is essential to character growth or change. In some cases, characters will be willing to face certain truths about themselves, and in other cases, they will shun these truths. As a novelist, Iromuanya believes it is her job to create the right circumstances at the right time for those who are willing to confront themselves and "chas[e] down characters who resist coming face to face with their truest reflection." For her, it's a matter of structuring the drama points just right for both kinds of characters.

If matters of character become important structural issues, certainly handling time, especially in novels that deal with historical events, requires careful structural decisions. "I am usually trying to write stories that span a longish time — decades," says Behrens, who has written two previous novels. For him, effective structure is critical in handling historical contexts. Behrens doesn't consider himself a historical novelist, but he does create social and psychological novels dealing with characters based on the past. He writes fiction to "investigate the various claims the dead generations seem to have upon me." Structurally, *Carry Me* centers on key historical events as Europe goes into its near-death spiral in between 1910 and 1938. Events in his work include the Declaration of War in 1914, Hitler's speeches in 1927, the Irish Rising in 1916 and Kristallnacht in 1938. While historicity isn't his main purpose, it provides the skeleton of his novel. He seeks an overall pattern that unifies his social-psychological themes with related historical contexts.

## Additional Structural Patterns

The journey structure is a classic organizing device, often serving not only character and plot but also theme. This was a useful device in Behrens' first novel, *The Law of Dreams*, which he calls "bare bones, simple and straightforward." Except for a short prologue, this novel is narrated from the point of view of a young Irish boy from the hills of East Clare. The journey motif allows Behrens to follow the boy over the course of a year as he makes his way to America. For Behrens, the journey structure worked because the story was about immigration and refugee flight.

Another approach is to use a circular structural element, as in Iromuanya's *Mr. and Mrs. Doctor*, in which an extravagant fur coat becomes not only symbolic but also crucial to advancing plot and character. Iromuanya builds on the metaphor of the fur coat as an organizing thematic pattern.

A structural feature can work in one section of the novel, if not the whole. In the prologue to her novel *Glorious*, McFadden uses an if-then refrain throughout. "While this is typical of a song or poem, it is not often seen in novels," she says. "I believe this technique was as powerful and impactful as an unforgettable opening sentence — except this wallop goes on for pages. The promise is made in those echoing lines and ultimately fulfilled at the close of the story."

## Multiple Points of View

You may decide that your novel calls for more than one point-of-view character, which is more complicated. The question becomes: Whose story is it? Once you do decide on point of view, the question of structure follows. How do you determine whether to divide the story into sections devoted to a specific character or to use alternating point-of-view chapters?

In her novels *Loving Donovan* and *Nowhere Is a Place*, McFadden found the characters were complex and layered enough so that she had to give them each a voice. A three-part novel, *Loving Donovan* is written in three point-of-view sections. *Nowhere Is a Place* uses alternating chapters to represent narratives shifting between the past and the present. In both novels, McFadden chose to handle point of view "in such a way that the personal and historical pasts wouldn't go unnoticed, because what happened 'before' is critical to what is happening in the now."

The two methods create distinct effects. Alternating viewpoints by chapter worked for Behrens as long as the shifts didn't occur within the chapter. "I want the characters, their voices and ways of seeing, to each own their own piece of ground within the book," he says. "Maybe I'm afraid of confusing readers or confusing myself if I blend different POVs in smaller fragments or alternate constantly within a chapter."

For Iromuanya, alternating points of view by chapter and even within chapters was the best choice in *Mr. and Mrs. Doctor*. "Most of the novel shifts back and forth between the perspectives of Job and Ifi, the husband and wife at the center of the novel," she says. "But there are also moments when the point of view shifts to Aunty and their son, Victor. When I started the book, I thought I would only be in the point of view of Job, but as I wrote, each chapter called for a different perspective." This difference in perspective becomes crucial to her novel. "So much of *Mr. and Mrs. Doctor* is about the differences between reality and dreams," says Iromuanya, "and in some cases the best way to magnify perception to the point of distortion is through shifting point of view." Thus, point-of-view shifts emphasize significant differences in Iromanya's characters' perceptions. With a different structure, the novel would not provide the emphasis she's after.

### Some Final Thoughts

Good fiction requires handling major story elements with careful artistic control. Most of what happens in good fiction happens in revision. You pound out your novel in scene, summary, and exposition; then, in revision, you go at it with an acutely critical eye, seeking the right balance — the right structure. And you may find your approach, in the end, defies every lesson of structural wisdom. Perhaps it's the five-stage plot structure. Perhaps it's the three-stage. Perhaps it's something of your own making. Whatever fits your project, go with it to create a structure to support your story and characters. Make sure that the various structural elements serve not only character and plot but also theme. After all, structure is the framework your whole fictional world stands on.

# Start to Stop

Writing a novel is a major investment of time and energy. Much of your time will be spent on the famous Aristotelian "middle" — the chapters that flesh out the beast with dramatic movement and power. Weeks, months and perhaps years you will give to this process: writing, rewriting, tuning, fine-tuning, making that interior world of your imagination as captivating, as engaging, as you can. Finally, the thing *lives* — words with blood, flesh and bone.

Be assured: If you want your novel to be read by an agent or a publisher, the opening must grab the reader's attention right off. It must pull the reader right in. Don't think to yourself, *It gets going around page ten. Bear with me.* You will have lost your reader by then.

Then there's the ending, which can be as challenging as the opening. Very likely you've woven numerous story threads, perhaps a complex intertwining of plot and subplots. How should you conclude? How do you provide a satisfying sense of closure? The novel *must* end — but where?

Answers to both openings and endings are partly genre-specific, but regardless of genre, certain basic novelistic principles apply. On your own, read the kinds of novels you intend to write. Also, look to professionals, including those surveyed here, because their experience can be a source of strong advice and useful tips.

## Discover the beginning

Let's start with your novel's opening. As with most aspects of fiction writing, creating a strong opening is not easily managed initially. It's often an experiment involving a number of false starts. Be open to change. Plenty of it.

"My openings are always in flux for a while," says Duff Brenna, author of *Too Cool*, a *New York Times* Noteworthy Book. "I keep a ruthless eye on them to make sure they're not luring me into a false sense of self-satisfaction." Developing the right opening is a matter of discovery, Brenna says. The second paragraph may be a better opening than the first. The second, third, or even fourth chapter may be a better place to begin than your present first chapter. Brenna advises rethinking both material and order. "Whatever you wrote before you found the 'real' opening should be deleted. Or, perhaps, put somewhere else. Maybe your first chapter or paragraph should be in the middle of your book. Then again, maybe it's the ending of your book."

Creating a striking opening line is also a matter of discovery for Mark Wisniewski, author of *Watch Me Go*. "I like to look through early drafts for the line that will grab the reader most," he says. "This might entail taking the second half of a sentence from the middle of paragraph four or five or even 15 pages in. A good opening sentence tends to come from the middle of a drafted scene, but not always. It's like a line of gossip that causes strangers to try to overhear it at a party: Everyone knows it's interesting as soon as they hear it."

Getting the tone right is crucial, and this can be quite difficult to manage. For David B. Coe, fantasy novelist, this is the hardest part of writing openings. "I want my openings to establish the voice of the narrating character," says Coe, "and the mood or ambiance of the novel, and that can take several drafts. I like to work linearly; I don't skip around when I write. So until the opening is just right, I can't move on." Coe ends up taking as much time to nail down a strong opening as he does to complete the first chapter.

## Choose the right type

There are four basic types of openings: exposition, description, narrative summary and scene. If you browse through openings of contemporary novels, you will undoubtedly find all four types represented. The question is which type of opening will best hook your reader and capture the basic thrust of the novel. Novelists often opt for the scenic opening, especially those seeking commercial publishers.

Opening a novel with dialogue or action can be a tad tricky, says mystery writer Elizabeth Craig, especially if several characters are talking. In this case, readers may lack the necessary context. But handled clearly, a dialogue opening can "pique readers' curiosity," says Craig, "and make them want to learn more." In *Quilt or Innocence*, Craig achieves this clarity by interspersing "short, necessary bits of exposition to set the scene" since barebones dialogue might confuse or frustrate readers. Typically, Craig's openings go light on description because, she says, "too much description often doesn't deliver the quick pace I'm looking for at the story's opening."

Coe also goes for scenic openings, ones that are heavy on action to give fantasy readers "an immediate rush of adrenaline." In *The Thieftaker Chronicles*, a historical urban fantasy series he wrote under the pen name D.B. Jackson, Coe uses his opening pages to accomplish several objectives. "Show a bit of magic, have my hero engage in a street fight with a thief or with his recurring nemesis, and introduce the historical events that will serve as the backdrop to my story." Beyond the adrenaline rush, his readers get a sense for his larger conflict, even if obliquely.

Ellen Sussman, author of *A Wedding in Provence*, tends to open her literary novels with a scene. "I want to ground my readers in my fictional world. It's as if I want them to jump right in and join the characters in action. I try to make sure that the opening scene captures some of the tension of the novel as well as introducing the main character and the setting. Of course, the tone gets established right away as well. Tall order for one scene!"

## Create conflict

"What I learned from writing and revising and selling *Watch Me Go*," says Wisniewski, "is that there should always be major conflict and development of plot. These two things should be in pretty much every sentence of the novel. So they'd darned better be in the opening lines."

"A good first page," says Brenna, "catches the reader's interest and makes him or her want to read on." And this means conflict, strongly suggested, if not dramatically played out. Brenna's *Too Cool* begins with vigorous dramatic action. His protagonist, a 16-year-old juvenile delinquent, is short on cash, his car is almost out of gas, and he's caught in the Rocky Mountains with a snowstorm on the way. There's no letup, says Brenna: "From the first paragraph on, it's one thing after another, boom, boom."

Do find a way to embed conflict, but it need not be action-oriented. It can reflect basic human discontent or disappointment, a rub or impediment. In *A Wedding in Provence*, says Sussman, the characters are on edge: "They want the French countryside, but they drive past ugly urban sprawl. All of this suggests the bigger fictional world to come." At the same time, as the novel proceeds, Sussman prepares the reader to view characters in a larger context.

Conflict is the engine that drives all fiction. In the case of genre fiction, readers may tend to have certain formulaic expectations about a novel's opening. With mystery novels, it is "helpful to open with a hint of trouble," says Craig. "The avid mystery reader is on the lookout for the story's victim, even at the start of the book. Readers are also keeping an eye out for the protagonist — the character they're supposed to identify with and experience the story world through." In a fantasy novel, there must also be a hint of trouble, but of a different kind. Readers should "know immediately that they have stepped into a world where they might encounter wonders, and also terrors," says Coe.

### Find the ending

As with openings, writing strong endings may take a discovery process. How do you know when to end your novel? "You don't," says Wisniewski, at least not right away. "Most published novelists I know don't. They write and write and write and revise and revise and revise. At some point, dozens of attempted endings later, they find themselves tweaking a final paragraph that just might possibly work."

The process can be arduous and exhausting. "I work as hard on my endings," says Brenna, "as I do on my openings. I will fiddle with the words until my eyes blur and my mind shuts down. I will read the last page over and over to see if I have overwritten it and left the heart-stop somewhere else. And frequently that is exactly what I've done." And then comes the necessary cutting, says Brenna: "I should have cut the last sentence or the last paragraph or page. I should have ended with the next to last chapter. Sometimes I get fortunate and the ending seems to write itself, and I know not to touch it. Only once in the eight books I've written has that lucky moment happened to me on the first draft." If characters sometimes experience epiphanies, writers struggling to resolve their novels perhaps can, too. For Brenna, knowing that ending, the *right* one, is on the order of an intuitive leap or grasp, accompanied by a joyful feeling of victory. "Endings can be endlessly frustrating, but you've got to work them until that 'Yes!' moment presents itself. When it happens, you'll know. You'll probably be smiling. And maybe you'll clench your fists, like a fighter who has knocked out his opponent. It's a moment of triumph."

For Coe, however, fantasy novel endings are actually easier than openings. "If I've plotted my narrative with enough care, the pieces fall in place rather neatly," he says. The process of discovery occurs incrementally over the writing of the whole novel, and it's like putting together a jigsaw puzzle. "The more pieces that are in place, the easier it is to fit in the next one, until at the end it all comes together very quickly," he says. An exception is a fantasy series, which is more difficult because you must know "which plot threads to tie up and which ones to leave at least somewhat unresolved for the next volume in the sequence."

### Tie up the conflicts

Endings are about "transformation," notes Sussman. "If the plot of the novel has successfully taken the character on a journey, then the end of the novel should hint at how that character has begun to change." This means a well-defined character arc driven by the novel's conflicts. "If the character isn't substantially affected by what's happened in a novel, then why tell that story?" asks Sussman. "The story, or plot, should be big enough and important enough to have the power to transform the main character."

Transformation is equally important to Coe. "My protagonist should be transformed in some way by all that's happened, and so should the world in which the books are set," he says. "Those transformations should cut both ways. My characters will have accomplished something of significance, but they also will have paid a price. It shouldn't simply be a matter of having pushed some sort of reset button and all is now butterflies and rainbows."

Given a novel's overall transformative movement, you must carefully consider any loose plot threads. This is certainly true of genre fiction. With the exception of fantasy novels in a series, Coe accounts for each of his numerous puzzle pieces and gets them locked neatly in place. Speaking of mysteries, Craig says, "The writer shouldn't leave the reader wondering regarding either plot or subplot. I feel good endings in mysteries tie up any loose ends: They shine light on the red herrings, connect the clues to the sleuth's deductions, and return the story's world to the idyllic state it was in at the start." Even with a series, says Craig, you have to "be careful about leaving too much unanswered at the end of the book. Otherwise, readers could get frustrated since the next book in the series could be as much as a year away."

But what about literary fiction? Should you make the reader work a little harder? Leave a few loose threads, add a little obscurity, perhaps close with a certain amount of ambiguity? Maybe with some indie presses, says Wisniewski, but not with commercial publishers. "If you want to write a novel that gets you a decent advance, embrace clarity and succeed and shine and excel within it — and do this all the way through your last word," he says. "Allow the narrative to end on its own terms and in the splendor of its voice. Perhaps, for your very last sentence, you might let your main character have one last surprising insight, or observe some detail loaded, at the plot's final moment, with thought-provoking meaning, so that the reader is both amazed and satisfied." A caution, though, about that final moment. "Whatever final bit you allow to shine, make sure it's from the soul of the story rather than yours, and deliver it smoothly and clearly, with a natural rhythm and in as few words as possible. The word 'wow' out of your reader's mouth is what you're striving for. Forget about typing 'The End.'"

It's worth emphasizing: Do not belabor the writing. Do not go on too long. "Often enough," says Brenna, "the ending is a few lines back, or a paragraph ago, or there on that penultimate page before you plunged on in hopes of something more uplifting. Avoid, avoid, avoid. I don't know of any axiom more penetrating than the one uttered by Isaac Babel that says 'No iron can stab the heart with such force as a period put just at the right place.' It is what all writers strive for, not a fade to white or a little lyrical thrill, but a conclusion that ties things up and feels inspired and leaves the author feeling he delivered what he promised."

Think of it this way — a good ending puts the final touches on a fine novel. It brings it all home. All the life you packed into your novel reverberates in the final moments. The opening captures the reader's interest; the closing makes it all worth it.

# Foreshadowing & Echoing

Writing fiction is a juggling act that requires you to keep several elements in the air at once. For instance, in a good work of fiction, characters undergo conflicts and change, developing in different ways and to different degrees. Readers should be able to trace the protagonist's overall character arc over the course of the story. As the plot develops, the short story or novel needs to build toward a final resolution that satisfies the reader and feels inevitable but not predictable.

Along the story's continuum, *foreshadowing* is instrumental in creating believable key events, especially the climactic one. "As a storyteller," says Barry Kitterman, author of *Baker's Boy*, "to make all the events of a story believable, my job is to go back to the early parts of the story and set everything up." Doing so, says Kitterman, avoids a *deus ex machina*, one that brings in "a big dramatic ending that hasn't been sufficiently set up."

While foreshadowing looks forward, *echoing* looks behind and reminds readers of what they've already seen, reinforcing a key element of a plot thread or a thematic idea. Both elements help knit a story together into a well-woven tapestry. Yet knowing the importance of each is one thing; handling them well is quite another. How do you avoid being too obvious? How many instances of foreshadowing or echoing should you include, and where?

## Being Too Obvious

When either foreshadowing or echoing are too apparent, they function like huge signposts in a piece of fiction. While we may want prominent signs in road travel, the enjoyment of reading a story can diminish when the writer intrudes with such obvious markers. Stephanie Cowell, author of four historical novels, cautions against "hammering it too much into the reader's mind."

Gary Fincke is author of thirty books of fiction, poetry, and nonfiction, including *Sorry I Worried You*, winner of the Flannery O'Connor Award for Short Fiction. About his most recent collection, *The Killer's Dog*, Fincke states that he doesn't think elements of foreshadowing and echoing are readily apparent in many of these stories. "I would like to think it's because they are there but not exposed until a close reading unearths them in the way that we discover significance in our lives." They are part of the overall design of the story, but it takes a critical eye to note and analyze the function of each.

How do you avoid being too obvious? One way, says Kitterman, is to "employ a little misdirection." For instance, in creating a prop detail that will serve a key role in plot development, try using a mix of different details so that, for the time being, the key detail will register "in a quiet corner of the reader's brain" and only be present "when the story requires it." The embedded detail will then make sense later, says Kitterman.

Fantasy writer Janice Hardy sneaks elements into the reader's subconscious "so they anticipate whatever emotion or event I want to prepare them for." At first glance, says Hardy, the reader may not pick up on the clue. "It's a hint of something that seems innocuous when they first see it, but then carries greater meaning or fits perfectly with something later." She cites as an example a scene from her fantasy novel *The Shifter*, in which her protagonist, Nya, returns home from work to discover she's been evicted from her boarding room. Hardy captures the moment in one, succinct line: "My door was pegged shut." This line plants a seed, Hardy believes, that will grow later in the reader's mind: "This one line foreshadows that she's about to lose all sense of safety and a place to run to. She's been kicked out, and no one will help her get back home. As the story continues, the number of 'safe places' for her dwindle."

Dropping in clues lightly, or "casually," as mystery writer Krista Davis puts it, helps avoid intrusive authorial sign posts. She cites an example from her novel *The Diva Serves High Tea*, in which a character is attacked in her home at night. "The victim spends the rest of the night with the protagonist. A friend hears about [the attack], looks around his house for a weapon ... and takes a decorative halberd with him to the protagonist's home. Of course, everyone makes fun of the halberd, but in light of the situation, it's soon forgotten." For Davis, it's best that this halberd is forgotten — temporarily, that is. "Because a halberd is unusual," she says, "readers will take note of it, but they're not likely to think about it afterward, as the story progresses. At the end of the book, the halberd makes a reappearance when a boy remembers seeing it and comes to the rescue with it when the protagonist is being attacked."

If you should avoid explicit, heavy-handed foreshadowing, you should do the same with echoing. There's no question that a story or novel ending that provides a well-turned echo has great value, says Kitterman. "Everyone loves a great last line. Everyone loves a final sentence or two that ties the story together, that brings the reader back to a beautiful moment, that moves the writing to the place where the story vibrates and becomes more than a story, becomes truth." But in an effort to end your story with stunning impact, you can overdo it, as Kitterman points out. "The danger here, as my old teacher Bill Kittredge used to say, is that it's easy to hit the nail right on the head, and hit it one time too many, really sink that nail a half inch into the sheetrock so nobody will ever miss what a terrific nail pounder you are." Achieving grandiose utterance comes at a price, then, if the echo comes on too strong. It cheats the reader of a rich sense of felt life. "The harder we strain to come up with the perfect last line — the perfect echo — the greater the danger the ending will feel forced," Kitterman says.

In considering this issue of the well-wrought closing echo, Kitterman looks back to a story he wrote some years ago, "In Dog Years." In this story, a little long-haired dog named Jack London dies midway through the story. "It was this loss," says Kitterman, "that started the main character down a road of a sad string of losses." These are substantive losses: his marriage, his job, and his prominent position in the community. At the end of the story, the protagonist offers a benediction for some young schoolchildren in his small town. Notice how Kitterman's closing line pulls everything together and also works in a subtle echo of the dog Jack London: "He hoped they would live contented and safe, with children of their own and dogs in their homes, celebrating one happy marriage per lifetime." With this "quiet reference to dogs," as Kitterman puts it, he is able to reinforce the role of Jack London, the dog, as emblematic of loss itself.

## Choosing the Number of Foreshadowing Instances

How many instances of foreshadowing are enough — or too much? Davis holds that one mention is usually sufficient. "If it's something that I feel might have been missed and is absolutely crucial to understanding the plot, then I might repeat it. But when you do that, you take the risk that you're signaling the importance of that item." Too much repetition risks, once again, that authorial signpost. If, in the service of plot, you need to provide this emphasis, do so, says Davis, but you're better off sticking to one mention.

Opinion varies on the ideal number of foreshadowing instances. Cowell says, "I think twice is enough, but it can be three times for foreshadowing. It's amazing how stronger things can register in a novel than they do in life. Since the reader expects everything on the page to have some meaning in the whole book, he or she will take it in and tuck it in her mind." Hardy follows the Rule of Three and says that each element of foreshadowing accomplishes a given goal: "The first mention is small, almost a throwaway detail that introduces the reader to whatever I want to foreshadow. The second mention connects it to the character in some way. The third mention is the payoff." For Hardy it's through these three instances that she can grab her readers emotionally and also assure believability: "I want the device to either create anticipation if I'm building toward an emotional payoff, or create a sense of inevitability if I'm creating a situation that needs to feel plausible." She knows she hasn't prepared her reader enough "when the details don't trigger the emotion I'm looking for in the reader." The number of times, if kept to three, isn't too much, Hardy says, unless one of the instances "shifts from a hint to a big neon sign saying, 'This is going to happen, wait for it.'" And so, a writer can be too obvious in two ways: in the manner of presenting the foreshadowing element, and in creating too many instances of foreshadowing, or, as Cowell puts it, in too obvious *hammering*.

## Where to Place Foreshadowing and Echoing

How do you determine *where*, exactly, to provide foreshadowing? Cowell uses it when she feels "the present scene is a little low on drama and wonder[s] if the reader's attention will drift." In Davis's murder mysteries, "something significant must happen in the beginning of the book to capture the attention of the reader before the murder." It's a matter of suspense — a mystery novel has to get the reader hooked early on. "That's the perfect time," says Davis, "to set up an incident that foreshadows what is to come. Additionally, you can mention weapons that might be used later or unusual behavior that will make more sense once your sleuth investigates."

Exactly where you put certain foreshadowing details is one question to consider, and the answer undoubtedly depends on the particular story or novel. How you *determine* where to put these foreshadowing details is quite another issue — a process question. Do you know in advance, or do you discover as you write where certain signals need to be placed?

For Kitterman, it's a matter of discovery. "I suppose," he says, "there must be some writers who, from the moment they begin a story, know exactly where it's going to end up." But Kitterman himself doesn't know, and, he says, "Everyone I've ever listened to has told me it's best for the writer *not* to assume she knows the ending of a story before she writes her way to that ending point." In fiction writing, for Kitterman, very little is nailed down, with unpredictable developments as he depends on his creative imagination. "If," as he says, "writing a story is a process of discovery, then any given story will make two or three unexpected moves along the way, and those unexpected moves will require the writer to go back later and do the work of dropping hints, making promises, leaving breadcrumbs for the reader to follow." For Kitterman, it's in the act of revision that one embeds any necessary foreshadowing details.

Hardy's process is akin to Kitterman's. "I don't typically plan my foreshadowing in advance. I let the story unfold during the first draft and then look for potential foreshadowing moments during revisions." For her, those foreshadowing moments tend to crop up in the initial draft, though in the revision stages substantive tweaking may be necessary. "Those elements tend to lurk in my subconscious, so they slip into a first draft all on their own," she says. "However, I *will* go back and revise to strengthen a scene that *would* work to foreshadow something. Often I don't see the perfect moment until I have the entire story written down."

We've already seen that an echo can come at the end of a story, providing a powerful reminder of its basic thrust. For Cowell, certain works may also call for echoing at various intervals in order to develop the plot as well as the theme: "In my novel *Claude & Camille: A Novel of Monet*, I keep echoing the theme of his water lily paintings and what they mean to him. As the book progresses, we understand that though Monet has lost his wife tragically when she was still young, he always has tried to find her essence in the water lily pond. Finally he has a dream that she is *in* the pond, and he goes splashing in it in the middle of the night calling for her. It's a scene I'm proud of in a book that was not easy to write."

Echoing can also serve a third function. In her fantasy novels, Hardy makes use of echoing in creating plot and thematic parallels. Echoing serves as the wheelhouse of the novel, the engine that drives her whole fictional universe, which is characterized by moral ambiguity. "I enjoy playing with ethical questions and gray areas," says Hardy, "and echoes work quite well here. I'll pose an ethical question such as 'How many bad things can you do and still be a good person?' and show how the various characters in the book will answer that question. Those individual choices illustrate how blurry the line is, and how there is no right or wrong answer." Hardy works consciously, but not forcibly, to create these echoes that unify a given fantasy novel, reinforcing examples of the theme and rounding out the emotional notes of the character arcs.

Foreshadowing and echoing are indispensable plot and structure devices. Yet one can overmanage them and turn them into glaring, too-obvious signposts that deny the reader the experience of felt life that fiction should provide. When they are labored or heavy handed, both are akin to the writer addressing the reader directly. As with most other aspects of fiction, subtlety is usually the best approach.

# Deriving Theme from Character and Plot

Any number of stories with different plots may have the same basic theme. We might say, "This story is about courage in the face of adversity." Or "This story is about mercy over justice." Or "This story is about reason gone mad." But does every story need a theme? Not necessarily, but most stories, if they're unified, have a theme, though it may not be as complex or as developed as the themes we find in literary fiction. The key to creating theme lies in knowing which story elements contribute to it, and how. Character, plot, setting, language (especially if it's metaphorical or analogical), and symbolism all contribute to the richness of theme. In fact, many writers must develop these elements first and then pull theme from them — or, at least, theme *emerges* from them.

## Creating Themes and Ideas

Let's say you begin your story or novel with a theme or idea in mind, hoping to empower your work with considerable range and depth. You're heavily invested in your thematic idea, and you want to make this theme quite evident so that the reader won't miss it. You're not intending to be didactic — you know good literature isn't — but you do want a work that is more than "a mere story." You want levels of abstraction that make this piece of fiction "real" literature. Should you go for it? Should you attack the creative process with a given theme in mind? Some top literary writers discourage it.

For Walter Cummins, co-publisher of Serving House Books and author of several story collections, this approach "invites the imposition of a heavy hand." Instead, he suggests allowing thematic ideas to come on their own, emerging "from the germ of a situation, character conflicts, and active scenes." When Cummins writes, he focuses on the "dramatic situation" and its resolution, his primary goal being "to come up with the right ending and to make that ending convincing." Once he's able to accomplish this, he states, "Whatever theme emerges from the ending is a shorthand simplification of what the story actually conveys."

Gladys Swan, author of four novels and seven collections of short stories, also avoids approaching her work with a theme in mind. Doing so, she says, "tends to make the story seem contrived or to make the theme obvious." Like Cummins, she believes that themes and ideas must emerge from both characters and plot. First she must come up with the right characters; she doesn't necessarily have them in mind. To get started, she draws inspiration from several things: "an image, an incident, a bit of interesting behavior, a chance remark, all of which I find the need to explore." Characters eventually come, and once they do, Swan says, "I can shape things, selecting what best serves the emerging unity of the piece." From this unity emerge the themes and ideas that inform a given story, but she doesn't try to put them into an abstract statement. They should be apparent to any perceptive reader, she thinks, in the various interstices and dynamics of the story.

For short story writer and novelist Jack Remick, themes must come out of character. Yet he first makes sure he isn't manipulating his characters. Once he has a character in mind, he engages in an exercise he calls "The Time Walk-Back": "I pick up the character, say, five minutes before the story opens. I don't know what the story is yet, but that's okay: [then I look at] my character ... one hour before ... one week before ... one year before ... five years before." Doing this exercise allows Remick to discover all kinds of things about his protagonist and other characters — "who they are, what they do, what they want" — before he allows them to speak because, he says, "when they do speak, you're sort of eavesdropping instead of making up stuff." Meanwhile, he interrogates his characters, attempting to discover "what Claude Lévi-Strauss calls 'polarities.'" Polarities include such opposites as: "open/closed; thick/thin; rich/poor; raw/cooked." These polarities, says Remick, serve not only a character-based function but a plot-based one as well: "The polarities lead to story arcs, and story arcs lead to character change and plot tracks. A plot track can be built on a character, an object, or an action." On their own steam, then, Remick's characters lead him to "plot tracks" that hint at one or more possible themes in a story or novel.

Emphasizing character as the locus of theme, Dennis Must, author of two novels and three story collections, states that he follows Faulkner's dictum. Faulkner once advised, "I would say to get the character in your mind. Once he is in your mind, and he is right, and he's true, then he does the work himself." For Must, theme and character are "mutually dependent." The true character, says Must, "invariably carries a story's theme inside his ineluctable heart." But there's more: To avoid the obvious, the writer must be "keenly sensitive to a character's inherent dualities and ambivalence." It's in these dualities that we'll find a theme suggested in Must's work.

Though Stephanie Dickinson, author of several books of fiction, works consciously in the revision stage by "editing and sculpting," she also makes certain that any themes that emerge in her work spring naturally out of the dramatic conflict of characters. For this conflict, she relies on "*hot-button* material or subject matter" about teenage girls, "the impulsive, rebellious years when choices can lead to mistakes that last a lifetime." With this firm foundation in dramatic action, she can avoid being heavy-handed with thematic ideas, no matter how ruthlessly she wields the revision pen. "As many threads as you can pull together," says Dickinson, "with almost the precision of needle-work, the stronger the writing, the more evocative."

Beyond the wellsprings of dramatic conflict, Dickinson also depends on "the textures of place, the light and dark shadings of a scene, in some ways a cinematic approach to thematic concept." With this highly visual method, she depends on specific details as well as the accretion of these details to suggest theme. Dickinson tries to unify the story around a central focus, working to "tie up loose ends or cut them, heightening those perceptions that evoke emotion and meaning."

## Handling Specific Themes in Fictional Works

As we've discussed, it may be risky to begin your fictional process with a given theme in mind. Instead, as you write early drafts, allow your characters and plot to unfold, letting thematic ideas come about naturally. They will certainly come, says Dickinson: "Gurus of how to write well tell us good storytelling will have a theme even if the writer hasn't consciously imposed one." It's a matter of letting it happen. The more you explore your characters and conflict, the more it's bound to happen.

It happened for Dickinson in *Love Highway*. Based loosely on the 2006 Jennifer Moore murder, her novel is a "duet for two voices: two Manhattan girls, one a murder victim and the other a passive perpetrator, each narrating authentically their half of the book." In writing this novel, Dickinson wanted to "explore and somehow understand this collision of the different worlds inhabited by two young women close in age." Of course, real-life events are only the springboard for fiction; it's what the writer does with the material that counts. Using stream of consciousness, Dickinson focused on the interior of her characters, peering deeply into their hearts and minds. As she did so, she discovered compelling intersections between them, suggesting parallel transformations that pointed to levels beyond the surface of character and plot. According to Dickinson, "Those plot-points of transformation where the girls most echoed each other in their perceptions and passions, becoming almost interchangeable, were freighted with thematic meaning." The themes in the novel are many, says Dickinson, dealing with sins of commission as well as omission. It was in the revision process that she felt at liberty to hone these themes: "Some points I emphasized by slowing the pacing of the action. Others I enlarged with dialogue and moments of epiphany, and then I stitched them back into the whole." Though she refined her material, she did stay clear of authorial intrusion: "I wanted to withhold judgment and allow the characters to reveal themselves." For Dickinson, fiction writing is a two-part process: in early drafts, she achieves a firm foundation in dramatic conflict; then, in revision, she refines any suggested ideas or themes.

Also in the revision stage, Dickinson refines theme through her cinematic approach. In *Love Highway*, her chiaroscuro added thematic texture to both characters and setting: "The two girls, victim and perpetrator, were profoundly connected as if Siamese twins caught between the Walks and Don't Walks, the millions of lit windows turning themselves off, letting the warehouses of grimy brick and scarecrow water towers do the looking out." Again, while Dickinson felt at liberty to explore the novel's language for its thematic possibilities, she remained faithful to the characters who had sprung full-blown from the drafting process.

If themes tend to stem naturally from the nexus of character and plot, sometimes a writer must depend on a process of discovery to unveil these two key story elements. In her story "The Old Hotel," Swan had neither characters nor plot in mind. All she had was a basic starting point: a striking image of an elaborate Victorian hotel in New Mexico. When she was thirteen and toured this hotel, it was no longer in use. Thirty years later, says Swan, this hotel "was completely gone from the desert landscape stretching away to the distant mountains." A sense of profound change moved Swan to write about the hotel. She worked with what she had: "I wrote about twenty drafts of a description of the hotel. Then the characters finally appeared." They were occupants of this mysterious hotel, once elaborately furnished: "Jack Whedon, a spineless and incompetent sort slickered into buying the hotel; his wife, Penny, hard-nosed and self-serving; and Jewel, their teenage daughter." Added to this family were two others: "Viny, a childlike, loving young woman, and a former music teacher with a mysterious past, who has come from Europe. Both have come to live at the hotel." Once she became immersed in the storytelling, Jewel became her focus. "The Old Hotel" soon became "a coming-of-age story with the time-honored themes of innocence and experience." But other characters also declared themselves and introduced the theme of illusions, including deception of "both self and others." Swan didn't impose these themes from without — they emerged in the telling. As she states it, "These motifs emerged as I wrote the story, coming from the interactions of the characters, who are not based on anyone I've ever known."

However you arrive at character, you should consider it, alongside conflict, as the wheelhouse of your story or novel. For Must, it's in the "ineluctable heart" of the protagonist where we find a story's theme and the possibility for universal, existential conflicts. In Must's "Dry Bread and Turnip Soup," the theme turns on the issue of personal identity. The protagonist, Peter Eckerd, is forced to question who he really is when his wife and her male companion strip him of everything that has defined him, including his library full of books, his manuscripts, and his clothes. Though he has admitted to accumulating too much, the wholesale carting away of his familiar possessions has caused him to wonder if he ever existed. By story's end, realizing that he surely must, by now, be a stranger to his wife, he opts for the guestroom. Yet Peter Eckerd soon becomes ambivalent, drawn between two personae. Says Must, the character "felt enlightened, for he realized he'd been an accomplice in perpetuating a static *I*. He'd become prisoner of his dormant self." On the other hand, he wishes to continue being his former self, hoping his wife will invite him back to her bedside. And thus, typical of Must's characters, Peter's duality provokes important existential questions such as "What is the nature of identity?" "What makes us who we are?" "Do we have a fixed or permanent self?" The story's theme is embodied in the questions themselves, not in pat answers.

If theme is not contrived by the author, it can give a work of literature much substance, as it does in Must's story. But it's possible, too, that a particular theme might not be quite as important as the literary devices that develop it. For instance, in Remick's *Gabriela and the Widow*, the theme is a familiar one of character transformation. While an important theme, Remick believes that his literary technique, his "structural scheme of polarities," commands the most attention. The novel's *spine*, as he calls it, is based on certain key polarities — in this case, *thick* versus *thin*. "This polarity," says Remick, "has a multitude of transforms, each transform linked to an object." For example, when Gabriela is first introduced to the reader, she represents *thin*: skinny, barefoot, in indigenous garb. But at the end of the novel she is *thick*, having come into the many material possessions of the rich Widow. Gabriela's plot track, says Remick, is represented by a "clothing arc" that represents her overall "psychological, physical, and financial transformation" in the novel. Remick's character and plot mechanisms gain more prominence than does the theme itself. The theme is important, but it's the symbolic handling of Remick's organizing polarities that mostly, he believes, grabs the reader's attention.

As interesting and compelling as theme can be, a good story, Cummins believes, cannot be reduced to it. There is so much more: all the felt experiences that radiate in it. In one of his recently published stories, "Celebrities," Cummins drew upon memories of a house in Brooklyn Heights where he'd lived as a young man of twenty-one. He recalled three of the tenants: a fledgling actor, a boat design hobbyist, and a young woman who met famous people at airports. "The characters that emerged from these real people were wannabe celebrities," says Cummins. But he went beyond these three characters to invent his protagonist, who "ghost-writes songs for a star and gets no recognition." Given the thrust of the story, Cummins states, "I suppose the theme that emerged was the shallowness of fame. But that is a cliché. Many, perhaps most, themes are. Stories have to be satisfying in themselves, much more interesting than the themes they can be reduced to." Even so, to develop this theme, Cummins says, "I had to invent character conflicts and, after several revisions, developed one between the actor and the protagonist. But what would be the ending, the climactic scene?" The ending scene is what Cummins depends on for his "shorthand simplification" to carry an idea. It has to be believable, convincing. He struck on the following: "I had the others in the building gather to watch the actor's last-minute appearance on a late-night talk show. He makes a fool of himself. Then I had to work out in a much-revised final paragraph how the protagonist reacts to his rival's humiliation. What does his action reveal about his own insight into his relationship with fame?" Cummins sees the theme of shallowness as only part of the story's fictional worth: "The story turns out to be about one man's unique response to that theme, which is more complicated than the theme itself." The story was nominated for a Pushcart.

### Developing Themes in Your Own Work — What the Pros Say

♦ **Read widely.** For Gladys Swan, appreciating themes and ideas in literature calls for reading beyond contemporary fiction to the classics, ancient drama, and poetry, as well as nonfiction: "History, psychology, science, and the arts, as well as literature, and whatever else interests you in the world around you."

♦ **Don't start with something to say.** "In my teaching experience," says Walter Cummins, "many beginning writers think they should have something important to say. Few writers do." What makes successful fiction, for Cummins, is not a particular theme but how theme is expressed, which calls for "characters and plots that engage and move us, and provide a sense of the complexity of human existence."

♦ **Feel the pulse that draws you in emotionally as well as intellectually.** "As I approach a narrative," says Dennis Must, "its pulse must arouse in me an acute sense of vulnerability or personal risk as to how the work may unfold." On the intellectual level, he says, "I also know that the effort will resolve itself ambiguously."

♦ **Find the *spine*, or key governing principle of the story**. "Unfortunately," says Jack Remick, "the spine always comes late in the writing. I would say that the writer has to wait for the story to reveal its spine. Some writers call it the *armature*."

♦ **Write flash fiction to understand theme as a unifying idea.** According to Stephanie Dickinson, "View the paragraph as a world-building exercise. It is a perfect structure with a beginning, a middle, and an end."

## Final Thoughts

Theme is the "unifying idea" of a story or novel. But be careful about approaching a work of fiction with a particular unifying idea in mind. You can do so, but as you write, be sure to let it hover somewhere up in the stratosphere, and focus on getting down into the dust of your characters' lives, into everything that makes them fully human. After all, if you want your themes or ideas to hook your reader, they will do so only through lively, flesh-and-blood characters, ones that seem so real they can step right off the page. Abstract ideas, though they can be quite compelling to contemplate, won't drive fiction. It's felt life that does this.

# Part III
# Some Story Challenges

# Writing Authentic Dialogue

Great fiction almost always includes great dialogue. As with drama we get to know characters by what they say and by what others say about them. If the dialogue is flat, the characters will be flat. If the dialogue seems off, or not believable, or real, we won't trust the characters as authentic beings. Grant Tracey, author of three story collections and editor of the *North American Review*, emphasizes the importance of dialogue in solid character development: "Dialogue is about giving characters space to breathe, to step out from the author's controlling voice to speak from a real authentic place of their own. Through dialogue characters are at their most autonomous and free." It's this distinct speaking voice, in the larger context of the story's narrative voice, that fiction writers need to master.

Writing dialogue of course presents many challenges, especially to authors whose characters tend to come from diverse backgrounds. Speech patterns vary from region to region of the country — and the world. Characters from different ethnic groups and social classes speak differently. Different trades have their own jargon. To create authentic characters and authentic sounding dialogue, writers can sometimes depend on their own background or experience, at other times on research of various kinds, and imaginative powers.

## Region and Culture

Robert Garner McBrearty, winner of the Sherwood Anderson Foundation Fiction Award, likes "doing 'Texans.'" He grew up with that language on his "ear and mind" and has a feel for handling the regional speech patterns. Still, he emphasizes, there's some skill involved — you have to make sure you don't overdo it. As an example he cites his story "Episode," the title story of his winning collection, which has a "distinct Texas flavor in the dialogue." The language is "fairly subtle," says McBrearty. "They don't sound like a bunch of hicks."

When it comes to handling regional dialect, Catherine Brady, co-winner of the 2002 Flannery O'Connor Award for Short Fiction and author of *Story Logic and the Craft of Fiction*, emphasizes that the writer has "to develop an ear — to be alert for the idiosyncratic qualities of speech and to respect them." She warns against such variant spellings as "I lak to be goin'" for "I like to be going" — word corruptions that are "implicitly condescending" as well as "sloppy." What's needed instead, says Brady, is a close attention to "the syntax and expressions that characterize a particular dialect or slang."

Steven Wingate, winner of the Bakeless Prize for his collection *Wifeshopping*, spots one thing writers tend to ignore about dialect — overall characterization: For one thing, says Wingate, writers need to attend to "body language, which can reveal a great deal about how a character communicates." And they should keep this principle in mind: "If a character is rendered well overall, dialect or jargony speech patterns will be easier to do — and more effective in small doses — because characterization doesn't depend so much on them."

Handling dialect well is one thing; making it fully accessible to your readers is another. Josh Weil, like McBrearty, has a close familiarity with his subject — the Appalachian south — along with the speech patterns or dialect of its inhabitants. Yet the challenge for Weil has been how to make the Appalachian dialect harmonize well with the rest of the narrative. In the first two novellas of *The New Valley*, which won the Sue Kaufman Prize for First Fiction, Weil connects dialect and speech inflections tonally with narrative voice. "So the rhythms and patterns and musicality of the way people speak in the mountains crept organically into the voice in the narration." At first glance, this may not seem all that important, says Weil, yet it is: "It creates a subtle connection between the music of the narrator and the musicality of the characters' speech." This tonal harmony between character speech and narrative voice "eases the reader into a more easy acceptance of the dialect in dialogue."

The writer's challenge might be how to handle dialect in another country, in a completely different culture. Midge Raymond, author of the prize-winning *Forgetting English*, drew on her experience living in Taiwan to write her title story, which required a strong sense for

Chinese speech patterns. Had she not lived and traveled throughout Asia, she wouldn't have known, for instance, which English words native Chinese speakers have problems with pronouncing and which articles (a, the, etc.), they regularly leave out of English sentences. Since she was learning Chinese at the time, Raymond says, this enhanced her understanding of Chinese speech patterns.

Yet authors sometimes have neither direct experience — at least not the sustained kind that Midge Raymond had — nor geographical or cultural roots to draw on. Yet a particular character they're introducing requires that they write outside their own language background. Doing this will take "comprehensive research," Catherine Brady states, "but it comes in the form of talking and listening rather than reading." Ellen Sussman, author of both nonfiction and fiction, most recently the novel *French Lessons*, says: "When I'm trying to learn a new voice, I try every possible way to first hear those voices. I'll rent movies where the characters speak that dialect. I'll find YouTube videos with characters from that world." David Hubbard, a short story writer from Carlsbad, California, even makes trips to different areas of the country to listen to the way people talk to each other. But as we've seen, getting a sense of the regional dialect, while absolutely necessary, is only the beginning. The rest is putting it into play — and not overdoing it.

## Ethnicity

Carolina De Robertis, author of the prize-winning *The Invisible Mountain*, speaks of the "added challenges" writers face in writing outside their own cultural or ethnic background. "There is the potential danger of falling into stereotypes — especially when the cultural group we're writing about is historically marginalized. There is plenty of bad writing, and even decent writing, that falls into this trap." Ethnic stereotypes need to be avoided, says De Robertis. "Stereotypes are not only sociopolitically problematic; they also bleed the vitality from fiction." This second result alone, De Robertis believes, should prompt writers to be sure their characters reflect as much "complex humanity as possible" — and dialogue plays a critical part in characterization.

It's this complex humanity that Irina Reyn, the Russia-born author of *What Happened to Anna K,* respects as she writes ethnic characters, and in her case it means opting for "very little dialect." She wants to develop her characters fully as individuals. "I usually allow speech patterns, tone and voice to guide presentation of a character," says Reyn. "I am very sensitive to the dangers of representing otherness."

So is Joe Benevento, author of *The Odd Squad,* a finalist for the John Gardner Fiction Book Award. Benevento believes that accurately representing slang, dialect, and words peculiar to a given ethnicity is quite important. He feels comfortable, he says, doing a Cuban store owner as well as an Italian-American grandmother but not a Cajun character since he lacks the sufficient firsthand experience to do so. But from what Benevento has seen, his own emphasis on verisimilitude is surprisingly not shared by a lot of agents, editors, and readers. For Italian-American language, for example, most people, says Benevento, seem to be ignorant of certain linguistic nuances, as when Mickey Rourke's supposedly Italian-American character in *The Pope of Greenwich Village* responds to the question *"Capisc?"* ("You understand?") with the ridiculous response *"Capisc"* ("You understand") instead of *"Capisco"* ("I understand"). As for fiction, "I've rarely seen working class dialogue done right — Italian Americans are always stereotyped, even though not all of us are Mafia wannabes, and the other dialects I also know about, Latino, black, Jewish, etc., are also usually botched. But it doesn't seem to matter." Why is this? Benevento explains that a "veneer of verisimilitude" is apparently enough if readers are sufficiently hooked by the characters and plot. Yet this is problematic for Benevento, who holds that writers who ignore verisimilitude create ethnic stereotypes and "botched" representations of ethnicity of several kinds.

Midge Raymond also believes dialogue should be accurately represented. She avoids writing dialogue for a given ethnic group unless she's sure she "can get it right." While extensive research might conceivably work, Raymond does believe the best way to capture the dialect of ethnic groups outside one's own is immersion: "hearing voices firsthand." But what if you can't gain such firsthand experience? There is one resource to consider, as a second option, says Raymond: the Library of Congress' Center for Applied Linguistics Collection has recorded 118 hours of audio documenting North American English dialects, and this is available online (http://memory.loc.gov/ammem/collections/linguistics).

One controversial issue that sometimes arises is whether or not a writer not of a given ethnicity even has a *right* to create a character from an ethnic background not the writer's own. Writers are sometimes criticized for doing this, just as male writers are sometimes criticized for creating women protagonists. Cliff Garstang, author of the award-winning *In an Uncharted Country* and editor of *Prime Number Magazine*, calls such criticism "ridiculous." For him, "A fiction writer is free to assume any identity he or she needs to for the purpose of telling a story; the only obligation is to do it well, and that's a whole other challenge."

## Social Class

DeWitt Henry, founder of *Ploughshares*, came from an upper middle class background, certainly not the working class that he wrote about in his novel *The Marriage of Anna Maye Potts*, winner of the inaugural Peter Taylor Prize for the Novel. Yet, growing up, Henry did have a good deal of exposure to different social classes and ethnic groups, including working class idiom and speech patterns. For his novel he was able to draw on this fund of language experience. The question for Henry was how to do it well.

"A primary focus for me," says Henry, "in writing *The Marriage of Anna Maye Potts*, was to translate articulate perceptions into the vocabularies and idioms of my characters." Since each character was quite different, Henry found this to be "painstaking, slow work." He found himself initially writing speech/thought in his "own literary vocabulary," then struggling for a "translation, which was sometimes silence and gesture and sometimes vernacular and cliché." The right technique comes, Henry believes, from developing "an ear" or "an eye" — and this takes a regular regimen, which he likens to the rigors of an athlete's training.

While Robert Garner McBrearty has sometimes depended on his

Texas roots, he's also done informal "field research" such as watching movies, TV, and the news to create working class characters. Working different jobs and eavesdropping on the way working class people talk has been one avenue that has really paid off. Then the challenge is to get these characters down in writing. McBrearty tends to start from just a little and take it from there, relying on his imaginative powers. "The idea is sort of like if one gets a little piece of the character, then the writer goes to work filling the character out." Once McBrearty gets that first line down, he's usually able to "tap into the way the person speaks" — that is, if he writes from "inside the character" versus "planting dialogue in someone's mouth." On the whole, he does feel more comfortable creating characters he's familiar with, and yet he's seen successes with material gained from eavesdropping too.

## Historical Fiction

The issue of realistic speech, along with dialect, naturally arises in historical fiction. But here the reach of years, when the writer goes deeply into the past, can present an additional problem. How does one obtain all the linguistic information one needs? And then, how does one handle it?

Edmund White is the author of many commercial press works of fiction, including *Fanny: A Fiction*, set in the pre-Civil War period, and based on the life of Fanny Trollope, mother of the famous novelist, Anthony Trollope. In this work White includes a runaway black slave named Jupiter Higgins. To handle Higgins with authenticity, he did extensive research, reading "slave narratives and fiction written before 1900 in which there were black characters." He didn't read "any technical linguistic studies on black speech of that period," but White says he would have if he'd come across them at the British Library, where he conducted his research. He did skim hundreds of books there. As far as Jupiter Higgins' speech patterns and dialect, White notes that he "had him quote from the Bible, from hymns and from the oratory of preachers." White did have one distinct advantage. He could draw on his growing up in the South, where he picked up the speech patterns of Southern Blacks, including "their ways of emphasizing a word and many of their vocabulary choices."

As with contemporary regional dialect, handling dialect in historical fiction can be quite demanding. In *The Circus in Winter*, some of which takes place before the Civil War, Cathy Day sought to capture her characters' voices "accurately, but not literally" — a difficult balance to achieve. With her novel-in-progress, set in the Gilded Age, Day faces new challenges. "How did people of that cultural milieu speak?" For answers, she's been doing considerable research: reading Edith Wharton, the first edition of Emily Post's *Etiquette*, and the society pages of *The New York Times*. The tone, as well as the vocabulary of this Edwardian era, is quite different from our own, Day points out, and she hopes to get a firm handle on "the lilt and cadences and rhythms of those voices." Day doesn't believe she needs to cover every base, though, just a few "dated phrases, old-timey words" — just enough to make her characters' speech sound real.

Josh Weil has wrestled with black slave dialect in his new novella *Solarium*. He feels comfortable with white southern dialect, picking this up from neighbors in Virginia. Handling slave dialect, however, has called for a lot of research. He finds this dialect "fascinating and wonderful and full of music." As a result, he says, "for a long time, I stuck to my guns, writing the first person slave sections in full-bore slave dialect." Yet this dialect led to problems: first, the difficulty of reading it; second, the fact that it was so "overpowering" that it caused readers to focus "on the way the words sounded instead of what they were saying." So Weil reduced the amount of dialect and left just enough that the dialect now adds to, versus detracts from, the story. In the current version of his novella, it isn't used in first person narration, but only "when a narrator is relaying the speech of *others*." This technique makes the slave dialect easier for the reader to accept, Weil believes.

## Workplace Jargon

Ellen Sussman has eavesdropped for a few days at a time at a garage in order to pick up "mechanic talk." To pick up jargon she believes you have to be in the language as much as possible: "The research is best when it's real immersion — then we can find our way to characters who really speak the language."

Once one's gathered the material, again the question is: how do you handle it? With jargon this means finding a way not to explain it.

For Grant Tracey it has to be "real, natural sounding." To make sure this happens, Tracey says: "Whatever job a character has let the dialogue reflect the milieu of their environment without worrying about explaining what they're talking about to readers outside that environment. Trust readers to get it through context." John Yunker, author of *The Tourist Trail*, solved the issue of exposition in his environmental novel by introducing outsiders to the world of penguin naturalists and animal activists so that the characters pick up the jargon themselves. This technique helped him avoid "overtly painful exposition."

## Taking the Challenge

As we've seen, sometimes you can depend on your background or experience when writing regional or ethnic speech patterns, or dialect, or group jargon, but you may need to do research if you lack the needed background. But wouldn't you be wise simply to avoid dealing with characters outside your own ethnic, cultural, or language background? Wouldn't that be playing it safe? Why risk being "off"?

Catherine Brady urges writers to take the challenge: "It's actually hard for me to imagine an American writer whose social world is so insular that s/he never encounters other dialects or speech patterns, and I also think that dialect and slang and regional (or even generational) speech patterns enrich dialogue — they're its 'poetic rhythm.' So I would encourage any writer to try to render differences in speech pattern while always remembering that s/he's not trying to create a sociologically accurate composite but a believable individual."

Mark Wisniewski, author of *Confessions of a Polish Used Car Salesman*, also sees a problem with writerly insularity, especially when it leads to autobiographical fiction: "I recommend using dialect that's not your own. It forces you out of your own manner of speaking and encourages you to write about characters unlike yourself. Semi-autobiographical (and certainly autobiographical) work, as most fiction editors will tell you, is often mundane, probably because the ego clouds the writer's perception of what engages the average reader. Anyway the use of dialect can keep you from falling into the I'm-so-interesting trap."

Skip Horack, author of the historical novel *The Eden Hunter*, reminds us of an important truth: If writers had always avoided certain kinds of characters, there would be "a whole lot of great fiction that never would have been written."

# He Said, She Said: Writing Strong Dialogue

To write great fiction, you must be able to create complex, memorable characters, engaging plots, and vivid settings. You must also be able to create scenes that move, ones that aren't labored or dull. Unless you're writing narrative scenes, this means handling dialogue — and handling it well. When dialogue is rich with energy, characters come alive on the page. The various complexities of the human being are made manifest in what is stated as well as in what is left unsaid — and in the apparent motives behind both speech and silence. It takes some doing to pull all of this off, but that's what it takes to write great dialogue.

## The Process of Writing Dialogue

Like every other aspect of fiction writing, crafting strong dialogue calls for a process. For T.C. Boyle, award-winning author of fifteen novels and ten short story collections, this process is mostly an unconscious one. He doesn't intentionally set out to energize his dialogue. "It just happens in its own energetic way," he says. "Usually it rides along with me in the way that narration does. All happens in the unconscious spell that overtakes a writer in the flow of composition." Novelist Amanda Filipacchi reports the same experience in drafting her dialogue. "It's something that comes naturally to me and requires very little conscious effort or calculation."

Of course, plenty of authors prepare to write dialogue by doing some field work. Virgil Suárez, author of several novels and story collections, regularly attunes himself to the various ways people speak. "I like to eavesdrop on conversations, and there are plenty of contemporary places where you can go and do exactly that and no one would notice you sitting there taking it all in." But when it comes to the actual writing, for Suárez this is largely intuitive: "It comes in a variety of ways, sometimes even in sleep. I also hear it as I am writing. The lines that come to me often evolve out of a character's need to speak, to be heard. It also comes from watching characters move from scene to scene. What would they say to themselves?"

All this is nonrational, a matter of feel. And yet Suárez has noticed a set of consistent features that energize his dialogue. Banter is an important one. "I am a big believer in banter between characters ... as it is a way to create dynamic tension through the way the characters speak." Suárez also plays with the margins between silence and sound. "Always present is the idea that silence is often much better for drama than dialogue itself. I like to punctuate my scenes with lots of quiet banter and have plenty of second-level (daily life noise) action going on in the background. My characters never speak in a vacuum; there's always something going on either in their minds or in their setting." Banter, silence, sound — these elements tend to pattern Suárez dialogue, elements engrained after years of writing, modulated to meet the needs of each new story or novel. It's his stamp of originality.

Originality is also important to Filipacchi, and for her this means avoiding the predictable. "Dialogue that foils readers' expectations, even in small and subtle ways, can arouse your readers' curiosity and make them pay closer attention. Misunderstandings and misinterpretations between characters can bring entertainment and stress to the reader — two forms of beneficial energy in fiction."

The more you write dialogue, the more you just let it happen, *listening* to your characters speak, you will probably discover your own distinctive approach: energized by the beat or rhythm of your characters' words, their utterances as well as silences, their back-and-forth, their complex, rich voices. Let loose your imagination, your intuitive side. Don't engineer your dialogue. If you force anything, it will come off as fake and inauthentic.

And yet there is always revision. Rethinking, redoing. Like every other element in fiction, you must, at some point, turn a critical eye to your dialogue and demand more of it. Does it reveal character? Does it reveal conflict? Will it keep the reader's interest?

For award-winning short story writer Laura van den Berg, revision strategies come down to several key questions: "Where is the tension? Where is the arc? What is happening underneath the surface?" As she reviews her dialogue, Van den Berg pays special attention to this latter issue. "It's crucial to think about what's crackling beneath the surface — where is the subtext? The layers? What is the end game for this conversation for the narrator? What does she want in this moment? These under-layers are a huge part of what brings energy to dialogue."

## Consistency of Tone and Character

To zero in on tone, you must capture the core of who your character *is*, his or her sensibility, and so forth. Capturing your character's essential nature takes an imagination that grasps what it's like to be another human being. It requires the writer to get outside herself — to experience empathy. John Keats called it negative capability.

Filipacchi says that, like an actor or actress, you must imagine yourself "in the skin" of your character. You must be aware of both personality and mood. "What kinds of remarks would that personality, in its current mood, utter at that moment? How would that personality and mood react to what has just been said to him or her?" As she writes, Filipacchi automatically asks these questions about all of her characters.

If you haven't pegged the right tone for your character in your initial drifts, do so in the revision stages. For Suárez, getting the tone just right ultimately calls for careful analysis. He tries to match behavior and mannerisms with language — is it a good fit? Additionally, says Suárez, character speech should reflect age, time, place, and thoughts and concerns. "The best trick is always to read the line out loud, play pretend. Block the scene the way a playwright might do it." As she revises, Van den Berg also analyzes tone with several criteria in mind. "I think a lot about tics and patterns and habits of speech — is this a polite voice? A voice that curses a lot or is partial to clichés or puns or bad jokes? This can be a way of getting a feel for a voice and distinguishing character."

T. C. Boyle states, "I don't typically work with accents or speech patterns, so it's just a matter of imagining what a developing character might sound like in a given situation." He cites as an example the narrator of *The Inner Circle*, John Milk, an acolyte of Alfred C.

Kinsey, the sex researcher. Milk, Boyle notes, "speaks and writes formally, a function of his shyness and uncertainty." Milk's formality is also established in his thoughts, his interior language. He tends to stumble when speaking, with a hesitancy, a sense of unease, which characterizes his speech throughout the novel.

## Breaking with Dialogue Convention

If you break with the traditional method of handling dialogue (double quotation marks), you need a purpose for doing so — don't break convention merely to be fashionable or trendy. As Boyle points out, "The trend lately has been to dispense with quotation marks, but trends by their very nature tend to give way to other trends, which inevitably loop back to standard procedure. Another way to look at it: Each story, each novel, finds its own mode of expression, which may or may not be reflected formally."

"Sometimes," says Boyle, "I dispense with quotation marks as a way (ask old Bill Faulkner) of total immersion, but generally I do use them for the sake of clarity." Most of the time Suárez sticks with quotation marks, too, though he did find reason to break with the standard method in his second novel, *Latin Jazz*. "I had a whole cast of characters to worry about, so I used different punctuation marks for the dialogue to signal which character was speaking." Van den Berg follows convention, but, she says, "I can think of many stories in which breaking the traditional standards is very effective — when you're trying to dissolve the barrier between thought and speech, for example."

And this is exactly what Filipacchi did in her first novel, *Nude Men*. "I wanted my main character to have imaginary conversations with his cat. I had to decide whether or not to use quotation marks for those conversations. I decided against it, in order to convey that those conversations are taking place in his head." We hear the narrator speak; we hear the cat speak. This is dialogue, but it's imaginary dialogue. Dropping the double quotation marks meets Filipacchi's purpose. It's not willy-nilly, and it's not employed merely to latch onto a trend.

## Typical Dialogue Problems

Few writers create polished work the first time around. Probably as you revise, you will discover some problems with your dialogue. These issues can fall into one of several categories.

### Giving Away Too Much

"Most obvious," says Boyle, "is giving away too much by way of dialogue exposition. We see this in poorly devised sci-fi movies but never, never, never in quality literary fiction. I'm not given to assigning long speeches to characters either, but obviously other writers really run with this (Dostoevsky, anyone?)."

### Inauthentic Sounding Speech

For Suárez, there is a distinct difference between character thought and speech. The former isn't a good fit for dialogue. "I prefer to always split the narrative into what the character is thinking and what the character is actually saying. It's a nice, quick way of getting to know my character right away. It's very true to real life. Ninety-nine percent of the things we think about are never spoken."

### Dialogue That Goes Nowhere

"Often I have dialogue in early drafts that is just blather," says Van den Berg. "There's language being exchanged, but it's lacking energy and weight and momentum. In revision, I think hard about the role of the exchange in the story — what is being revealed here? Why does this matter?"

### Repetition

"A common mistake a writer can make in an early draft," says Filipacchi, "is to make dialogue too long, not only in the back-and-forth between characters but in each individual utterance by each character. Cutting down the nonessential and repetitive portions is the easiest way of energizing dialogue. Ask yourself if the information delivered in that dialogue is crucial. If yes, are there other ways of dispensing that information, throughout the novel, in a less tedious way?"

## Tips from the Pros

◆ **T.C. Boyle:** *"Follow your instincts*. You create and absorb a billion bits of dialogue in your life off-screen. Ask yourself if what you've put in the mouths of your characters sounds real — i.e., as if someone would actually say those words and use those expressions in the very particular situation in which you've put them. I like to set my socks on fire once in a while just to see what sort of expression will emerge from my own vocal apparatus when the flames reach my ankles."

◆ **Virgil Suárez:** *"Listen. And then listen some more*. Crisp, real dialogue comes from watching carefully how people behave, move, and punctuate with gestures. Silence is extremely dramatic and should be reverted to as often as possible. I like to listen to people talk; I like to watch their expressions. Nervous tics and mannerisms are golden. Realistic dialogue is *never* spoken in complete sentences. Fragmented dialogue sounds real, timely, urgent."

◆ **Laura van den Berg:** *"Dialogue is more than speech*. It's about what's passing between two people. Condense as much as possible. Be as precise as possible. Think about what the characters want and need and fear and love and hate."

◆ **Amanda Filipacchi:** *"Add tension and energy*. Pique your reader's interest by paying close attention to what a character chooses to divulge to another character. How truthful will the information be? How tactful will a character be? How carefully will she choose her wording? Will the character exercise self-restraint or blurt things he will regret later? Playing with these elements can add tension and energy to dialogue."

## Summing Up

Think of it this way: When dialogue fails, it's because the language of your character seems contrived and doesn't sound real or authentic. It lacks energy. Given your particular character, the tone is off. Powerful dialogue makes us see and hear characters in their own voices, not the author's. It's high octane. It fuels character conflict, and it has an ultimate destination.

# Putting Words to Work

No story will make it off the page if story, character, setting — and a host of other elements — are not deftly handled. But there's one important aspect of fiction writing that isn't talked about as much as character or plot, but is just as essential to the story: the language itself. Language drives the work. Language makes everything happen. Language that falls flat makes characters fall flat.

No matter the style, when the language really works, it charms us. It hooks us. Some writers find that figurative language in particular — language that works on a different level than a purely literal one — grabs the reader in ways unadorned writing never could. It functions, in part, to meet that old saw: *Show, don't tell.*

Yet how does figurative language come to writers? Does it come naturally, or is it something we must work at? And what specifically does it contribute to a story?

## Using Figurative Language in Your Fiction

What are some examples of figurative language? How is it used? How does it work in context with a scene or the whole story or novel?

Susan Tepper, poet as well as fiction writer, used figurative language as a structuring device for her novel *dear Petrov*. "Even the title is figurative," she says, "since this is not a book of letters." The novel is set in 19th-century Russia during wartime. Nearly every sentence — actually, they tend to be sentence fragments — is figurative, says Tepper. In one chapter, "White to Blue," her unnamed female protagonist meditates:

> From the parlor looking inward to the hall, when the winter sun is nearly over, the blue hall paper turns the ceiling white to blue. As if a sea had passed on through these walls. Pressed in such a way as I'm unable to, unaccountably...

Notice the imagery of white turning to blue and then the analogy of the sea. "I set this story in a cold, remote land, during a tumultuous time period. It lent itself quite naturally to the figurative style," Tepper says.

For Stephanie Dickinson, author of *The Emily Fables* and *Flashlight Girls Run*, the use of figurative language is a natural tendency in Homo sapiens. "We are a meaning-making animal," she says. As a writer, she finds herself drawn to making "comparisons between disparate entities and substances, between what is beautiful and what might be considered ugly." Notice, for instance, this passage from "The Hermit," part of her flash fiction collection *The Emily Fables*:

> Beside the hut, rabbit skins hung drying. Why was the hermit's mouth lost inside his beard forest, lips grey like a pitchfork handle? Standing, he was a blackjack oak, yet kneeling and frozen he was tall still.

A beard is not literally a forest, but it becomes a forest in this passage. Two disparate entities — lips and a pitchfork handle — are likened to each other in a simile. The hermit is not literally a blackjack oak, yet the passage metaphorically continues to place him in the context of nonhuman nature. The figurative language is compelling itself, but it also serves a function, says Dickinson. "Here I use both simile and metaphor to suggest the hermit's physical body merging with the woods surrounding him," she says. He is not separate from nature; he *is* nature.

For Rosalind Palermo Stevenson, author of several works of fiction, figurative language is important not only in description but also in developing thematic ideas. This is the case in her recently published novel, *The Absent*, set in the second half of the 19th century. Note this passage from the point of view of her narrator:

> There was a wolf with us on the floor...Sprawled on its side like a dog sleeping, but it was a wolf that had been skinned and stuffed. I began petting it in the dream, though Lucie Beale refused to pet it, and as I was petting it, it came back to life and leapt up and ran away.

The visual experience of this passage is important to Stevenson, but also what the imagery suggests. The language works on at least two levels: The wolf in this dream stands, she says, for "the wilds," for wilderness, for "the power and naturalness of the earth, [which are] important elements in this novel." But since the wolf is "skinned and stuffed," the imagery also suggests "the destruction of the wilds." When the wolf leaps up and runs away, this action suggests "regeneration and a kind of redemption — an important thematic undercurrent," says Stevenson, in a novel that deals, in part, with the violence of Westward expansion.

Sometimes one word can take on several meanings. Donna Baier Stein's novel *The Silver Baron's Wife* is written from the point of view of an 83-year-old woman facing death. Note the word "snarl" in the following passage: "There, by the bed, with its snarl of gray blankets." Baier Stein chose the word "snarl" for two key reasons: "The woman who sleeps there sleeps restlessly, and the dreams and thoughts birthed there are tangled and uncomfortable." But there's also a third reason: "I also chose that word because the rest of the paragraph talks about intangible things, like the spirit of the character's dead mother hanging nearby. I thought the sound of the word was a good, abrupt reminder that even if Lizzie may be seeing a spirit, she is still rooted in a physical environment."

Not all writers use figurative language. It's certainly possible to use nouns and verbs and to be strictly literal while still allowing the reader to "see" or "hear" from accumulated prose detail and voice intonation in dialogue. This is generally the case for Barry Kitterman, author of *Baker's Boy*. Yet he admits that a given character may seem to call for a bit of figurative language. "The amount of figurative language depends on the relative eccentricity of the narrator," he says. Consider the thoughts of this failing minister in "Wedding Day," from Kitterman's collection *From the San Joaquin*:

> He had nothing new to say from the pulpit. It was difficult enough on a Sunday morning. By Sunday evening, the words he hoped to use felt as heavy as the air in the church, burdened with the scent of floor wax and old hymnals. Some days he thought about his future with sadness and uncertainty. Other days, like a middle-aged pitcher sent to the showers, he felt the sweet anticipation of release.

Notice the economy of language in the two similes: The first likens the "words he hoped to use" to the heaviness of the air in the church, "burdened with the scent of floor wax and old hymnals." Captured here in succinct olfactory imagery is a sense of how terribly sluggish this minister feels, how uninspired. The second simile gives us a tactile image, the fresh shower water washing him clean of the futile past, giving him a "sweet anticipation of release" because the struggle's over, finally, and he can move on.

## Where Figurative Language Comes from

Where do those good metaphors, similes, those clever analogies come from? Is it a native ability you're just born with? Or do you just reason it out? Do you do a little planning here and there?

"I would say that my figurative language comes from that same place that all my writing comes from: that place of deeper consciousness," says Stevenson. "When composing, I don't write from a contrived idea of what I want to say. I don't approach my work from the standpoint of 'I'll use this here or do that there to achieve some desired effect.'" What she does do is attune herself to her emotional, intuitive side: "An internal voice and rhythm are what tend to move the flow of words onto the page for me."

"My use of the figurative style comes as naturally as breathing," says Tepper. "I never control a story. First, I see a picture or a scene in my mind, and the resulting language and style come out of that. Any other style, for this particular book, would have failed the characters and what they are trying to convey. The writer has to listen to what the characters want."

"When I was writing in Lizzie Tabor's voice," says Baier Stein, "the figurative language flowed naturally onto the page. I intentionally put myself in the mind of a woman who was either a very eccentric old woman or an American female mystic. I knew that this character would see things in ways others might not. Her perception, and thus her language, would be more fluid and surprising."

But perhaps it's not the characters that you listen to or are drawn to, but some sort of existential need, or perhaps an artistic one. "I write to order chaos, to survive," says Dickinson. "I write to recreate calamity and beauty; I write to communicate my time on the planet to readers." For Dickinson, figurative language is an "essential tool kit." Much of her orientation toward thinking figuratively comes out of her roots in rural America. "I was raised on an Iowa farm, and the lushness of the fields and sloughs, the flourishing insect and bird life that enveloped me heightened my observation skills. I listened and I looked. I daydreamed. I read everything I could, and I loved the quicksilver words themselves — the metaphors and similes."

Dickinson soon began honing her craft. "When I began writing, I found the connections came somewhat naturally, and I practiced them, sometimes losing myself in similes." Yet there's a risk with that, she says. One mustn't overdo it.

"I have to discipline myself, as I am almost too drawn to figurative language," she says. "Too many similes and too much metaphor-making can cancel out their power or surprise."

If the appeal of figurative language for Dickinson comes out of her native appreciation of concrete, sensory detail, the same is true for Steve Sherrill, author of *Joy, Pa* and *Ersatz Anatomy*. "I have been drawn to, compelled by, sensory details for as long as I can remember," he says. "Sounds, sights, smells, etc., capture my imagination. Sometimes for a brief fleeting instant, but other times these details lock into a story or poem, underway or brand new."

Similes and metaphors have to come naturally out of these sensory details, says Sherrill. He doesn't work at "forcing" them. Nor does Kitterman: "I would never strain to fill a story with figurative language. That strikes me as a way of showing off, of authorial intrusion. If I work at anything along these lines, it's to keep the fancy language from getting the best of a story."

But isn't it likely that a stunning simile or metaphor, a just-right analogy, won't always appear in early drafts — even when you give your imagination full rein? "I often *wish* startlingly beautiful metaphors and similes would always flow naturally, but sometimes I have to work at it," Baier Stein says. Yet she saves this conscious effort for the revision stage, when she tends to "massage or play with the language more." If the language doesn't "magically appear on its own" in the first draft, she doesn't worry about it. There's always time in later drafts.

This can be the case for Stevenson, too. "Once all of that 'material' is on the page, then the critical phase of the process for me begins," she says. "So it is in this phase that I have to 'work at it' to make certain that all the language, both figurative and literal, is organically true to the work as a whole."

## Benefits of Using Figurative Language

First, it should be noted that the use of figurative language, like any tool in fiction writing, has to be appropriate — it must serve a useful function. In some stories, it may not. It can depend on the narrator or the nature of the protagonist.

"I've been writing a series of stories with children narrators," says Kitterman, "and they tend to see the world in a straightforward, if naïve, way." Consider this example from "The King of Okietown," which will appear in *The Green Hills Literary Lantern* this summer:

> He rode the bus home that afternoon, and he learned the bus driver's name, Mr. Harry. In the days that followed, Davey saw Mr. Harry take care of other tasks, sweeping and mowing and raking the schoolyard leaves in his brown shirt and brown pants. That was being a custodian.

It's a simple, ordinary style, yet concrete, creating images in our minds. It reflects the consciousness of the young point-of-view protagonist. "The language paints a picture," says Kitterman, "but not through the use of the poet's metaphors and similes." For this particular character, the simple, straight-forward language is authentic.

But when it's appropriate, figurative language can have a decidedly positive impact on the reader. "For me as a reader, figurative language excites me almost as much or more as the story being told," Baier Stein says. "Since words are the tools of writers, anything a writer does to manipulate those words brilliantly simply adds to the pleasure of the reader." The language becomes something to dwell on and savor: "Well-done figurative language makes the reading experience, for me, multi-dimensional. I'm not just following the plot to see what happens next but also relishing the visceral experience of being in the hands of a masterful writer. The language itself brings enjoyment moment to moment."

Figurative language can be truly poetic. "The link between figurative writing and poetry is pretty intense," says Tepper. "Figurative writing is also generally musical. It ebbs and flows, rises and falls, crashes, offers periods of silence." These periods of silence are significant, says Tepper, since they are openings into the text: "I believe it's the silence, a bit of the dark unknown, that snags the reader, invites the reader to step in. To become a character or even part of the narrative landscape. After the flood of language, the silence worms its way into the reader's unconscious."

Knowing when to create those moments of silence takes insight, she says: "When a writer can pull that off, knowing exactly where to drop silence into a piece, where the reader can become introspective, well, that's the ultimate: granting permission to join in the story. Where the really personal stuff lives and dreams. Because what the author offers, and how the reader absorbs, is the crux of storytelling. The greats, Tolstoy, for instance, knew how to make this happen instinctually."

As we've already seen, figurative language is also used for its capacity to point to something larger than the literal, or specific.

"I love the larger context for using figurative language, which frames it as a way of enabling one's writing to go beyond the meaning of the words themselves, and by doing so to deepen or enhance both the language and meaning of the work, as well as the reader's insight and appreciation of what is being said," says Stevenson.

"Whether it is personification, hyperbole, or understatement, whether an allusion or a simile, figurative language is the life raft that carries the writer's voice, the whole work itself," says Dickinson. In her story "Jesusita," from *Flashlight Girls Run*, "A girl-child of three is let out of a car next to a closed gas station and abandoned," Dickinson explains. "Alone, she waits for the car's return. The reader is not enlightened as to the girl's identity or where she comes from. 'The night surrounds her like hunger' is a simile I chose to use in this particular context, as its placement colors the text around it. The elaboration suggests a child's confusion of the senses and is immediately followed by, 'She licks the bottom of her shoe, where leftover motor oil clings.'" Through the simile combined with the incongruous action that follows, Dickinson steers her reader "toward the story's thematic significance or unifying element, its message." Modern readers no longer seek a story's moral, she points out, but they do "look for the subject that dominates the writing." Similes and metaphors can function, then, to "illuminate and enrich what is of consequence in a text and are often central to the overarching framework."

## Tips from the Pros

♦ **Susan Tepper** — "Nothing in the artistic realm should ever be forced. If the writer is struggling, something is off."

♦ **Stephanie Dickinson** — "Just because there are Instagram photographs of every conceivable thing, don't assume description isn't necessary or welcome. Everyone knows what a table at the coffee bar looks like, but not your particular table, not the unique people around you, not you/your narrator."

♦ **Rosalind Palermo Stevenson** —"Don't depend on overly familiar phrases, often bordering on or being actual clichés. I believe that the most important thing for a writer is to be authentic and to write from a place of their own interior vision, and to develop and discover the language and writing style that best serves this vision."

♦ **Barry Kitterman** — "If it's language that is natural to your protagonist or your narrator, then it will work. If it's the flowery exuberance of the writer himself or herself, then it won't."

♦ **Donna Baier Stein** — "Look for concrete, specific, visual imagery that is unexpected. Pair two things that aren't commonly paired."

♦ **Steve Sherrill** — "Reach for the extreme, the excess, the outrageous. Using bad metaphors will never kill you, but you might learn how not to get bitten by them again."

## A Few Final Words

Language is what makes writing — it makes story. It's the words themselves that mysteriously create character, plot, setting; in short, everything. To create interesting writing, you don't have to use figurative language. But it does have its appeal. It can suggest larger ideas beyond the literal. It can create beauty, poetic beauty. It can help put your reader into the world you imagine in your head, the world of the five senses, creating the very pleasure of sensation.

# Developing Your Prose Style

Prose style. It's the language of the story, involving such varied elements as diction, tone, and rhythm. Style can be formal or informal. It can be edged with irony and sarcasm, or it can be straightforward and direct. It can be opaque or accessible. It can be lyrical or jarring.

But there's certainly another way to think of style, and that is the extent to which it is "dense" (without the pejorative connotations) or "spare" in terms of detail. Dense here meaning full-bodied, richly textured. Spare meaning lean, sometimes cut almost to the bone.

Dense: James, Faulkner, Bellow.

Spare: Hemingway and Carver. Cormac McCarthy's work can be provocatively spare.

Certainly prose style is often a writer's signature, yet beyond this, we do need to keep in mind that style, like any element of fiction, is not separable from the various other story elements. "The notion of appropriate prose," states Sven Birkerts, Editor of *Agni*, "assumes that all elements are integral, organically interconnected." Robert Stewart, Editor, *New Letters*, states the matter categorically: "A writer should put nothing into a story that does not have its own role in the over-all impact." Every word, that is, and every device used in the creation of the story, must somehow contribute to the whole — and relate to each part. Style, says Grant Tracey, Fiction Editor, *North American Review*, "always relates to character. A lean prose can suggest inarticulateness, repression, hard-boiled sentiment. Violence hovers. A more heavily textured prose invites a closer proximity to the character and a sense of things being shared, confessed. I know that's simplifying things somewhat, but those are some possible moods created by these choices. Of course there are others too."

Or, in other words, regardless of the style, dense or spare, prose style is expressive of what's happening at all levels of the story.

"Form must follow function," as Caitlin McGuire, Managing Editor, *Berkeley Fiction Review*, points out — which is another way of speaking of organic unity.

### Editorial Preference

As a writer, you probably have a preference when it comes to prose style — at least you lean more toward one style than another. Readers often have preferences. What about editors?

For some literary magazine editors, organic unity is all that's important. Each story dictates its own style. Brock Clarke, Fiction Editor, *Cincinnati Review*, emphasizes the different demands and needs of each story, pointing out that editors have "to recognize those needs and demands and adjust accordingly: some stories are surrealistic, some premise driven, some realistic, some intensely devoted to details of the natural world, etc. We love them all, as long as they're well done." And "well done" is judged by appropriateness to subject, character, etc.

The same standard applies at Pocol Press. J. Thomas Hetrick, Editor, states that his press accepts "both thoroughly descriptive authors such as Brian Ames (*As Many Hands as God*) and Thomas Sheehan (*From the Quickening*) and the sparser prose styles of Paul Perry (*Street People, Lost People*) and Robert Garner McBrearty (*Episode*). The commonality of each of these authors," says Hetrick, "is that every one of them are expert storytellers."

*Nimrod International Journal* has absolutely no preference at all, states Francine Ringold, Editor-in-Chief: "Through the 52 years of *Nimrod*'s history we have published stories and prose poems that demonstrate our openness to many different styles. We neither prefer a heavily textured style, nor a severely spare approach. Quality is all, and quality (aside from appropriate spelling, grammar, and word choice) is a result of the style supporting and crystallizing the content: characters, setting, action."

Grant Tracey, *NAR*, can also appreciate both prose styles. "I like lyrical prose full of poetry, and harder, crisp prose full of Anglo-Saxon words. I probably prefer the latter, but realize that is more of a 'scene-driven' Hemingway and Carver style. Lately, in my own work," says Tracey, "I've been interested in summary and voice and the art of telling. Lyricism and details of the heart (what a character thinks and feels) lends itself more to that voice. So I'm waffling here. I like both."

Some magazines are not as open; they do have distinct stylistic preferences. *Agni*, for instance, goes for a "rich, textured presentation." For Sven Birkerts, prose style "represents something of the complexity of the character's psyche/thought process, and while we respect and admire many writers who prefer a more pared-down Carveresque mode, we don't feature it as part of our 'vision.'" A magazine can do "only so much," says Birkerts, and thus "it must strive for a certain distinctiveness."

*New Letters*, says Robert Stewart, doesn't generally publish minimal fiction, though he points out that all fiction today "in some way probably has been influenced by Hemingway." While the range of fiction published by *New Letters* is "unusually wide," including the traditional, the short-short, and "tightly satirical fiction," the prose style isn't likely to be the Carver type.

For some editors, like Fred Schepartz, at *Mobius*, "less is more." He adds to this a concern about prose that gets too detailed, that becomes "overwrought, overdone, or just flat out pretentious." Some writers tend to believe that the more detail, the better. Schepartz is concerned about where this thinking might lead: "I just want to stress that elegant, beautifully written prose need not be wordy."

Mary Wharff, Fiction Editor, *Coal City Review*, also prefers a spare style. She admits that this preference may be due to the fact that she herself writes "lean prose." That fact aside, Wharff does believe that "the right details can make a great bare-bones story much more satisfying for readers." Yet writers should be careful to leave some flesh on the bones, cautions Wharff: "There's a danger in being too lean, in losing readers by leaving out clarifying details, or losing the heart of the story by being too terse. There's no vivid world where every character speaks in one line, three-word sentences." On the whole, what Wharff looks for are "stories that are sparely vivid, where details are few, but are so right-on that each one interests me."

The matter of preference could depend on the editor who considers the story — this is true at the *Bellevue Literary Review*. Three different editors, working in democratic fashion, make final choices. Danielle Ofri, Editor-in-Chief, tends to "favor narrative detail over minimalism," though she does "shy away from stories in which the author's hand (or author's thesaurus) is too heavily felt." Ronna Wineberg, Senior Fiction Editor, is more open. For Wineberg, "it's a question of whether a story with a minimal style develops character sufficiently and also has narrative movement. This is my consideration for a denser style, too."

## Editorial Critiquing of Style

It is highly unlikely that an editor will take a well-wrought Carveresque piece and try to turn it into a Faulknerian one — or vice-versa. If the magazine or press tends not to take the lean, spare kind of writing, they will simply reject the work as "not right for us" because it doesn't fit with the taste or vision of the editors. Suggestions about style — about cutting, adding, or rethinking the language in some way — come either as a final condition for acceptance, or as final editing for an accepted piece. Prose style editing at this stage is one of chopping "excessiveness," on the one hand; or, on the other, adding necessary material to make the writing clear.

So what can you expect?

At *Agni*, says Sven Birkerts, any editorial changes on prose style are handled on "a case by case process, and we do both, but always in close consultation with the author." Barbara Pezzopane, Foreign Editor, *Storie*, writes: "In terms of editing, we are more interested in the dramatic syntax than in doing a lot of scissors-work. Much more than each word the writer uses, we're concerned with the overall composition of the story."

Grant Tracey, *NAR*, states: "I rarely mess with a writer's prose. I think writing is sacred and I don't want to impose my will or aesthetic to a writer's craft. That being said, I will on occasion challenge writers to make language more striking when I feel they've resorted to clichés or stock expressions. And I have, now and then, suggested cutting a paragraph (usually at the end of the story) that I feel 'sells' too much."

The ending is also fair game for Brock Clarke, *Cincinnati Review*: "Writers, despite some evidence to the contrary, are like most other humans in that they tend to go on too long, and when this happens, I often suggest cutting the ending. And sometimes, although not as often, I suggest additions that might add what the excised material lacked."

At the *Bellevue Literary Review*, final editing is fairly routine. "Sometimes," says Ronna Wineberg, "we ask an author to condense parts of a story, take out paragraphs or words, to make the prose leaner. And sometimes we ask a writer to add more description, to anchor a story in time, or to work on the dialogue. This, of course, depends on what we believe a piece needs. So we may ask for cutting in one story and expanding in another story." An editor "works closely," says Wineberg, "with the author on revisions. If an author objects to some of the changes, we try to respect the author's wishes." But editing can also be a requirement for acceptance. "There are times we accept a piece with the understanding that certain revisions must be made before the story can be published."

At *Berkeley Fiction Review*, editing is mainly a matter of meeting a condition for acceptance: "Typically," says Caitlin McGuire, "the only stories that we have any follow-up correspondence on in the way of workshopping are the stories that get a divided vote from the staff. Sometimes, we accept the submission if one section is cut; other times, we need additions to the story to make it flow better."

Robert Stewart states the policy at *New Letters*: "I frequently suggest cutting words when working with prose writers, especially writing that I want to accept for publication. William Zinsser says that clutter is the disease of the American language; and even when an essay or story has good material, it often contains redundancy or other clutter. Most of the time, the cutting takes the form of individual words or short phrases that slow down the pace and bore the reader." As to making the writing more descriptive, that's an entirely different matter, says Stewart: "If I need to suggest that more descriptive writing would be helpful, the story or essay probably is not close to being accepted. Most of the work I would do as editor occurs with writing that is already mostly complete."

P.T. McNiff, Editor-in-Chief, *Southern California Review*, makes the same point about stories under consideration: "At our journal, we don't heavily edit the material before publishing it — if we feel that the story needs either paring down or beefing up, we end up passing. If that's the only hold-up, we include a note when we return the story encouraging the author to continue working on the piece."

## Prose Style That Works

As we've seen, some editors have their own stylistic preferences. Other editors do not — if the style performs its function, that's enough. But, as we've also seen, outside of this question of preference, prose style issues may come up for editors in the acceptance or final editing process. Editors may suggest cutting or adding. Whatever stylistic changes are made, the final governing principle for style is that which governs short story composition as a whole: the organic interrelationship between all elements of the story. Different stories make different demands.

Character is, of course, a key element.

Francine Ringold recalls two prize-winning stories published by *Nimrod* that were radically different in style. Ann Forer's "Adolescence," which won a Nimrod/Katherine Anne Porter prize, was one sentence only, "as breathless and complex as the speaker. Oh, of course, the reader (aloud or in the theatre of her mind) knew when to stop or pause just from the lilt of the language, but the overall effect was to wind the reader into the mind of the narrator." The second award-winning story, "Verge," by Laura Louis, consisted of "spare, short sentences, and words that you hit and drop." Style is closely related to character, says Ringold, as a Chinese mother "chopping, always chopping vegetables, fruit, meat" gives "abrupt commands to her daughter: do this, do that!"

The lesson here? Style must relate to character, as Grant Tracey has pointed out. Organically. Form following function.

## Developing Your Own Style

To develop your own style, read and study good fiction, both contemporary and classic. Study both styles closely: the richly-textured, full-bodied style; and the lean, spare one. Which style works better for you? Be open to change as you develop your style over time. Be open to change with each story you write.

That is, for each story, be sure your style works at all levels as the language of character, place, action, mood, and idea. If you go for a richly-textured style, is this right for the story you're now working on? Or is a leaner style better? And what about other stylistic features? Should the language be ironic or direct? Should it be somewhat elliptical, or should it be plain-spoken, accessible? What about the rhythm or pacing? As you consider the specific elements of your story, you'll wonder about these stylistic features — and more. Working in this manner, with your vision of the story as an organic unit, you'll be well on your way to developing a strong prose style, regardless of the kind you choose.

# Exploring Exposition & Summary

Fiction depends largely on strong scenes and heightened dramatic moments, but it also requires solid narrative summary as well as exposition. Narrative summary telescopes time. Exposition — and by this I mean *expository prose*, not the first part of a five-stage story structure — is used, among other things, to delve into characters' feelings, thoughts, and reflections. The risk with either of these modes — narrative summary or exposition — is that the writing can become very dull. How do you prevent that? How do you craft strong exposition and summary that keeps readers engaged?

## Handling Exposition with Dramatic Appeal

Let's begin with exposition, one of the toughest fictional modes to handle well. To energize your expository prose, start by finding ways to create vivid imagery. Christine Sneed, author of the novel *Paris, He Said*, states, "I try to do a kind of literary braiding in expository passages — that is, along with hinting at or saying outright what a character's emotional state is, I bring in visual or other sensory details so that readers can clearly picture the character and/or the setting." She does as much as she can to represent "both the interior and exterior lives" of characters. In "The Virginity of Famous Men," the title story of her recently published collection, Sneed provides an abundance of precise detail in one short paragraph: First, we discover that her characters' apartment is in the eighth arrondissement of Paris. We know its size — a three-bedroom flat — and, more to the point, we know its style — a Haussmann-era building. In a nice little detail, we learn that it overlooks the "effusively floral Square Marcel Pagnol." No need to draw a map for the reader; anyone can search online for Paris and find the location of Square Marcel Pagnol, but stating a particular location fuels interest. More interesting details follow: The characters paid three months' rent upfront for a place with an out-of-order elevator and leaky windows. Her writing isn't just cerebral or abstract; the descriptions conjure pictures in our minds. Concreteness is vital in pulling readers in, says Sneed, but she cautions against overdoing it. "No word should be superfluous."

If handled deftly, exposition can function to create a rich, interesting voice. For Lori Ostlund, author of *After the Parade*, your voice will fall flat if you "over-report." She states: "The more that readers are *told* that a character is sad and is crying, the less sad they tend to feel." Instead you must get *inside* your characters, not view them from the outside. To do this, to reveal what Ostlund calls your "character's internal landscape," she suggests "transferring the emotion to something external." This means an objective referent that subjective feelings and emotions can be attached to. According to Ostlund, "What a character is observing and how he or she chooses to interact with the environment can help to keep the exposition interesting." In *After the Parade*, the point-of-view character's sense of loss isn't stated explicitly but instead is suggested by his noticing the absence of his personal things in a particular room: remembered books, gifts from students, an Indonesian night table, and the teak it was made from. A lamp illuminates the sheer lack of these things. As Ostlund points out, it is much less effective to dwell on a character's emotional state — here, a sense of loss — than it is to focus on specific things linked to this state. The external associations help the reader feel the emotion more intensely.

Another hallmark of strong exposition is an interesting pacing or tempo. Award-winning author Robert Garner McBrearty cautions against the use of prose that monotonously plods along, prose "which makes readers feel like they're wading through weedy passages to get back to a more interesting scene." McBrearty's recommendation is either to speed up the prose or to vary its rhythm "so that the exposition is just as lively and intense as the scenes." Consider making your prose lyrical, says McBrearty, "creating a kind of music that carries the reader along." If the writing is lyrical enough, it will pull readers in so that they can hardly stop reading, "one line pouring effortlessly into the next as the music builds to a crescendo." And here, at this heightened emotional moment, says McBrearty, the surprise suddenly comes: "Exposition reveals something unexpected before we drop into the next scene, a little breathless now, and eager for more." With the right pacing, as with other well-handled techniques, exposition can be a great benefit, not a burden.

But now for an important process question, perhaps one you hadn't imagined. Should you limit exposition as much as possible in early drafts? Is there a disadvantage in opting for exposition at critical junctures of your preliminary drafting? For Angela Pneuman, author of *Lay It on My Heart*, there can be. In her own fiction, says Pneuman, if she depends very much on exposition in the formative stages of her story or novel, she will find herself "trying to figure things out too quickly — steering the story towards meaning too early." Instead, states Pneuman, "What I really need to be doing is watching, listening, and trying things out." Once she understands her characters' motivations, she feels "more sure-handed with interior exposition, more sure about where it belongs."

Good exposition is critical, but Pneuman has taken us beyond the question of how to create strong exposition. To avoid authorial shaping and engineering, should we avoid it in early drafts and save it for later? Writers have to decide this issue on their own, but Pneuman has raised a significant question related to the early stages of the drafting process.

### Handling Narrative Summary

First, let's distinguish between scene and summary. With scene, you focus on one event, achieving as much dramatic intensity as possible; with summary, you cover more than one event, or perhaps several, over time. "As writers," says McBrearty, "we don't want to, or shouldn't, dramatize each passing moment or day, so we give just a sense of what is occurring." Yet McBrearty reminds us that, fundamentally, all writing must be dramatic, and narrative summary is no exception.

The question is: How do you invigorate your narrative summary? One way, says McBrearty, is to include "a conflict of interest" between your characters. This conflict can certainly be backward-looking at times, but mostly it should be forward-looking. Above all, McBrearty states, we need "to care about what's in store for them in the future."

In his novel *The Western Lonesome Society*, two young brothers, Tom and Will, are taken captive by Indians. Over several years, Will has grown to prefer Indian ways, but not Tom, the older one: "Tom fights for him, reminds him of the old days, but Will runs from him and covers his ears. He does not even like the old language anymore." In a short summary passage, with his typically forceful style, McBrearty captures the young boys' deeply felt conflict. Strong summary, like strong exposition, pulls us inside characters, enabling us to sense their emotional lives.

For Dennis Must, author of two collections and two novels, drama is as important in summary as it is in scene. To achieve rich, dramatic power in his own fiction, Must draws on years of writing and directing plays. But in addition he depends on the quality of his creative imagination. He states, "It's how close I have gotten to the pulse of the vision and/or recall that is occurring in my consciousness." This vision is informed principally by his growing up in the Rest Belt in the 1950s. According to Must, "Having grown up in the industrial belt and worked in a steel mill and on the railroad, these images are as familiar as family voices." He finds the need to "conjure them awake in the imagination." As Must emphasizes, "I must be inside the experience of my characters if the narrative is to come to life for the reader." In *Hush Now, Don't Explain*, he places the reader there, vividly, in this tight summary passage: "Yet we saw hundreds of men working through the night, tending the maw of these leviathans of commerce. The bells of industry, metal clanging against metal, never ceased ..." Here, with fine economy of language, Must captures the characters' witness of this industrial leviathan through the long, dark, clamorous night. The language is specific and concrete, not vague and general. The energetic language keeps this summary from being a dull recounting but instead a piece that is experientially *alive*.

Summary collapses time, whether it's several years or a single night. The best summary is energetic and vivid. It burrows into character, just as scene does. For Pneuman, it's this character function which summary must absolutely satisfy. For her, good summary creates the most "scenic points of entry" as possible. "Usually," she says,

"I keep narrative summary close to a character. I admire writers who navigate a greater distance, but in my own work, summary feels like it's in a character's head. So it becomes a matter of characterization and voice."

## Scene or Summary?

You can know the difference between scene and summary and still wonder: When it comes to the actual writing, which portions of your story or novel need scene, and which require summary? Ostlund has discovered that her creative writing students often choose summary when they really should choose scene: "It's hard to build tension with summary; key moments, especially at the end of a story, shouldn't be summarized. I also think of scenes, particularly the accretion of scenes, as the primary way that we have to show changes in characters. Scenes allow us both to see what caused a change and also what the change is (the effects on the character)." But summary *is* needed at times, says Ostlund, as a way of moving certain necessary events along quickly — and quite often at section or chapter beginnings. When it is needed, the writer has to know how *much* summary to use because, as Ostlund points out, "too much summary or unclearly sequenced summary can weigh down the beginning."

## Helpful Tips from the Professionals

No one can tell you everything about writing good exposition and summary. But certainly the professionals can give you some useful tips on handling exposition-related issues.

♦ **The merely factual:** Dennis Must has come to embrace this passage by Boris Pasternak: "What is laid down, ordered, factual is never enough to embrace the whole truth: life always spills over the rim of every cup." For Must, regardless of fictional mode — scene, summary, exposition — the burden of the writer is to create a character whose life spills over beyond the mere facts of daily existence. What we need, according to Must, is a character who desperately *needs* and *wants*. As Must expresses it: "I believe to embrace the 'whole truth' in fictional narrative art is to create a character who *yearns*. It is simply not enough to narrate the troubles one is confronting. It's getting inside the ineluctable heart of a character that causes a story to resonate in a reader's mind."

♦ **Interiority of characters:** Exposition can be used to capture the interior lives of characters. But when, and how much? How about in scenes? In her creative writing classroom, Angela Pneuman helps her students learn to judge the impact of interiority in scene writing by doing a three-part exercise. First they write "entirely in scene, with dialogue, gestures, little descriptions if necessary, but no interior." Then she invites them to include "all interior — memories, evaluations, private thoughts, impressions." In the third exercise, they play around with both the external (actions, speech) and internal (thinking, memory). "There's no right or wrong," says Pneuman, "just degrees of the effect the writer wants to produce. It can be a great joy to tinker in this way, trying out different things."

♦ **Mood and tone:** "Consider the mood you're trying to set," says Robert Garner McBrearty. "Is it funny? Sad? Ironic? Foreboding?" Too often, he says, writers tend to equate exposition and summary with "providing necessary information," but, he points out, that shouldn't be the only goal, or even the primary goal of these two fictional modes — the goal should be to keep readers enthralled. You can accomplish this feat by developing a compelling mood and tone. McBrearty offers a few interesting scenarios: "Maybe your main character says cheerful things in a crowd but secretly views the world through a dark inner lens. Or maybe the seemingly cynical person is filled with hopeful inner longing."

♦ **Backstory:** Backstory, which may call for exposition, is often essential for context, as Christine Sneed points out, because you can't rely only on the present time frame of your story. But be sure to prune out what *isn't* necessary and to be fairly ruthless about it. "You have to be pretty unsentimental when you're editing backstory, exposition, or narrative summary," says Sneed. Knowing what to prune, and what not to, comes in time, she says. It's a matter of learning "the right balance between backstory and the story's present, but eventually I think it becomes easier."

♦ **The "thesis-statement syndrome":** Exposition can be a real spoiler, says Lori Ostlund, when a writer sums up everything that's about to happen in a scene. Her example: "He then told her about the time that his best friend pulled a gun on him, destroying his faith in friendship." This kind of exposition, says Ostlund, will kill any tension, and any reading pleasure, in the scene because "the reader already knows about the gun and has also been instructed how to interpret this scene." Ostlund does grant that this syndrome can be useful as a story planning technique, but she suggests that if you want to make your writing vibrant, you must delete expository spoilers as you revise.

## Summing Up

Exposition and narrative summary are difficult to write, but if you find ways to make these prose modes dramatic, they can be a benefit to your storytelling. Don't laboriously tell. Do find ways to create vivid imagery for your readers and enter the minds and hearts of your characters. Be careful to choose the right places for exposition as well as narrative summary. Probably the best way to learn how to handle these modes well, and when to use them, is to find good models from the professionals. See the craft in action.

# Setting the Tone: How to Handle Voice in Your Fiction

In real life, we often speak of tone of voice: "What's with that tone of voice?" Perhaps because it sounded impertinent or disrespectful; we picked up on an attitude we didn't appreciate. At any rate, we know that *the way words are said* matters just as much — if not more — as the words themselves.

In fiction, as in real life, we listen carefully for voices: both the author's and the characters'. The authorial voice is the voice we hear when we're reading the author's prose, whether it's exposition, narration, or description. Think of the difference between a Hemingway narrative and a Faulkner one: Hemingway's prose is lean and stripped down, whereas Faulkner's is intricately and richly embellished.

Characters also clearly have distinctive voices that establish personality, attitudes, and disposition. Think of Huck Finn, Holden Caulfield, Moll Flanders. A character's voice can be apparent in both thought and speech. And speech in fiction, as in real life, clues us in to a character's take on self, others, and the world at large.

As a writer, you may have been urged to find your voice. The idea is that once you do this, something "clicks." You've found the right voice for your narrator or your protagonist. Maybe initially your voice sounded amateurish, bumbling, uneven, wrong for the story or wrong for the characters, but now it's got authority, it's just right, it's tuned in.

But how do you find that voice? And what about from project to project: Should you work toward creating a consistent voice, one that readers will recognize as uniquely yours?

## The Nature of "Voice"

Walter Cummins, former editor of *The Literary Review*, emeritus professor at Farleigh Dickinson University, and a short story writer, points out that a voice's sound is created by such elements as "sentence rhythms and patterns, word choices, enunciations, syntax, and pauses." Voice must work in tandem with key features of a character or story: "In addition to sound, the details that a writer chooses to note imply a distinct worldview. There's also an attitude toward people and places, situations and events that emerges."

It's a complex process, says Cummins, especially since fictional voice consists of both the basic authorial voice and the occasional, or contextual, voice, which depends on the particular story elements. "I consider the voice underlying the occasional voices [to be] one that develops unconsciously, but a writer can be more deliberate about adjusting that basic voice to one that suits the narrative situation," he says. For instance, in his own work: "As far as I'm concerned, I just write in a manner that's natural to me. But people have commented on what they find are distinctive sentence patterns and rhythms, a voice I hadn't intentionally planned and didn't realize I had."

Robert Garner McBrearty, author of several story collections, likens voice to the style of a good actor. "Somehow with the great actor, we're feeling not only the acting style but the 'voice' of the actor," he says. Everything about this actor's performance, says McBrearty, reveals an authentic style/voice: "The delivery of the lines, the facial expressions, seem called forth from some deeper, authentic place, as if the actor has *become* the character rather than simply pretending." In fiction, a distinctive style and personality must come through as well, he believes. While his work is often comic on the surface, there are serious layers beneath. It's the deeper layers, he believes, where we discover the real character, and it's essential that voice, whether it's first person or third, convey this deeper level.

Voice is contextual. The voice that suits Alex Cavanaugh, a sci-fi novelist, is also a comic one, but pitched to a specific readership, those who aren't into the technical side of science fiction. He goes for "light humorous passages, especially those with a more rapid-fire delivery." A light-humorous voice is nicely suited to his space opera readership.

For Joanna Campbell Slan, author of the cozy mystery novel *All Washed Up*, voice is "the humanity behind the words that connects the reader to the character on a personal level." For historical novelist Stephanie Cowell, author of *Claude & Camille: A Novel of Monet*, voice has to do with capturing the deepest recesses of her characters' emotional and spiritual lives. Her protagonists are people with great stature, with profound artistic potential. What are the wellsprings, the inner life, of a character like Monet, fiercely driven by his art?

## Finding Your Voice

So how can you find your own voice in a particular work?

Cavanaugh believes if you want to find your voice, you must discover a unique way of telling your story. This may take years of practicing the craft. One problem beginning writers must overcome, he says, is the tendency to write with "proper language," making one's work "correct" according to the rules of formal grammar — but if you write like a schoolmarm, your fiction will be lifeless. Cavanaugh says it's best "to just throw it out there with no inhibitions." With practice, "eventually your personality will start to come through."

In her own work, Cowell wants to be sure that the personality that comes through is her character's only, never an authorial voice. "I've never really tried to find my voice because *I'm* not in the story, except that I am making the characters come to life on the page, but I never feel they are mine. I feel they come to me as a child is born to you, and you do your best to shape that child to go into the world."

Slan says finding your voice takes trusting your abilities as an author. She recommends writers do a lot of reading and have plenty of life experiences. "It's a maturation process," says Slan. And then, at some point, you'll experience an 'aha' moment when you find your voice.

"I like to think of a musician tuning an instrument with a tuning fork," she says. "Until the pitch of the instrument and the fork matches, there's a discordant vibrato. When the instrument and the fork are perfectly in tune, they create one pure, unwavering sound. That's what I aim for, creating a pure sound that resonates with my readers."

Like Slan, McBrearty also suggests reading a lot. "Notice when you find something distinctive about the writing voice," says

McBrearty, something that makes it sound "authentic." Whenever you're in the midst of the creative process, he recommends "getting in touch with your deepest thoughts and emotions, even if they are never directly stated on the page." In fact, he says "what is unsaid" might be "what is authentic."

Authenticity is equally important to Cummins. As a professor, he says, "I get a sense of an inherent voice from my first readings of their work. Yet they haven't shaped that voice at this early stage. They may even want to emulate someone else's, a successful writer they admire. But while they can learn elements of craft that way, they can't force a voice that isn't inherently their own." Finding their own voice comes, says Cummins, from "pruning excess, developing scenes and characters, finding the hearts of their stories." Once writers improve and understand the writing process, they will gain confidence. "Then their true voice will start to emerge," says Cummins. It's a misconception of voice, he believes, to think of it as something separate from everything else in a story. "It's one aspect of a whole, one revealed as a writer finds how to master other aspects of story writing."

## Handling Multiple Voices

How many voices can a work of fiction have? And what about the voice of the authorial persona versus the voices of the characters?

"The most obvious multiplicity is found in dialogue," says Cummins, "whether the basic telling is in the first or third person." And "characters should be distinctive when they speak," he says. "But if the story is conveyed by one narrative voice — typical of most stories or novels — that voice must be consistent."

Cowell believes a work of fiction can have many voices, but "I think all the voices must be used to expound one major theme or plot." She uses her novel *Marrying Mozart* as an example, where she has a total of six different voices: "the 21-year-old Mozart, the four pretty unmarried Weber sisters, and their controlling mother." This novel consists of "variations on a theme," with each character's distinctive voice related to the central issue of the novel: the marriage to Mozart.

Slan also strives for a unifying voice in a given work of fiction. "By my definition, there will always be one authorial voice within a book, unless the book is an anthology. However, just as each character has an arc within the arc of the book, so does each character have his/her own voice within that over-arching voice of the author."

## Creating a Consistent Voice

What about a continuing voice from story to story, or novel to novel? You don't want to sound like Stephen King in one work and John Grisham in another. Readers can know you by a voice that is consistently *one* voice. But how important is consistency in a writer's voice?

"A distinctive voice that carries from one book to another gives readers a sense of familiarity," says Cavanaugh. "They know what to expect. It will grow and develop over time, and changing genres alters it some, but I think authors should focus more on overall voice."

He suggests practicing to maintain a consistent voice. "A good exercise is to take one written page or passage, and write it completely different. The more times you rewrite it, the more possibilities you'll see — and the more voice will begin to develop. You'll start to recognize what is comfortable and natural for you. Plus, you'll learn how to maintain that natural style even when the subject matter and genre change."

Cummins encourages adaptation. "A writer can and probably should modify his or her essential voice to suit the tone and circumstance of a particular book," he says. Yet there are limits, he points out: "I recall meeting a British writer who had a successful first novel but felt a need to write in a totally different manner in his next, with a voice closer to that of another writer he longed to emulate. He shared part of that attempt at a public reading, and it sounded strained. It wasn't him."

When adapting your voice to suit a particular work, Slan suggests listening to recordings. "When I wrote my Jane Eyre books, I listened to snippets of *Downton Abbey* before settling down to write. This infused my thinking with the cadences of the British accent." As to changing genres, she points out that your voice must be adaptable if working on vastly different projects: "When I wrote a textbook, my voice was more professorial and removed. When I wrote nonfiction about scrapbooking, I could be more friendly. When I write about Jane Eyre, I have to be more formal and erudite." And her other fiction? "When I write about Kiki Lowenstein, I'm very much a figure in mom jeans, but when I write about her friend Cara Mia Delgatto [from *All Washed Up*], I have to think like a businesswoman. These are all facets of my personality, revised and weighted to shape the message I want my audience to receive."

It's true that certain genres call for certain kinds of voices. Wouldn't it be misguided, absurd, even, to adopt your James Joyce style in a company memo? One has to remember audience and purpose. But within a given genre, you can maintain a voice that is relatively consistent, and hopefully one that comes natural to you. Always remember: If you force it, it will *sound* forced, not authentic.

### Voice and Subject Matter

How do you pitch your voice to the subject matter? According to Slan, "To select the proper variation of your voice, you must first put yourself in the place of your reader. What does he/she expect? Then go on to ask yourself, 'What does the genre demand?'"

But how can you be sure it's effective? Beta readers can help, says Slan. But do be careful, she cautions: "They must be fans of the sort of work you're hoping to create, or they won't be able to discern a misstep."

Cummins sees the matter differently — in fact, oppositely: "The voice should come first and drive the way the subject is handled rather than the subject dictating the voice.

"Shakespeare wrote comedies, tragedies, and histories with very different attitudes toward his stories, and yet the voice behind them is always Shakespeare's. F. Scott Fitzgerald wrote *The Great Gatsby* and the social satire fantasy story 'The Diamond as Big as the Ritz.' He made both approaches his own. That's the point," he says.

Whichever comes first — voice or subject — the tone of a story can be way off. "I mean, if you're stuck with a style where all the world is light and happy, [that] voice will not do to describe a brutal murder," says Cowell. And so, if that's your usual style, it behooves you to pick your subject, genre, and characters well. What's your temperament? What's your general take on the world? What kinds of characters suit you?

"I choose mostly very sensitive characters," says Cowell. "I think I would not be good at describing the deeds of a serial killer! I have a gentle, sensitive style. It would not be good for thrillers or mysteries or traditional romance or science fiction or fantasy or whatever. It is me, and it suits what I do."

Sometimes it's possible to take advantage of a discrepancy between voice and subject matter, such as in black humor or farce. "If you are writing comedy, it's that unexpected fillip that makes us laugh," says Slan. "If you are hoping to surprise the reader or to keep the reader intrigued, a disparity between voice and subject matter can create interest."

## Now, Go Find Your Own Voice

An interesting, compelling voice is the engine that moves readers from sentence to sentence, from paragraph to paragraph, from page to page. A flat voice will cause us to close the book. With practice, you'll discover a voice that is true and authentic to you, and it's crucial in your journey as a fiction writer. After all, finding your voice in a work of fiction is finding its core, its center, the heart of it.

# Avoiding Clichés: Recognizing Them & Getting Beyond Them

If there's one criticism most writers have received at one time or another in their writing career, it's that their work is clichéd — in some way. It might be their story's premise, or it might be a character or two, even the protagonist. Whatever happens to be clichéd is old, well-tilled soil, the road we've been on before, old hat — all clichés to describe clichés. In a word, a cliché lacks freshness or originality, and even the word novel means new, different — not the same old thing we've seen and heard over and over. So of course if writers want their work appreciated, valued, and accepted for publication, they must find ways to avoid clichés of various kinds.

## Clichéd Plots

Plot is an important fictional element and one that is subject to cliché. Certain topics garner a lot of attention at different times. They're in the news, so to speak. Cliff Garstang, author of the award-winning *In an Uncharted Country* and editor of *Prime Number Magazine*, tries to stay away from some plots that turn on topics that are "just too familiar," and among these he lists "senile parents, cancer victims, cheating spouses, partner dying of AIDS." Even so, as he points out, these human ills and problems do certainly make up real life, so why should a writer "completely ignore them?" And in addition, "all of them are useful metaphors for other aspects of life." So if Garstang tends to avoid plots that turn on these overused topics, he does believe writers shouldn't utterly avoid them — yet to handle them well is clearly a challenge: "The trick, I think, is to layer stories effectively. Okay, so someone in your story has cancer. That can't be all that story is about, but perhaps the cancer is in the background and what's really happening is . . . something else."

Robert Garner McBrearty is a recipient of the Sherwood Anderson Foundation Fiction Award. McBrearty's solution to "predictable" plots, akin to Garstang's, is "to take the story elsewhere, not to deliver the expected trajectory or ending." This mustn't be done, though, at the expense of "internal consistency and authenticity." For McBrearty, surprise is the key element, but this comes with a caveat: "Merely being surprising for surprise's sake is almost its own cliché. The surprise has to be earned; it has to feel right."

Tikvah Feinstein, editor of *Taproot Literary Review*, has tired of coming across two predictable plots: the "long estranged and then reunited" one and the "I fell in love again plot, often after a long pulling apart and a sudden maturing." Feinstein explains her antipathy toward these two plot-lines: "At *Taproot* we read a lot of stories with hospitals and nursing home settings where the 'end of life' drama is played out by a survivor who has lost a last chance to say something he/she should have said long before." This plot becomes too reductive, Feinstein suggests: "Writers should keep in mind that it's easy to fall into a let's fix-it story line. But conflict in the reality of relationships, unpredictability and surprising resolution is the plot and story line we seek." Like Garstang, Feinstein doesn't rule out using such plots, but she does emphasize that they "are hard to write in an unpredictable style." The payoff is that when the writer freshens them up, "they can be fantastic."

Ronna Wineberg is senior fiction editor of the *Bellevue Literary Review* and author of *Second Language*, a story collection which won the New Rivers Press Many Voices Project Literary Competition. Wineberg points out that "almost any situation can seem clichéd" — typically tied to the "great topics" that writers so often turn to: "love, sex, betrayal, cruelty, death — to name a few." To avoid clichéd treatment of these topics, what the writer must do, says Wineberg, is make the situation "unique and surprising, give the characters depth, create authentic individuals on the page."

## Clichéd Characters

If it's difficult to avoid clichéd plots, it's also difficult to avoid clichéd characters — or one-dimensional stereotypes. "Sometimes one can play with stereotypes," says Garstang, "but it's a dangerous game." The dilemma the writer faces is this: "On the one hand, char-

135

acters should be recognizable, but characters who are too familiar will fail to surprise."

As with clichéd plots, there is a list of overused character types editors reject and writers try to avoid. Lydia Dishman, editor, *Emrys Journal* says: "We've run the gamut including hooker with a heart of gold, abused wife, surly teenager, etc." Barrett Bowlin, editor, *Harpur Palate*, sees as especially risky those characters having "difficulties with disease (especially cancer); male characters as alcoholics, and female characters with eating and/or body-image disorders." These character types themselves are not deal-breakers for publication, says Bowlin, but authors must find ways to "push past" such ready-made clichés. Some of Bowlin's favorite stories have, in fact, worked with these very character types. "I love stories about disease. I love characters who wrestle with alcoholism, eating disorders, and problems with self-image." Bowlin loves writers who "find a way to kill the cliché while simultaneously working within it." But how do you do this? Bowlin's answer: "I'd encourage authors to be extremely careful in areas in which they feel comfortable. If your writing feels safe, or if your plot or characters or settings or images feel reliable, get rid of them. The people who read your stories want you to surprise them."

Stated simply: with character, as with plot, if you settle for clichés, you won't surprise. And you must find ways to surprise your reader, or your work will fall flat. Overworked character types are off-putting if that's all you have, but writers who are somehow able to "push past" the cliché can delight readers with their insights and creativity.

But it's not just the overused character types that present traps. Gary Fincke, winner of the Flannery O'Connor Award for Short Fiction and author of many books of fiction, believes that avoiding the typical character clichés like the "drunk daddy" really isn't all that hard. What *is* hard, says Fincke, is "to avoid the clichés that form because they're so personally accessible from the writer's experience." Fincke has found ways to avoid these in his own work. "One of my revision steps is always to try to complicate characters and working to vary situations."

Robert Garner McBrearty can speak to the problem of avoiding clichés related to what's "personally accessible" — in his case, it's the university scene. "Maybe because I teach, I have to think about avoiding clichés about teachers and academia" — which means the potential for both a clichéd plot and clichéd characters. A typically comic writer, McBrearty states: "One always wants to do a certain 'take' on academia, to reduce it to an absurdity. Because much of it really is absurd, one is in the precarious position of trying to depict the very real absurdity of academia while simultaneously trying to avoid reducing it to a cliché about academia." Clichéd treatment equals one-dimensional characters — characters that seem cartoonish, not fully alive or real. To deal with this problem, McBrearty struggles "to get inside the character, to sense the character almost like a living human being." Don't "impose characterizations," McBrearty cautions: "I will now create a hard-boiled detective who has a kind spot for dogs and orphans." This strategy of working from the outside, of artificially rigging things, won't work to create multidimensional, real-to-life characters, asserts McBrearty. Instead, you need to reach down to a "much more subliminal level."

Linda B. Swanson-Davies, co-editor of *Glimmer Train*, is also troubled by one-dimensional characters. She states: "I suppose, because we publish literary fiction, we are most aware of character-related clichés. We see stories with pimply runaways, used-car salesmen, diner waitresses with Southern drawls, and people described only by nationality, as though those descriptions are all we need to understand who the labeled person is." She doesn't believe writers deliberately set out to "diminish their characters in this way" — such stereotypes result instead from a lack of knowing "anything of consequence about them." And this kind of knowing does take time. Swanson-Davies suggests this litmus test for clichéd characters: "To help figure out if your character is a cliché, imagine that someone you personally know and *care* about actually matches the description of your character. If you cannot imagine yourself and your character sharing similar types of concerns with love and family, personal and occupational goals, fears and secrets, your story has probably not yet found its footing."

Not knowing characters well enough to avoid clichés may stem from a lack of direct personal experience, believes Barry Kitterman, author of two story collections. "Sometimes, the problem arises from our only knowing a subject through stories we've read, movies we watched, or worst of all, television. So we can't easily rise above cliché." Kitterman's solution is to choose protagonists who are closer to us in terms of their basic background and knowledge so that we are able to write about them with authority and believability.

## Other Clichés

Clichéd language is, of course, a big offender. In fact, clichéd phrases are often one of the first things writers are cautioned about, and many writers work on clichéd words and phrases even if they never get beyond clichéd plots and characters. Even so, clichéd language does persist, as Michael G. Czyzniejewski, author of *Elephants in Our Bedroom*, and editor at *Mid-American Review*, can tell you, and clichéd language absolutely kills a story's chance for publication at *MAR*. Writers better shun "dead as a doornail" and "green with envy," says Czyzniejewski, but, in more general terms, they need to watch out for "any set of words commonly found together." Put another way, writers need to be careful about depending on "commonspeak." Czyzniejewski attributes this dependence on predictable phrasing partly to laziness, but partly also to not knowing that clichés make for bad writing — that good writing has to be "original, not to mention musical, persuasive, and full of life."

"Shock openers," "blatant cleverness," and "open endings" are three story features that Barrett Bowlin, at *Harpur Palate,* says are currently on the rise in the submissions he receives — and rapidly becoming stock clichés. He attributes this to the workshopping of stories, which, on the whole, does produce better submissions but paradoxically carries with it certain problems. "What I mean by this is the act of being clever for cleverness's sake in the story, or the author feeling the need to start off with an attempt at being shocking (so as to catch the attention of the editor) and then failing to earn the value of that shock factor for the remainder of the story, and so on." Clearly, the lesson here is not to depend on special effects and arty devices but instead on solid, well-developed plots and genuine characters.

## Rethinking the Cliché

There's still another way of thinking about clichés — not, in this case, as a specific story weakness or problem as we've seen so far. To Karl Harshbarger, whose many stories have appeared in high-profile literary magazines, including *The Atlantic Monthly*, it's the clichés that go to the core of the story's very premise that are the most off-putting. When Harshbarger begins to read a story or novel, he says, "I sense (or at least believe I sense) whether this author has a legitimate world view, or, perhaps I should say, an inner integrity, which can teach me something about this universe I live in. When I find this quality I will accept whatever particular approach the writer decides to use: flowery language, simple language; bizarre characters, run-of-the-mill characters; wild, improbable plots, old, exhausted plots, and so forth. If, on the other hand, I sense the author has a limited world view or a limited inner integrity I find myself rejecting his or her work in its entirety as a cliché."

Harshbarger's concern is not, then, with clichéd plots, clichéd characters, clichéd language, or any other story element that might be clichéd. His concern goes to the heart of the matter, to the story's fundamental ideas or themes — and whether this work can "teach" him something about this universe he lives in. Harshbarger's view here is akin to a poet-priest kind of view of literature versus a more aesthetic one. This may not be a viewpoint that has a lot of currency today, but it is certainly something to reflect on if one considers how it's the basic conception of the story that is the wheel house that governs the whole. If Harshbarger finds the story's core itself stale, he doesn't care how good the execution is. Technical performance plays a supporting role, at best, in Harshbarger's concept of a story or novel's primary function. While one may reject his belief that if a story or novel doesn't enlighten us somehow, it's clichéd, it does seem reasonable to consider to what end the criteria Harshbarger mentions, if met, might have possible pay-offs for a story or novel's success with readers, agents, and publishers.

### Hovering on the Brink … yet Avoiding the Cliché

As we've noted, fiction can hover on the brink of plot and character clichés, and yet still avoid them. This takes a skillful maneuver or two, a new emphasis, a re-shifting of the story's focus from a hackneyed plot or character to new, fresh ground. Seasoned writers report battle successes on various cliché fronts.

#### The Dying Mother

Ronna Wineberg's story "Second Language," the title story of her prize-winning collection, deals with a woman and her dying mother. The problem Wineberg faced was how to keep this topic from being utterly predictable. A writer friend gave her some helpful advice: "You have to make this different from all the other stories that people write about dying parents." As she revised, she "decided the daughter would be married, have an affair, and think about this while she was visiting her mother in the hospital." She also found other ways, namely humor, to shift the attention away from the obsession with dying. She made the hospital experience absurd in places: "a doctor wanting to perform an operation he'd already done, the difficulty of getting a nurse to come into a patient's room." These humorous plot developments weren't all, though, says Wineberg: "I tried to give the characters very particular voices, dimension and their own struggles, so the frailty of the mother wouldn't overwhelm the story." With her added story devices, Wineberg's story was now much more than a Dying Mother story.

#### The Bipolar Disorder

Robert Garner McBrearty considers his story "Episode" (from his prize-winning *Episode*, Pocol Press, 2009) a good example of a story avoiding the Bipolar Disorder cliché. The story's basic plot is about a younger brother intervening in one of his brother's many bipolar episodes. "I wanted to show that the brother having the episode is actually being fairly logical at times, rather than presenting him as a raving maniac." Further, McBrearty wanted to cast the bipolar brother as "more than his illness," and in doing so he believes he was able to beat the cliché: "I think too often writers overplay illnesses like depression, bipolar disorder, alcoholism. They reduce their characters to representative of the disease." McBrearty, on the other hand, wanted to create "a fully-individualized character, suffering from his disease, but not consumed by his disease." He believes because he put the emphasis on the family's struggle "with the disorder at this particular time," he was able to avoid making the older brother merely a specimen of the Bipolar Disorder.

### The Bully

In "Someone like Me" (from *From the San Joaquin*, SMU Press, 2010), Barry Kitterman was struggling to create a character "very similar to a kid who bullied me when I was a boy." The problem to overcome, says Kitterman, is that "Bullies can easily be cartoonish." To avoid the cliché, he needed to make sure his character, like all good characters, was three-dimensional. Kitterman offers a general guideline for character creation, based on the principle of difference: "A beautiful woman needs an ugly character trait; a striving self-centered stock broker needs a butterfly collection. A bully needs a weakness of his own." Kitterman overcame the clichéd bully problem by giving his character something you wouldn't normally associate with a bully — "a speech impediment." The result? "He started to seem halfway human."

### Angry, Cold Father & Smart, but Passive Son

Gary Fincke says: "At a recent reading, I was fifteen pages into a story called 'A Room of Rain,' which has an angry, cold father and a smart, but passive son, when I arrived at a scene where the father admits to heartbreak and the desire to hold on to sentiment." Fincke was pretty well into the revision process when he wrote this scene, and once he'd read it out loud, he realized that it alone made a great difference in helping him avoid the cliché: "the father is more than what the son believes he is, and now there is more at stake if the son chooses to dismiss him — there's ambivalence, which lies at the center of every solid story."

## A Final Reminder

If it's a subject or story-line that everyone's familiar with, if it's a character type we all recognize, if it's an expression on everyone's lips, be careful. Don't necessarily steer clear of potentially clichéd plots and characters entirely, but do find ways to freshen or liven them up — to make your fiction as fresh and as original as you can make it, but at the same time believable. This is certainly a hard balancing act to perform, but certainly well worth it when you are successful at it.

# Part IV
# Fiction Short and Long

# Jumpin' Jack Flash

Flash fiction goes by many names: microfiction, sudden fiction, short-short, postcard fiction, etc. Its word count runs anywhere from 140 characters to over a thousand, generally capping out at 1500. Any number of famous writers have written flash, including Langston Hughes, Raymond Carver, David Foster Wallace, Jamaica Kincaid, John Updike, Joyce Carol Oates, Amy Hempel, and Margaret Atwood, to name only a few.

Since the 1986 appearance of the landmark *Sudden Fiction*, an anthology edited by Robert Shepard and James Thomas, flash fiction has become a special genre for many fiction writers, with quite a few magazines and journals as well as small presses open to the form. While commercial presses aren't generally receptive to single-authored flash fiction collections, W.W. Norton published *Flash Fiction* in 1992; *Flash Fiction Forward* in 2006; and *Flash Fiction International: Very Short Stories from Around the World* in 2015.

Other than being short, what's at the heart of flash fiction?

For Randall Brown — author of the award-winning flash collection *Mad to Live* and editor of Matter Press, which specializes in flash — it comes down to what the form says about the nature of the world and human experience in it.

"The world — shattered and lying in shards — has grown tired of its pieces being glued together to create the illusion of something complete. Instead, the world hopes someone will pick up a single fragment and create out of it something whole, something that fills that compressed space with the entirety of all that there is," he says.

Michael Martone, whose flash fiction has been widely anthologized, sees flash "as a corrosive genre." He states: "I think its cultural appearance corresponds, along with other events and historical occasions, with the move of literary writers and poets into the university, the university that is an ancient scientific sorting critical machine. This world wants rigor. This form, 'flash,' wants play. It can't be categorized. It can't be taught. It knows not to know."

Still, there must be certain identifiable properties of flash. How is it different from, say, a prose poem?

"I used to say that the difference between a prose poem and a flash story is that in a flash story something happens. Now I have pared back 'something happens' to 'movement,'" says Pamela Painter, award-winning author of the flash collection *Wouldn't You Like to Know*.

Whatever flash fiction is, or how it differs from other forms, it has a large following.

"There is a really mighty, supportive flash community these days. It's great to see people holding each other up and supporting each other's work through publication and review and word of mouth. It does seem like there are more full-length flash collections and anthologies being published in the small press world, which is exciting," says Sherrie Flick, author of *Whiskey, Etc.* and the award-winning *I Call This Flirting*.

## Writing Flash Fiction

Why write flash fiction and not the traditional short story? The short story itself is a compressed form, so why seek even greater compression?

For some it may be in the demands of such extreme brevity, the challenge of handling a whole piece of writing in such a short space.

"It's a great artistic expression," Kim Chinquee, author of *Oh Baby: Flash Fictions and Prose Poetry*. She sees flash as both a challenge and a gift: "Compression is a challenge when the story goes spooling out of control — 'Spooling off to where?' the writer might timidly ask. But then s/he acquires some backbone and welcomes the gift, self-bestowed largesse though it may be, to write short — to end the story in a flash. The challenge and the gift both nourish flash writers — I wish they occurred simultaneously more often."

Flash fiction can be an opportunity for experimentation, as it has been for Stuart Dybek, winner of many awards and author of two short-short collections (*Ecstatic Cahoots* and *The Coast of Chicago*). Dybek notes that he never set out to write flash "as such." Back in college, he tried out the short-short form "in relation to the prose poem." Because of its compression, he found it "a good form to work out prose rhythm, to play around with fragmentation, to inhabit the no man's land between fiction and poetry."

The experimental potential of flash has also attracted Flick, who enjoys "messing with craft elements, tuning in and tuning out of ways that traditional short stories are written." But her interest in flash fiction goes beyond using it for occasional experimentation. The form itself has attracted her, with most of her stories running 500 to 1500 words, though she didn't set out intentionally to write in the genre. "Writing short came naturally and early in my career," Flick says, "so it wasn't so much a decision as a revelation that this was the type of work I should be writing."

## Good and Bad Flash Fiction

A short-short story has to handle all the fictional elements seamlessly within an extremely tight space. Given these extreme parameters, what makes a piece of flash fiction truly great? Chinquee provides a sweeping list of key attributes: "Language. Imagery. Surprise. Things that are left out. Elements such as tone and point-of-view can fill in for the plot. Rhythm. And a smashing title and ending." For Painter, too, good flash has certain essential ingredients: "Density, texture, tension, forward movement, the necessary end." Related to texture, Flick stresses quality of language: "Excellent sentences. A kind of internal rhythm to the language." For Brown, "A myth of flash fiction is that *every word counts* (they don't), but that being said, the compressed space does put more focus on the language choices writers make."

What about mistakes, pitfalls, or problems in writing flash fiction?

Language problems, for one. With Flick's emphasis on compelling language, she warns against "lazy sentence structure." For Brown, the language pitfall includes "choosing the too-familiar word." For Painter, "dull language." And for Chinquee, a "lack of sensory detail."

Another problem area for Painter is a "static story." Flick, too, is concerned about this problem: "I don't think a piece of flash should rest on a gimmick or a joke or a super-long extended metaphor. I do think there should be a story inherent in the piece, and this is what separates it from a prose poem to some degree." But she does warn against trying "to bring too large of a scope to a tiny story."

Other pitfalls in story content and development, according to Brown, include choosing the too-familiar "setting, situation, and/or resolution; playing it too safe and relying too much on the same tired form and the same tired content; and going for the twist at the end rather than the deeper significance." As to endings, Chinquee warns against ending your story too soon. But above all, she cautions against "ending the piece by saying it's a dream."

But there's another way to look at this matter of overcoming mistakes in writing flash fiction. There's the position that the writer shouldn't be thinking in terms of "good" and "bad" at all. The goal of flash fiction isn't about achieving either dynamic. Consider what two leading figures in this field say:

For Dybek, the question of "good" or "bad" flash fiction must be seen within the context of fairly recent "anthologies, workshops, contests, etc." that have provided a set of criteria for the present generation of flash-fiction writers — criteria that wasn't in place when he began to write this form. "The genre — if it is a genre — was never about *shoulds*. It was about taking a chance, giving yourself permission to call something that might be a fragment a right to exist, the way a painter might decide to leave a painting at some point not quite finished, because it interests him more that way," he says.

Martone thinks along similar lines: "The truth is I really don't think about 'goodness' or 'badness.' That is the critic's job. The key element for me is not that a piece gets better, but that it gets different. I enter a text with curiosity for what this thing is: Is it a 'giraffe?' Is it a 'lion?' I don't make a distinction that the lion is better than the giraffe. You might as well ask what are the elements of a 'good' mammal? *'Yes, that groundhog there is looking a bit sketchy,'* " he jokes. "No, all pieces are interesting, different, fruitful."

### Submitting to Magazines

Hundreds of publications are open to flash fiction. What draws so many magazine editors to this form?

For online magazines like *Atticus Review*, "the online format is better suited to shorter fiction," says fiction editor Michelle Ross. It makes sense: Bite-size chunks of text in this medium are very reader-friendly.

But it's not just about convenience. "I confess to having a special fondness for flash fiction," Ross says. And so does Sue Walker, editor of *Negative Capability Journal*. Hers is an enthusiastic welcome: "Flash fiction is the way you fall in love. Someone is sitting at a bar, in a coffee shop, at the corner table in the library. You look up. Eyes meet — and *voila*. That flash, that momentary gleam in the eye is exciting. It is the promise of what is to come."

Though flash has its devotees like Ross and Walker, others simply treat flash the way they would any other fictional work.

"The reason to publish flash fiction is the same reason to publish fiction of any length — it takes hold of you and won't let go. I don't treat flash fiction as a special genre of fiction that is exempt from the same qualities that I look for in other short fiction," says Phong Nguyen, co-editor of *Pleiades*.

## Publishable Flash Fiction

Nguyen's remark takes us to the question of quality, of excellence. What makes good flash fiction from an *editorial* standpoint? The criteria come down to compression, language, character, story, and context.

For Ross, publishable flash requires adept handling of the form's restraint. "Good flash fiction is sharp, tight, and precise. It's immediate, cuts to the chase. One unneeded word or wrong word, and the reader's trust in the writer falters. There's great beauty in flash's compression. This compression tends to lend itself to great depth, too. The best flash fiction deals with big ideas, big emotions," she says.

For Laura Broom, fiction editor of *The Carolina Quarterly*, it's that "immediate impression," which flash is so well known for. There should be no delay, says Broom, "no time or words wasted in diving into the fictional world. Ideally, this brevity should work in tandem with evocative, deliberate language."

For Tara Laskowski, editor of the flash fiction online magazine *SmokeLong Quarterly*, the elements of good flash are covered by the magazine's guidelines. In general, it should begin with language that surprises and digs deep, generating narratives that strive toward something other than a final punch or twist. It should contain pieces that add up to something, oftentimes (but not necessarily always) meaning or emotional resonance. And it should be honest work that feels as if it has far more purpose than a writer simply wanting to write a story.

Good flash, according to Laskowski, situates richly developed characters in a well-delineated setting: "It makes the reader feel like the characters are fully formed people with histories and pasts, in a fully formed world that exists beyond the moment we are experiencing." Walker emphasizes not only strong characterization, but story as well: "Think inventiveness," she says. "Think surprise. And don't forget the importance of a title that says: *Stop. Come in.*"

Suggestion of a larger context is important for Nguyen. "This sets it apart from prose poetry in a way — that it renders more than a moment but a world," he says. A strong voice helps accomplish this: "I have a special fondness for strong voice stories in general, but if you can suggest a character through a compelling narrative voice, that goes a long way towards establishing wider context."

Anthony Varallo, fiction editor of *Crazyhorse*, values getting into the heart of the story quickly. "A good flash fiction leads the reader into a world already in full swing — if the story isn't already underway by the first punctuation mark, forget it — and builds to a moment of change or transformation."

In keeping with these standards for strong story development, Varallo lists three key elements of good flash fiction: the first line, the last line, and the title. He points out that all of these elements must work in tandem "in ways they don't necessarily have to in a traditional 5000- to 7000-word story, where you have more room to let the story's impact arise slowly, gradually."

Tara L. Masih is the founding editor of the new annual series *The Best Small Fictions*, which honors the best flash fiction under 1,000 words from journals and presses around the world. She notes that what is deemed as "good flash" changes based on historical and cultural context. "If you asked someone of the O. Henry period what a good flash was, they would have insisted on twist endings. Literary writers have gotten away from the twist in the United States, but it is still valued in other countries, such as China. I see many stories come from around the world that don't fit what we believe is a 'good flash' in the States, and our team of mostly U.S. editors must overcome our own prejudices and open up to different formats and approaches to telling a small story."

Masih says editorial staff must be open or receptive to cultural differences. "We try to judge each story on its own merit and use more of an emotional and stylistic rubric: Does the story have power and resonance in a small space? Does each word count? Does the writer offer us something new in terms of language, structure, voice, point of view, punctuation use, worldview? Is it concise (not just short)?" she says.

## Unpublishable Flash

So where can flash fiction go wrong? What kinds of problems do magazine editors note in the slush pile?

"One of the most common mistakes I see in flash submissions," says Ross, "is that the writing just isn't tight. The sentences are flabby. The writer wastes words on details that are not important to the piece." Varallo also rejects manuscripts that "spend the first few lines clearing their throat." Walker presents another problem related to flabbiness: "A story fails," she says, "when it falls into explanation, into redundancy."

Treatment issues can be a problem. For Walker, "A story fails when it tends to preach or become sentimental. This editor, then, leans over and, with a flourish, drops it into the round waiting can."

Another problem is a failed attempt at ambiguity. According to Nguyen, "It's very easy to mistake obfuscation for ambiguity when writing a flash fiction story. In an effort to suggest a wider context, some writers can fall back instead on vagueness and obscurity." He turns to Anton Chekhov for clarification: "I think Chekhov's old saw about the task of the writer being 'not to solve the problem but to state the problem correctly' applies here, but some writers forget the second half of that burden, which is to be as sharp and lucid with your prose as possible."

Lack of development can be another pitfall. "A lot of the stories we get don't feel like flash," says Laskowski. "They feel like scenes from a longer work. Or they are short stories cut down to 999 words to meet our guidelines. Or they are just character sketches, with no narrative arc or story."

Endings can present another problem, says Brown. "As a reader, I want an ending that takes me somewhere — that moves beyond where the story began. A description of a moment without significance is unmemorable, however lovely the language may be."

## Submitting to Small Presses

It's one thing for a magazine to take a few pieces in an issue and another for a book publisher to invest in a volume of flash fiction, whether an anthology or a work by a single author. But there are a fair amount of small presses that regularly publish book-length microfiction collections.

Rose Metal Press is one of the leading publishers of flash fiction. The press publishes two full-length books a year and also holds an annual chapbook contest for flash fiction as well as flash nonfiction, with the winning entry being one of the two genres.

"At RMP, flash is one of our flagship genres, an exciting form that inspired our focus on hybridity and mission to promote innovative writing in the first place," co-founders and editors Abigail Beckel and Kathleen Rooney tell me in a jointly written email. Rose Metal Press's book-length works include the novella-in-flash form, composed of stand-alone pieces that work toward a larger whole — a win-win for both the individual piece and the volume as a whole: "The flash pieces allow for the immediacy and punch associated with flash writing, but they have recurring characters and plot points that connect them to a longer narrative arc," Beckel and Rooney say.

Red Hen Press is another venue for flash fiction. According to editor Kate Gale, the press is "interested in the future of hybrid fiction, especially flash fiction. We've been publishing one book of flash fiction a year, and we hope to continue to do so." Given readers' fleeting attention spans, "flash fiction seems ideal," says Gale.

BOA Editions is also open to flash fiction, though publisher Peter Conners says he doesn't actively seek it: "We publish two fiction collections per year, and if there is a flash fiction collection submitted that stands out among the other submissions, I'm more than happy to publish it."

## Creating a Collection

Unlike magazines and journals that publish individual pieces, a book publisher must decide not only on the integrity of each story, but also how it fits in the overall work. So what kinds of unique problems do book publishers see in their submissions?

"Most of the neat tricks that brought flash fiction to our attention in the first place are now old hat. So it's not enough to simply give very good interpretations of flash fiction as you know it," Conners says. "You need to infuse it with something new, something surprising, something that is uniquely your own." He's noted too many manuscripts that demonstrate "mastery of the form," but lack anything "singular to that particular author."

Even if the individual stories pass muster, what about their place in the volume as a whole? What must transpire in a book-length work of flash fiction to be publishable?

"With flash collections, you want them to speak to each other across the collection without having them all say the same thing or compete for space," says Conners. "It's very tricky, and it's why there are few flash fiction collections that can sustain compelling interest across a single reading session. That doesn't mean they're not good — they just need to be read one piece at a time, with breaks in between."

He adds that a successful volume is a matter of masterful layering. "The best flash collections can be read more like short story collections — with meaning, symbolism, tension, etc., accruing as one reads deeper. Ultimately, you want the reader to end the collection and then start it all over again feeling compelled to read the early pieces with the gravity and understanding they've accumulated along the way."

Masih, who mines many single-authored flash collections for *Best Small Fictions* each year, agrees. "I often feel collections would be more powerful if some filler stories were dropped. Just as each word needs to be important in flash, each story should be important in a collection so the whole achieves a narrative or emotional arc in order to be memorable. It's easy to recall a novel as you spend hundreds of pages with one story. [It's] harder to recall a flash collection with hundreds of small stories. Better there be fewer, with more quality and resonance."

Beckel and Rooney note the power of order: "It's common advice, but worth following: a flash collection should open with a super-strong story, one that sets the tone of the whole manuscript and that hooks the reader so that they want to keep going and read the entire thing. A weak first story can harm the chances of an otherwise accomplished manuscript."

As to the matter of overall cohesion, the editors state, "Even if a collection is not linked in terms of plot and characters, per se, we look for stories that are made cohesive by some other aspect: voice, atmosphere, and so on — traits that make it feel as though the stories take place in the same universe and go together because of some over-arching sensibility."

Books of flash that lack this overall unity risk rejection, say Beckel and Rooney: "If the individual pieces don't have at least some resonance with one another across the whole set, it's hard to want to publish them as a collection."

### Summing Up

It's easy to see the appeal of flash for both writers and editors. The form calls for adept handling of language, depth of development, and movement, resulting in richness yet restraint. So much is accomplished in such a short space. Remember, though, to keep in mind Martone's and Dybek's position as well: flash may not be about "should" or "good" and "bad." Perhaps it serves the writer in finding something *new* and *different*, and leaves the question of merit to others.

# Beating Out the Stiff Competition in Fiction Writing

What are the five most important things you can do to get your work accepted at a high-profile literary magazine — or to get your novel published? Answers from professionals vary considerably from submission issues to craft issues, from knowledge of the genre to the highest quality fiction possible, to the right attitude and the need for dogged persistence.

Let's begin with magazine editors at three prestigious magazines. As a writer what should you do if you want to get your stories accepted at these magazines?

## What Some Top Literary Magazine Editors Say

**Anthony Varallo, Fiction Editor, *Crazyhorse:* "Publishable" Isn't Enough!**

If you want to beat out the best fiction submissions, there are, to begin with, some bottom-line things you absolutely must attend to, says Anthony Varallo. First, proofread your work. Second, read the magazine you plan to submit to. Third, if you're submitting fiction, you should read plenty of fiction. "If you wish to write short stories, you must read short stories and read them massively." Fourth, says Varallo, it's important to read your work out loud — especially the opening pages — watching for anything that doesn't "ring true." Fifth, Varallo cautions writers not to submit a first draft — because this is "work that simply isn't ready yet."

But why *these* five? Varallo explains: "The five points above all congregate around a single idea, namely that writing is *work*, and you must work hard if you want your stories to go out into the world. There can be nothing careless, sloppy, inattentive, or thoughtless in the stories you submit — instead, your stories must show, sentence by sentence, that you've done the work of writing."

Yet work can be good — but not *great*. And *Crazyhorse*, Varallo makes clear, is looking for great, memorable work — work that lives on: "A 'publishable' story is perhaps one which gives the editors little to do, but — and this is important — a publishable story is not necessarily the same thing as a story we're going to accept." Out of the hundreds of "publishable stories" *Crazyhorse* receives each year, only a "handful," Varallo says, are accepted for publication. These stories are the ones "that we can't forget, that speak to us, that we love, and that we hope our readers will love, too." What's *publishable*, then, "is too low an ambition for publication" at *Crazyhorse*. "The story has to do more than just be 'publishable.'" What it in fact has to do is linger in the memory of readers for a long time after they put it down.

### Susan Burmeister-Brown, Co-Editor, *Glimmer Train Stories*: Stories That "Matter"

The story that lingers on, the one several cuts above the merely "publishable," is also what *Glimmer Train* editors are looking for. Susan Burmeister-Brown, Co-editor, sums up the editorial criteria succinctly. "The reader cares about the characters, and thinks about them after the story is over. The story is rooted with some detail so that the reader has something to envision and hook into. The dialogue, if there is any, is believable. The story offers a deep and fresh view. It matters and it lingers. At the end of the story, the reader is satisfied. It doesn't mean everything is wrapped up nicely, but that this piece of the journey has come to a sense of closure."

What *Glimmer Train* is looking for, then, is the truly knock-out story. And here's why: The first three criteria Burmeister-Brown includes relate to the adept handling of key elements of fictional craft — character, detail, dialogue. The last two editorial standards surely depend on an artistic handling of these elements, though with any story, as any serious student of fiction knows, the sum of the parts is never equal to the whole, and while it's hard to pinpoint *all* of the elements that must be added to the three elements of craft Burmeister-Brown focuses on, it's clear that the finished story must accomplish just what she says it must. The story that provides a "deep and fresh view" is the kind of story that illuminates the intricate meanings integral to felt or lived experience. The writing is "deep" because the story is layered, not surface-level or superficial. The story is "fresh" because it doesn't depend on clichés or platitudes. It's not predictable; it's absolutely new. And for this reason, it gives intelligent readers "satisfaction," both intellectual and emotional. It's indeed the story that "matters" that meets these tough demands, and yet this is high quality literary fiction, and that's what *Glimmer Train* editors want.

### Susan Mase, Fiction Editor, *Nimrod*: Stories That "Dazzle"

Editors at *Nimrod International Journal*, a prestigious literary journal that is among the oldest in the country, are also looking for that great short story, and Susan Mase, Fiction Editor, describes what this looks like: "The story that quickly rises above the rest, the sure thing, often grabs our attention at the first sentence, delights or compels in some way after a paragraph or two, and sends us racing to the finish, our senses heightened with the promise of discovering a stand-out piece." Such a find, says Mase, "speaks to us, dazzles or connects us."

If Mase admits she cannot provide a precise definition of this "stand-out piece," it does have certain recognizable qualities, she says — a distinctive voice being one. *Nimrod* editors are sensitive to this voice, the kind "that captures our attention from the first word to the last." They hear it in the story's "rhythm, turn of speech, personality." A second quality is "fully alive characters." Mase emphasizes that editors "see a character emerge from the way he or she talks, gestures, acts, and not necessarily by what we are told by an omniscient narrator." In other words, this is a character that comes alive before them — realized through dramatization: by showing versus telling. Third, regardless of the kind of story, it must be layered, giving the reader something to delve into, or "explore" — or, in Burmeister-Brown's language, it must be "deep." And, as with *Glimmer Train*, descriptive detail is also essential. Mase points out that such sensory detail delivers two payoffs: "Precise, vivid details bring your voice and content and characters to life, and carry us below the surfaces to reveal a keenly observed interior or exterior world." Fifth, a strong sense of place is vital, but it "must be a seamless addition to voice, character, and content and not included at the expense of narrative interest."

*Nimrod* editors often find stories that contain most of these qualities, stories that come close, says Mase, and they may reject the piece but suggest some revision. She urges writers to make these revisions promptly and re-submit, that "many of the stories we publish are the result of a second or even third try."

As we've seen, writers hoping to beat out the tough competition at the top literary magazines need to address a number of issues. Pay attention to submission standards. Bottom-line: proofread your work. Know the magazine you're submitting to — a marketing essential. Know the genre. Become a voluminous reader of fiction, especially short fiction. Your work itself needs to be finished, polished — with a strong sense of craft, of storytelling techniques, of story sense, evident from the first page of your manuscript. And go for the great story — not the merely "publishable." A lot of stories fall into this bare-minimum category; they're competent, but they don't "dazzle" the reader. Great stories have the power to linger with the reader long after the story has been read. Maybe it's due to the story's multi-layered complexity. Maybe it's the compelling description. Maybe it's the voice the readers remember. Maybe it's all of these. Top literary magazine editors know professional work when they see it, and also when they *hear* it — when they listen to your voice on the printed page. And that's from page one on.

## Short Story Writers & the Tough Competition

Naturally, writers see publication from a different perspective. They're at the creative end, and what makes a work great is often hard to judge, to be totally objective. Still, writers who have been at the game for some time certainly have developed what it takes to get their work accepted in the top markets. They know their craft. They know their genre. They know the submission game well. They know how big the slush pile is — and it's very big at the top literary magazines. They've developed hard-won strategies to beat the odds, and they've also developed the right attitude — a positive one. Rejection doesn't defeat them.

### Gary Fincke: "Read the Magazine"

Gary Fincke, whose work has been published in innumerable prestigious literary magazines as well as in a number of collections, including *Sorry I Worried You*, winner of the Flannery O'Connor Prize for Short Fiction, hits several of the same issues we've already seen: knowing the magazine, basic proofreading, and story quality.

First, says Fincke, "Read the magazine — it seems so obvious, but it's where to begin — editorial tastes matter to your chances — I began by sending my stories to magazines that had published writers I admired — there's a connection in that equation."

Second, proofreading: "Send a clean copy — again, so obvious, but a large number fail this test — I've judged contests where entries are obviously not proofread."

Third, "Give the story room — don't rush it out the door the day you believe it is finished — it's always revealing to read the story 'later.'"

Fourth, having authored several short story collections, Fincke offers some sound advice to those planning a collection at some point: "For a story collection, pay attention to the order of stories, the points of view and their varieties — the subjects — for example, unless you want the collection to be all coming-of-age stories, make sure that you don't have the bulk of them in that territory or they might seem redundant."

Fincke ends his advice on a familiar and crucial point: persistence counts. But he makes some important distinctions: "Be persistent — as long as when a story is rejected and I can read it again and still believe in it, I'll keep it in circulation; and the other side of that — sometimes when a story is returned I read it again and see it new — revision follows, or even discarding it." Persist with a story as long as you "still believe in it." Otherwise, revise some more — or … just put it away. You should consider "discarding" a story that's fatally flawed, or maybe there's no story there at all. That's not giving up; that's doing something positive. That's putting your energies in work that's worth your time and attention.

### Karl Harshbarger: "Write the Highest Quality Stories Possible"

Karl Harshbarger, who has published sixty stories in many of the top literary journals in the country, including the *Atlantic,* knows about beating the odds in literary magazine publication.

"My first suggestion is by far the most obvious," says Harshbarger: "write the highest quality stories possible." His other suggestions, he states, "pale beside this one." He explains: "The editors of the top ranked magazines are simply looking for the best material they can find (as are, I hasten to add, the editors of most 'lower ranked' magazines). If your writing is of high quality, eventually you will be accepted in one of the best journals."

In other words, it's just a matter of time? Well, no. Because there's certainly more at hand than a mere waiting game, as Harshbarger makes clear. There's the rigorous process of continual submission: "Be diligent and methodical in sending your stories out. This would seem to be an obvious suggestion, but I know a number of writers who work very hard on their writing but are seemingly haphazard in submitting their material. If the journal doesn't get your story they obviously cannot consider accepting it."

In the highly competitive world of publishing, it doesn't hurt to have a sense of realpolitik, notes Harshbarger: "When possible (and, of course, within limits) cultivate some kind of personal relationship with editors and/or members of their staffs. Since there are a lot of fine stories being written, sometimes (as in the rest of life) who you know can make a difference." In other words, a foot in the door can't hurt. Schmoozing might get you a reading with a senior staff member. But the story had better be good.

Fourth, for Harshbarger, read the good journals and know what they want. There's an obvious difference, he points out, "in what the editors of *The New Yorker* seem to want as compared to some other literary journals." That is, magazines reflect different sensibilities, different tones. This is another way of saying know your market.

Finally, Harshbarger warns the writer not to be naïve about the nature of the game: "Be aware that the market is highly capricious and the damndest things happen or (more often) don't happen." The upshot? "It's not your fault! At least 50 percent of the time it's the gods up there!"

And yet, while there's an undeniable subjective component in creative writing, Harshbarger does urge writers to persist in developing the highest quality stories possible. In the midst of a battery of rejections, you can be assured, Harshbarger believes — despite the mysteries of capricious fate — that top quality work will ultimately find a good home.

### Robert Garner McBrearty: "Write!"

Robert Garner McBrearty is the author of three story collections, including *Episode*, winner of the prestigious Sherwood Anderson Foundation Fiction Award. His third story collection, *Let the Birds Drink in Peace*, was published in 2011.

First, McBrearty emphasizes being the professional that the business requires: "Write! This sounds obvious, of course, but the writer who writes regularly, who works hard, has a much better chance than the writers who don't." Send your work out regularly, Harshbarger tells us. Make sure you have plenty of it to send out, says McBrearty.

Second, "Develop something distinctive in your work, whether it's the type of stories you tell or your own distinctive writing voice. Easier said than done, but this is where the combination of work and inspiration comes in." Hard work "increases the chances you will become inspired," says McBrearty. If you plod along for a while, uninspired, you need to realize that "writers often make breakthroughs, have sudden insights that transform their writing for the better." It's these insights, surely, that are needed for the story with a "deep and fresh view" that *Glimmer Train* calls for — and for the story that "dazzles" the *Nimrod* editors. Stories without insights are dull. They are flat and one-dimensional and offer no surprises.

Third, McBrearty turns to the opening page, which must absolutely grip and pull the reader in: "You need a strong opening page. If the first page isn't appealing, the story doesn't have much of a chance. I don't mean you have to have a great hook or something extraordinary. I just mean the prose has to be smooth and sharp." It must suggest a page-turner, says McBrearty. You have to gain your editor's interest — and confidence — right off.

Fourth, attitude. "Have a positive attitude but be realistic. (Though a certain amount of fantasizing comes naturally to fiction writers and may be a healthy thing! If one didn't dream big, why bother?). Accept that you're not going to beat out the competition most of the time. For every story published or award won, most writers have many rejections in between." We understand McBrearty correctly when we see the difference between being realistic and being defeatist: Acknowledge the odds, but don't give up.

Fifth, says McBrearty: "Build a backlog of drafts, fragments. That way you always have something to work on. You may have a story or partial story that's been sitting around for years and you pick it up and suddenly see it anew. Inspiration isn't just about creating something new — it can be about finding the treasure in something old. On the other hand, don't spend too long going down a dead-end road. Writers need to sense when it's time to let a story go and move on." There's a time to "discard," as Gary Fincke advises.

## Beating the Competition with Both Stories & Novels

Mark Wisniewski can speak to both short story and novel publication. His stories have been published widely in the top magazines in the country, and his novels have been highly acclaimed, though these accolades have required patience on his part. His short story "Straightaway" appeared in both *Antioch Review* and *Best American Short Stories 2008* after having been rejected for nearly two years; his first novel, *Confessions of a Polish Used Car Salesman*, was compared to *Huckleberry Finn* by the *Los Angeles Times* and sold out two printings after having been rejected for ten years; his second novel, *Show Up, Look Good*, was rejected for seven years before its recent publication by Gival Press, after which it was praised nationwide and likened by numerous reviewers to *The Catcher in the Rye* and *Bright Lights, Big City*.

According to Wisniewski, the five things needed to beat the competition for success in the best publishing venues include, first off, a great story. He speaks of his recently published novel: "To beat out the competition, a writer needs to be open to finding a great story. I try to keep my eyes, ears, and mind open. I was lucky to hear *Show*

*Up, Look Good's* narrative voice in my head, and luckier still to have been open to it."

Second, says Wisniewski, the writer needs the "ability to recognize a great story as great." He points out the difficulty of doing this. "There are so many mediocre stories in print that it becomes difficult to recognize a great story as such. Ask yourself: Has this story been told before? What makes it different? Does it make me uncomfortable? If so, maybe that's a good thing."

Third, a writer needs the "guts to write a great story." This might sound a bit odd, but Wisniewski explains: "There are plenty of reasons why a writer might be afraid to write a great story. Political and social agendas of editors, publishers, writing teachers and English professors affect would-be boldness. It's probably true that to write a great story is to risk failure, loneliness, harassment, and/or ridicule."

Fourth, Wisniewski stresses the "ability to revise optimally." This takes some doing, he points out: "Most writers are too impressed by themselves and their work in general to revise a great story sufficiently. And sometimes the knock-dead core of a great story will exist in the writer's head but not completely on paper. Alternately, a great story can be whittled away by too *much* revision. At times I worry about this regarding *Show Up*, which, thanks to an agent, ended up being only half of its original length, leaving so much of it implied that some readers don't 'get' it. Optimal revision is a matter of balance, and ultimately a matter of serving the story above all else."

The fifth and perhaps most crucial must for Wisniewski is persistence in the face of rejection. "A great story is more or less guaranteed to face significant rejection. This might be because agendas in publishing do indeed result in the success of 'safe' work, but it's also because of huge slush piles, poorly trained or motivated editorial assistants (who are, in their defense, paid little or nothing), editors' desires not to offend sources of funding, and so on. In any case, the writer of a great story might need to withstand rejection for months if not years before publication, and even then, publication might bring modest financial reward."

These are indeed hard-hitting comments about the market

from an author who has served his time in the trenches. But what Wisniewski sheds light on here is the average reader's desire to read the great story — and yet the writer's difficulty, first, in knowing exactly what the "great story" really looks like, given the abundance of less-than-stellar work found in print. Whether or not one shares Wisniewski's view of the state of published fiction — and of the lack of good models for the "great story," given the market's frequent opting for the "safe" — his idea about needing *guts* to write the great story must surely resonate with many writers. Greatness, Wisniewski suggests, is revolutionary. It challenges the staid, the conventional. It makes us uncomfortable. And given Wisniewski's experience, trying to get great work published may mean years of rejection. Yet shouldn't writers stick to their guns and write only what they know is absolutely outstanding? Wisniewski believes they should, and he encourages them to both develop and value the "guts" to do so.

Great fiction means work of very high artistic quality — meeting the kinds of standards we've seen from three top literary magazine editors. If you as author deem a piece of your fiction great, and you've written and revised it to enhance its greatness, don't give up on it, regardless of any apparent scarcity of payoffs. If it's truly great fiction, it will *eventually* find a good home, as Harshbarger tells us. And publication in the best places, the venues with the toughest literary standards, has always been validation for writers, and great work eventually gets there, though the route may be long.

# Rise of the Novella

The novella goes way back to *The Decameron* by Boccaccio, to *Candide* by Voltaire, and, within the last hundred years or so, to Thomas Mann's *Death in Venice*, Franz Kafka's *The Metamorphosis*, John Steinbeck's *Of Mice and Men*, among many others.

So what exactly *is* a novella?

As a form, the novella combines the compression of the short story with the sprawl of the short novel, and many writers as well as readers find this attractive. The novella typically runs about a hundred pages, though it can run a bit longer. But usually the novella is designated by word count, not page count. A novella typically starts at about 20,000 words and tops out at 50,000, which is the minimum length for a short novel. There's no mathematical exactness about this word range, but generally speaking, when a work falls a few thousand below 20,000 words, it's a novelette, and when it falls under 7,000 words, it's a short story. When it's 50,000 and climbing, it's a short novel, until it hits about 80,000 words, and then it's a standard novel.

But here's the catch: A work of fiction falling below 80,000 words is a long shot to be published by a commercial press.

Excepting digitized romance and sci-fi/fantasy novellas, novellas are a hard commercial sell even if you bundle two to three of them or include your novella in a short story collection (story collections typically don't sell either). Unless you're a well-known author, you'd probably do better going for a small or independent press. You won't stand to make big money, but if your novella is good and you persist, you *can* eventually find a good home for it. There are plenty of small presses that are highly respected for the good work they publish. Your 30,000-word novella may even be published as a stand-alone, either in regular print or digital, at a small press.

However, small presses often don't publish many novellas, perhaps one to two a year at the most. Why? The reasons vary. Price point can be an issue because, like their commercial counterparts, small presses do have to stay afloat. Like other forms, novellas must earn their keep, and this may come down to having a viable marketing strategy.

But it's not just financial considerations: Some smaller presses may publish only a few books per year, and novellas aren't the only form they publish. Some presses, though welcoming novellas, simply haven't received any they like. Some, like Brooklyn Arts Press, haven't received any novellas at all — but the press is really open to them. Publisher/Editor-in-Chief Joe Pan says, "I'd love to publish a novella at some point, but people don't submit novellas to me. They submit short fiction, flash fiction collections, collections of prose poems, or novels. For me, a small press publisher, a novella would be a perfect sale, because fiction sells better than poetry, generally, and shorter novels cost less to produce. Win-win."

Green Writers Press has published just two novellas, with one in the works, but Publisher Dede Cummings says that "it is a great form for us that we want to publish more of."

Jon Roemer, publisher/senior editor of Outpost19, also hasn't published very many novellas, but he particularly appreciates the form. "We publish novellas because they pack a good punch. They also take remarkable concision and all-round artful storytelling."

Furthermore, several magazines, including the *Alaska Quarterly Review*, *Seattle Review*, *McSweeney's*, and *Novella-T*, publish novellas, either serialized or in full.

Some magazines have created a platform to publish novellas outside their pages. Under its Working Titles outprint, *The Massachusetts Review* publishes novella e-books (7,000 to 25,000 words), and *Ploughshares* now offers its digital-only Solos (7,500 to 20,000 words). There is a novella contest hosted by the prestigious *Quarterly West* and novella options in the Drue Heinz Literature Prize, which offers $15,000 plus publication by the University of Pittsburgh Press.

So there are homes, then, for your novella. But let's go back. How does the novella happen? Do writers plan it in advance, aiming for a certain number of pages or words? What special features does the novella form have for writers, and what story elements determine its length? How do editors view this form, not only from a marketing angle but also for its special capacities? What tips do both writers and editors have when it comes to the novella as a form? Four novella writers speak out, followed by four small press publishers who have found a place for novellas in their lists.

## Author Bios

### ♦ Tara Deal

Author of *That Night Alive*, winner of the 2016 Novella prize from Miami University Press.

Her previous novella, *Palms Are Not Trees After All*, won the 2007 Clay Reynolds Novella Prize from Texas Review Press.

*photo by D. Constin*

### ♦ Jane Smiley

Author of 14 novels, three novellas, two short story collections, five works of nonfiction, and five YA novels.

Her novel *A Thousand Acres* won the 1992 Pulitzer Prize and National Book Critics Circle Award.

Member of the American Academy of Arts and Letters. Won the PEN USA Lifetime Achievement Award in 2006.

### ♦ Robert Garner McBrearty

His short stories have been widely published, including in the *Pushcart Prize*, *Missouri Review*, *North American Review*, and *Narrative*.

Author of three short story collections, one of which won the Sherwood Anderson Foundation Fiction Award.

*photo by Norm Rehme*

*The Western Lonesome Society*, published by Conundrum Press, is his first novella.

### ♦ Josh Weil

Author of the novel *The Great Glass Sea* and the novella collection *The New Valley: Novellas*, published by Grove Press.

A Fulbright Fellow and National Book Foundation 5 under 35 honoree.

He has received the American Academy of Arts and Letters' Sue Kaufman Prize, the Dayton Literary Peace Prize, and a Pushcart Prize.

*photo by Jilian Carroll Glorfield*

## Small Press Summaries

### ♦ *Alaska Quarterly Review* (*AQR*)

One of America's premier literary magazines and a source of powerful new voices.

Founded in 1980 and published twice a year, AQR's global perspective is influenced by the people, cultural traditions, and environment of Alaska.

Michael Dirda wrote in *The New York Review of Books* that *AQR* "remains one of our best, and most imaginative, literary magazines."

### ♦ The Chicago Center for Literature and Photography

CCLaP (cclapcenter.com) is a full-service arts organization that publishes original books and produces a weekly online magazine and monthly podcast.

Sponsors semi-regular live events and local classes and workshops.

### ♦ Nouvella

Founded in 2011 by Deena Drewis, Nouvella is an independent publisher dedicated to novellas by emerging and established authors.

Nouvella titles have been selected as a National Jewish Book Award winner, a Lambda Literary Award finalist, and an Amazon Best Book of the Month.

Nouvella has helped launch the careers of *New York Times* best-selling authors such as Edan Lepucki and Emma Straub.

♦ **Outpost19**

Award-winning book publisher committed to delivering provocative reading.

List includes critically acclaimed novels, memoirs, biographies, short fiction and essay collections, novellas, and anthologies.

Titles are distributed by Ingram Publisher Services.

## Part One: Writers speak out

*When you begin a work of fiction, do you know if it's going to be a short story, novella, or novel, or does the story just take you and seem to determine its own length?*

**Tara Deal**: I don't write short stories, so my choice is usually between extremely short flash fiction or the longer novella form. I really love the novella form, and I turn to that when I feel I have an idea that depends on a character's development or philosophical investigations rather than a single point to be made about something emotional or aesthetic. For example, a recent flash piece I wrote uses a Delmore Schwartz quote as a starting point, about how the mind is a city like London, and the piece tries to embody that idea in a short space, in a flash of thought. But for my novella *That Night Alive*, I was thinking about "art and failure, persistence and success," as the back cover copy says, and I needed the expanse of a longer form to work it out. And as a reader, I need the time that 100 pages provide to think about those ideas.

**Robert Garner McBrearty**: I'm a short story writer, and I normally have in mind a pretty clear trajectory — but not so with my novella. I started writing *The Western Lonesome Society* in very much an exploratory sort of mood. I really didn't know what I had on my hands, but I conceived of a writer writing to his imaginary literary agent with various ideas he has for novels. As I did that, I realized each of those ideas the narrator was mentioning to the agent actually had to become stories in their own right, so I used the story within story concept. In this case, there are several stories within the main story. I didn't really see it turning into a long novel, though. It seemed to me that the concept would only be interesting for so long. Early on, I knew I was writing a book of about 100-150 pages.

**Jane Smiley**: I wrote all three of my novellas in the 1980s. All three of them were explorations of particular emotional experiences. I have not written any novellas since. I think they were triggered by the emotional complexity of having children, and juggling them with marriage and a career involving students and writing books. All three presented themselves as novellas, and I wasn't tempted to make any of them longer or shorter. The ideas seemed to need focus and concentration but also a degree of length. I think that a short story works sort of like a lightning strike, and I felt that I needed more time to develop the situations. But at the same time, I wanted to explore the feelings of the characters with greater focus than I thought I could in a novel.

**Josh Weil**: It depends what we mean by 'begin.' I map out my stories over a long time in a process that feels to me almost as creative as a first draft. In the initial stages of note-making and scene-imagining, the story tells me what it needs to be, but by the time I'm putting words on the page, I have a pretty good sense of the story's general shape. I have been surprised, though: I began my novel, *The Great Glass Sea*, as a novella, but as I got deeper into it, elements (for instance, the main character's relationship with his mother) took on import that I hadn't foreseen and that I hadn't supported sufficiently and that led to the need to rethink the scaffolding — which pushed it into something larger.

*For you, what is possible in the novella that isn't in either the short story or the novel?*

**Deal**: In a novella, nothing is a distraction. There is no filler. Not that a novella has to be spare — it can be a burst of luxuriance — but nothing can be superfluous. And if you read it in one sitting, which you can, you can become immersed in the world of the book from beginning to end. And I think this allows the writer to build up some resonances and reflections that might get lost in a longer format. It also allows for some experimentation that might get tedious in a longer book. For example, in *That Night Alive,* the sentence that ends one chapter is the same sentence that begins the next chapter. I liked using that device as a link between seemingly disconnected material, but as a reader I wouldn't want to deal with that for 500 pages or so.

**McBrearty**: The novella opens up a lot of possibilities, including more scenes and a larger cast of characters. The short story may take some asides, flashbacks, flash forwards, but most of the time the use of these is much more limited than in the novella. *The Western Lonesome Society* also allowed me to take several different points of view. Though of course there are exceptions, the short story usually takes one point of view. In *The Western Lonesome Society*, I went into the heads of various characters, and I saw the novella form as providing an opportunity to experiment with narrative structure. There's kind of a manic intermingling of stories, starts, stops, sudden cutting away from one storyline, veering to the next, which I think would have lost its appeal in a full-length novel. So the novella was the right form.

**Smiley:** A novella is more like a play or a movie — you can follow one character or small set of characters for a hundred or 120 pages without shifting focus to the larger world around them. You can follow their changing situation and emotions from the beginning to the end of a fairly complex event or set of events (unlike a short story), but you don't really have to give much of a larger context for the set of events. So you can focus on feelings and give the novella a lot of complex emotional impact. Novels always explore the world that the characters live in, and so the emotional impact can be large, but it also might be mitigated by context — there is a constant balance that a novel must strike between the personal and the impersonal. I like that, and I love writing novels, but for intense feeling, I think novellas are the best.

**Weil**: The novella can combine the intensity of a short story with the generosity of a novel. It can be read in one sitting and focus fiercely on one corner of the world or of a character's life, and yet submerge the reader in that focus more completely and deeply — which can be a particularly powerful experience. But because it's short enough, it can allow for some of the experimentation of a short story without losing the reader. My novella *Sarverville Remains* (from *The New Valley*) is narrated in a fairly difficult and particular dialect, something that was vital to the tone of the story but that I don't know I could have maintained over 300-plus pages. More recently, I wrote a novella that was particularly dark and painful and, while there are certainly novels that plunge their readers into that for many hundreds of pages, I felt the level of emotional difficulty and intensity would have to be leavened over a work longer than a novella — so the form felt necessary to stay honest to the tone.

*What tips do you have for beginning novella writers?*

**Deal**: My advice is to read some novellas and see if the form suits you. Because you wouldn't want to write what you don't enjoy reading. Some of my favorite classic ones are Dostoevsky's *Notes from the Underground*, Melville's *Bartleby, the Scrivener*, and Thomas Mann's *Death in Venice*. Melville House has a wonderful series of reissued novellas.

**McBrearty**: If the storyline feels tight, it's probably a short story. If there are various places to expand, it sounds more like a novella. Consider your characters. In short stories, writers usually create characters in a sparse way. In a novella, you need to develop them, to go into more depth. Also visualize particular scenes in your mind. Plan several important scenes as well as thinking of the book as a whole. Expand the scenes. In short stories, we may cut the scenes short, but the novella allows you to more fully develop them. Fully describe the action. Let the dialogue build. Add some twists and turns to the plot. Surprise the reader! At the same time, though, one allure of the novella is that it's a faster read than a novel. Keep the pace lively and brisk, the story moving swiftly along.

**Smiley:** Because a novella is only about a hundred pages long, the reader will give the writer a little more leeway for different types of complexity — but you can only choose one type of complexity. I chose clarity of style and plot in my three novellas so that I could explore complexity of feeling (characters don't know or can't decide how to deal with the feelings that their relatives are giving them). But once you choose which type of complexity you want to focus on, you can really make that complexity intense and almost overwhelming, because you have to put it on the page, explore it and wind it up in a fairly short time. A good model is Kafka — much of his work gains intensity because it is focused and not very long. He immerses us in strange situations, explores the situations, and leaves the background out. He explores with such particularity that each story seems to pop off the page and take over the reader's mind.

**Weil**: Focus relentlessly on whatever the core of your novella is. For me, that's often a character's particular emotional wound that leads to a specific narrative question. I don't stray far from that. But it could be any other aspect of fiction; the key is, whatever it is, you can't scatter your focus away from it. But, in focusing on it for such a sustained period, you have to look a little harder, almost as if you're peering through layers, so that you are hitting the same thing in more complex (and simply *more*) ways than you would in a short story.

## Part Two: Editors speak out

*How many novellas have you published in the past few years, and what are your publishing goals for the novella in the future?*

**Ronald Spatz, editor, *Alaska Quarterly Review*:** *Alaska Quarterly Review* (*AQR*) has published three novellas between 2013 and 2016, and has another forthcoming in *AQR's* winter and spring 2017 edition. *AQR* publishes the full range of fiction — from short-shorts/

flash fictions to novellas. We take our role as a *non-commercial* publisher seriously, and therefore we are open to all of those forms. In that sense *AQR* is among the scarce platforms that publish works that are generally too short or too long to be published in mainstream magazines. Other than the practical consideration that we do not have unlimited space in our print editions, the length of a work is certainly not what primarily drives our decision-making.

**Jason Pettus, owner, Chicago Center for Literature and Photography**: Since starting up our trade paperbacks in 2014, we've been publishing one or two novellas a year, and then another couple of short-story collections the size of novellas. We will likely continue in this vein for the time being, although that number mostly depends simply on how many great manuscripts we get of that size, not any predetermined quota.

**Deena Drewis, editor, Nouvella**: We've published nine novellas since we started in 2011. For 2017, we've got a four-title list planned, which I think is really fitting for Nouvella. With our emphasis on helping launch the career of new writers specifically utilizing the novella format, we like to keep our focus really concentrated. In the future, the annual list could expand to six or eight titles maybe, but I think it's this idea of focus and intimacy between new writers and their new readers that makes Nouvella special.

**Jon Roemer, publisher/senior editor, Outpost19**: Six. Ideally, we'll publish four more next year and maintain that pace going forward. It's an opportunity to diversify the formats on our list. We market them in our Short-ish series, which includes extended essays, as a way to highlight them. But they're also part of our general list, sitting alongside novels, memoirs, and biographies, and are otherwise given the same marketing and promotion as any other title.

*The novella is a kind of middle-child between the short story and the novel. Do you see any strengths or special qualities in this form when well-handled?*

**Spatz**: At their best, these longer stories provide opportunities for narrative complexity and extended development in service of character in ways not possible in the shorter forms. James Joyce's *The Dead* and Jane Smiley's *Good Will* can serve as diverse examples why the traditional short story length would not have been adequate to develop the necessary scope and depth for these pieces. By the same measure, pushing those works to novel length would gravely dilute their power and focus. It really comes down to the fact that the novella is neither a lesser form of the novel nor a padded version of the short story. When the novella succeeds, it is because the additional length of the work is *required* to tell that particular story and bring it to its fullness of feeling and effect.

**Pettus**: I don't particularly see the novella format as especially different from full-length novels when it comes to specific strengths. I'm one of those people who just feels that every story out there has its natural length, with some of those being shorter and some being longer.

**Drewis**: The best thing about novellas is that they're exactly the length they're supposed to be. Because they've been more or less declared "unpublishable" by larger outlets and the big publishing houses, no writer really sits down with the intention of writing a novella. It ends up that length because there is no more to cut and no more to expand upon, which I think indicates a very thought-through, intentful manuscript. As for the strengths of the form itself, I always love looking at what Alice Munro is able to do with that medium-form length; her ability to move through vast swaths of time and space is proof over and over again why it's not only a valid form, but a necessary one.

**Roemer**: Novellas are the ideal vehicle for literary authors who like to drive their own way. They can do things in a novella that readers wouldn't tolerate in a work of 200 or 300 pages. The limited length lends itself to more intensity, sometimes with breathtaking concision, sometimes by sustaining a style or technique over a spectacular duration. It's a virtuoso's game, and readers win big. That's probably why they've lingered in classrooms, from *The Metamorphosis* to *The Awakening* to *Daisy Miller* to *Chronicle of a Death Foretold*. They've been career landmarks, too, like Saul Bellow's *Seize the Day*, Philip Roth's *Goodbye, Columbus*, or Cynthia Ozick's *The Shawl*. I've seen novellas eyed almost enviously, like the way John Irving used *The Pension Grillparzer* inside *The World According to Garp*, or Roberto Bolano's *2666*, which he originally mapped as five connected novellas. We've been reading them all along and maybe didn't always know it.

*What tips do you have for writers submitting novellas?*

**Spatz**: The novella as a form is problematic for print publishing primarily because of space considerations. So there are implications when *AQR* invests in a novella-length work — a number of traditional length stories have to wait for a later slot in our publication schedule. But *AQR* does not have a higher standard for novellas than stories. We expect the same compelling level of freshness, honesty, and development commensurate with the form. For writers submitting novellas to *Alaska Quarterly Review*, I would emphasize that it is generally *not* plot that ultimately hooks us but rather the voice of the piece. The voice must be *strong* and idiosyncratic enough to create a unique persona and drive the piece forward.

**Pettus**: As far as what we in particular look for in novellas, I encourage writers to see them more as shortened novels instead of elongated short stories. My advice for novella writers is the same I would give to writers of full-length novels: Pay close attention to how your piece balances plot, character development, and dialogue; and don't bother submitting it at all if you have't come up with a truly unique idea, because no editors in their right minds want to read their million-and-first tender coming-of-age story or generic technothriller.

**Drewis**: Stand by (and be proud of!) the fact that this is the length your work *must* be; novellas are becoming an increasingly viable format, and there will be more and more opportunities to publish your work.

**Roemer**: Novellas should be exceptional acts of craftsmanship, be it showy or subtle. Readers see them as something different, approaching them with heightened expectations, so we should do what it takes to meet them where they're at.

## Wrapping Up

If you've written a novella and are seeking a publisher, you can be confident that a small press is a good option. Don't be put off by the fact that not a lot of novellas are published by small presses. Publishing is always a tough act, but if you've got a great novella, you'll see it published if you keep at it. There are strong believers in this form, advocates, enthusiasts, and often, like anything you submit, it's just a matter of finding the right publisher at the right time.

# Part V
# Two Genres

# Writing Historical Novels

R eaders devour historical novels, and if you're setting out to write one, perhaps what motivates you is a compelling interest in the past. British writer Edward Rutherfurd speaks of how his strong interest in the past arose from several early influences: historical novels, his reading of history, family stories that went back for centuries and — a big influence — his parents moving to Salisbury southern England within walking distance of Stonehenge. And in Salisbury itself, an 800-year-old cathedral. In Salisbury, noted Rutherfurd, "The past didn't seem like a distant place."

Rutherfurd's story offers an interesting and useful paradox: The distant past can be imaginatively present. Making it seem so is precisely the accomplishment of historical novels: maintaining the attraction for the distant "then" as you bring this deep pastness alive in the dramatic "now." Clearly, it takes considerable research to pull this off. After all, so much from the past is lost to us — customs, fashions, modes of transportation — and yet all this must be recovered and made concrete. But how do you go about it?

## Researching Historical Novels

Adequately researching a historical novel means uncovering as many primary and secondary sources as possible and also traveling, or, as Lynn Cullen, author of *Mrs. Poe*, says, getting your "feet on the ground."

Primary materials include both print and non-print sources. Print sources can include diaries or journals, letters, maps, atlases and city guides. By reading diaries and letters, Stephanie Cowell, author of five historical novels, is able to flesh out a world with "things a character would see, would use or taste." Maps are important to C.W. Gortner, author of *The Tudor Conspiracy* and numerous other works of historical fiction. Gortner finds the Internet particularly useful for images and scans or re-creations of historical sites and maps. For *Paris: The Novel,* Rutherfurd made careful use of atlases, because, he says, "Paris has the finest set of historical atlases." Not only do they provide great visual material, adds Rutherfurd, but also precise historical detail: "I could tell you practically who was living on every street." For *Mrs. Poe*, Cullen used New York City guides and other accounts written during the mid to late 1840s. For these, the New York Historical Society Library was an invaluable resource.

Family histories can also be a rich primary source. When Rutherfurd was researching the medieval period for *Paris,* he turned to French people he knew for ancestral family stories. Some family stories, he notes, are available on the Internet. Social and cultural material is, of course, important in situating the reader in the time and place. Cowell pays close attention to fashions, recipes, and the art or music of the period.

The Internet is, more and more, a useful vehicle for researching primary sources — Google Images and Pinterest are two rich sources of pictorial information. To Cowell's delight, the Browning correspondence — and even images of the envelopes the letters came in — is available on the Web. This is a rich find for her novel-in-progress on Elizabeth Barrett and Robert Browning. The Internet has also been a great source for period music, including early wax cylinders with people's voices and even Robert Browning's voice on YouTube.

If primary sources are important to novelistic research, so, too, are secondary sources. In her acknowledgments for *Claude & Camille: A Novel of Monet*, Cowell lists a number of books she read about Monet and his fellow Impressionists while preparing to write the novel. Gortner reads biographies and social and political histories. Rutherfurd loves working with historians and museum curators. Here again, the Internet is useful, especially with biographies. Cullen values the "luxury" of Googling the people and times connected with her project. While she goes straight to the bibliographies of the entries on sites such as Wikipedia, she does caution novelistic researchers not to depend entirely on the Internet. Consider it a "springboard in finding printed matter," Cullen says.

A critical part of a historical novelist's research is travel. "I make a point," says Cullen, "of going to every single scene in my books, even if the place has completely changed. It's important to know what the air feels like, what color the soil is, what the topography is, what birds are around, and so on." Cowell has traveled widely to England as well as Europe to walk the streets where her characters walked. Although Rutherfurd had been to Paris innumerable times since childhood, in writing *Paris*, he felt he must "walk the place." Gortner also makes it a habit to visit places where his characters live: "I've been to the Tower of London several times, including a personalized tour to view apartments usually closed to the public. I have also toured the Alhambra in Granada, the alcazares of Segovia and Seville and the châteaux of the Loire, where a special tour of Chenonceau taught me how Catherine de Medici had designed the original gardens to grow vegetables."

It's vital, then, to situate yourself in the world you intend to write about. Do so in as many ways as you can to place your reader there as well. Of course, this is a task that takes serious commitment. But the more you like your subject, the more you'll be ready to take on the heavy load of work. "Do fall in love," says Gortner. "I cannot emphasize this enough. Without true passion for your subject, the research will become both daunting and overwhelming."

What about all the research materials you've gathered? How much will you end up using? More than half of the research Gortner has done on his novels he never uses. "Wear your research lightly," he says, "focusing instead on telling a magnificent story." Cowell takes the same position: "A few details mean more than a whole lot of them."

## Juggling Research with Writing

A question remains: When, during your novel project, do you do all the research, and when do you start the writing? One way to manage research with writing is to do some initial research, get started on the novel, then continue researching as you write.

For his very long novels, Rutherfurd does enough research to be able to produce a 40-page synopsis. "It's like an architectural plan for a building." In the case of *Paris*, this took him three months. As he moved into the writing itself, every time he came to a different historical period, he did more detailed research.

Gortner spends three to five months on "initial binge-research," then starts writing as soon as he gets a grasp of his character. As he writes, he continues to research, especially when he encounters "an unforeseen obstacle." His research can go on beyond the first draft into the revision stages. Get started writing early, he advises. "Research in and of itself can be seductive." Cowell agrees: "At one point," she says, "I have to stop looking at history books and just write the novel. I have to take all I have read within me and combine it with my own loves and longings and losses and let the character be born."

Cullen is particularly quick to get to the writing. After only a few weeks of "preliminary research," she's hard at the computer keyboard. She's anxious to get into her characters. Not that she does short shrift on the research: She continues researching as she writes. This approach, she finds, "results in the story coming slowly to the page since I'm learning as I go along, but the voyage of discovery using this method gives me such a creative high. It's a real treat to put together the puzzle of a story page by page, bit by bit of historical research. In this way, I experience writing the book much the same as a reader experiences reading it."

## Sticking to or Altering Historical and Biographical Facts

One issue in writing a historical novel is whether you should stick faithfully to historical and biographical facts or, at times, alter them to create a more interesting character or workable plot. And what about creative license?

Rutherfurd toes the line on major elements related to historical settings – kings, governments, key events. These major things the historical novelist must, without exception, get right, he says. Students of the French Revolution shouldn't find one's novel about this period off-track as to events and dates. But within these basic parameters, "You're free," he says, "to do what you like," as long as the work captures something essential about human nature, and *that*, as he points out, doubtless hasn't changed over the many millennia humans have trod the earth.

What about famous people? If you're using a historical figure, must you be bound to everything factual about this character? It depends on what you intend to change, says Cowell. She opposes changing what she calls "large facts," but she's willing to reduce the number of brothers a character has from six to four to avoid confusing the reader, and she's willing to "manipulate time" by reducing 37 love scenes to three because a "plot has to race along, whereas life is repetitive." As Cowell sees it, if she changed things radically, her characters would end up being fictional, not historical. In *Marrying Mozart*, she stuck as closely as possible to the biographical facts. But *Claude & Camille* was another matter: Much less was known about her characters, and she created them from as many historical snippets as she could find.

Cullen is adamant about sticking to biographical facts: "One of the little games that I play with myself as a writer of novels set in history is to never consciously alter facts to fit my story." Since her main goal is to write a novel about the human condition, she admits that she could surely play fast and free with the facts. But she finds this somehow untenable, and so she chooses people with biographical information gaps. Cullen's novelistic method is to "find these gaps and to fill them with what *could* have happened."

Gortner is one who generally does his utmost to adhere to established record. His practice is to alter facts only when he doubts their veracity or a particular motivation or reason behind a statement or action. Gortner is careful to document any significant changes he makes in his afterword. If the choice does come down to historical fact or fiction, the latter, he believes, must win out: "One of the principal challenges of writing a historical novel is that you are, in the end, writing fiction: You must always keep in mind that your reader wants to both learn and be entertained."

## Creating Historical Settings

To situate readers in another time and culture, you must first "soak in the atmosphere," Rutherfurd says, and then to create setting, as with all fiction writing, place the reader in the world of the five senses. Your process will involve a careful selection of historical details that bring the world you're attempting to create experientially alive for your reader.

For Cullen, it's important to use as many of the five senses as you can, and, during research, writers should "look for as many sensory historical details as possible." In her own reading on New York, she turned up an interesting fact — that sailors complained in the 1800s that they could smell the stench of the city six miles out to sea. She couldn't pass that up: "I knew I would be popping that little gem into *Mrs. Poe*."

"One technique I use," says Cowell, "is to set my scenes in as many places as possible so as the plot goes along, I can also show the characters moving through their lives." In *Claude & Camille*, using setting to develop both plot and character, Cowell simultaneously gave the reader a strong sense of young Monet's experience of 19th-century Paris, including several cafés or restaurants, streets, studios, a wealthy home, a tenement, a blizzard, galleries, artist supply shops, walking by the Seine, gardens, inns, train stations, the cheap balcony seats in a theater.

To situate his readers firmly in historical settings, Gortner makes judicious use of sensory detail, depending more on suggestiveness than profusion. A good example, he notes, occurs in *The Queen's Vow*. In the story, says Gortner, a scene describing Isabella's awe upon arriving in the alcazar of Segovia shows the Moorish arcades and waterways in the palace. "She also hears caged leopards," says Gortner. "Her brother the king kept the leopards as pets — an eccentricity I incorporated." For Gortner, strong settings can serve a function beyond placing the reader in the historical past — they can also be melded into the narrative in ways that propel the story forward.

Like all fiction, writing historical novels takes time and commitment. With historical fiction, there is the added component of research, without which you cannot hope to place your reader in the time and culture you have chosen. Doing the research is no guarantee that you can pull off a successful historical novel. You must find ways to include strong details of every kind. When you've accomplished this effectively, the past becomes dramatically and compellingly real, and its ghostly mystery becomes as present as today.

# In Good Humor

**M**ost people enjoy a good laugh. Most people enjoy a good joke, a witticism, an unexpected twist or a good "snapper," as Mark Twain put it. Fiction can be laugh-out-loud funny, as it was for Ben Fountain reading Joseph Heller's *Catch-22* for the first time. "I still remember reading it on the bus, trying not to laugh hysterically and, of course, failing," he says. "People could see what I was reading, and they all understood." But humor in fiction doesn't have to be hilarious. It can be dry or deadpan, as in Nathaniel West's work, offbeat or quirky as in James Thurber's, dark as in Flannery O'Connor's. The authorial sensibilities vary, but all are known for their humorous take on people and the world. It's the sensibility rather than the particular breakdown of comic writing that makes the humor work.

If you're interested in writing humorous fiction, the first step is to decide what your own lens, your particular slant on life, is. What makes people, human experience, and the world at large, funny, odd or bizarre to you?

## The Humor Impulse

Sam Lipsyte, author of *The Fun Parts* and *The Ask*, has his own take on what works. "Every writer has a slightly different filter," he says. "Every person does. We are always creating narratives from the information we absorb through that filter. The shape and tone of these narratives have much to do with our temperaments and our world views. There happens to be a comic streak in much of what emerges from me. I see the world as collisions and mergers of the comic and tragic."

Elizabeth Stuckey-French, author of *The Revenge of the Radioactive Lady* and *Mermaids on the Moon*, also believes that her penchant for humor writing comes from a native sense for the comic, originating, in part, from extended family stories "about people and the weird, funny, awful things they do," she says.

Amanda Filipacchi, author of *Vapor* and *Nude Men*, speaks of her own sensibility as "a slightly unusual way of looking at people and at life." If she has an artistic mission of any kind, it's "perhaps to slightly alter people's perception of reality," she says. "I'd like to help people see things in a fresh way. I am often also naturally drawn to writing satire."

Knowing what your particular sensibility is can help you clarify the narrative voice in your work. What does this voice suggest about your take on the world? Do your characters tend to view things in this way? If you tend to use humor in your fiction, it's important to consider what the purpose is. Do you want to be funny, or does your humor serve another, larger goal? If so, what is it?

## Purposes of Humor

Perhaps the most popular purpose of humor is to entertain, and clearly this is one key purpose of fiction itself. But if humor's sole purpose is to entertain, it may lose its effect, especially if it depends on one-liner jokes or slapstick. If it's "simply slapstick, it's not satisfying," says Stuckey-French.

Humor can certainly entertain, and should, but it can serve a much larger purpose. It can illuminate something about humans and the world in which they live. For Fountain, whose *Billy Lynn's Long Halftime Walk* was a finalist for the National Book Award, humor has a fundamental place in contemporary realistic fiction. "Practically every human situation is shot through with humor of one kind or another, if not inherently, then by virtue of the human animal's need to play, to amuse itself, to be entertained, to cope," he says. "Including humor in even the most 'serious' kind of story is, to me, simply a way of staying true to the experience." Humor is a matter of rendering human life authentically. Fountain rejects an attitude in contemporary American fiction that equates utterly depressing writing with the "profound and serious": "The best fiction, the fiction that stays truest to how complex and ambiguous most of human experience is, is fiction that weaves humor into the characters and narrative. Because it's there, usually, the funny stuff, along with everything else, the sadness, the tragic, the pathetic."

Jack Pendarvis, author of *Awesome* and *Your Body Is Changing*, underscores the close link in human experience between funny and sad. A comic mode allows him to explore what is true of humans and their struggles to achieve happiness in an imperfect world. As a comic writer, he enjoys exploring how silly the deepest longings can make us. "My hope is that people will respond to the characters with empathy — because we're all in that boat — though that doesn't always happen," he says. "Sometimes people will think I am being harsh with a character when in fact I completely identify with him or her."

Dark humor, also called black humor, is a literary mode that finds the comic in the bleak, the devastating and the miserable. One expression of this mode is hard-boiled realism. Stuckey-French judges her own fiction to be somewhat dark because she often pairs it with serious issues. But the purpose of humor in her work isn't, she points out, to make light of the issues themselves, which include sexual abuse and nuclear poisoning. The humor comes "in the way that people cope with those things." In doing so, they reveal their basic humanity, which, as Stuckey-French shows, is in itself at times humorous.

Black humor can be a response to the primal nature of human existence — a complex conjoining of the comic and the tragic. "Comedy and drama," says Lipsyte, "are about looking unflinchingly at our condition as doomed beings who still, out of some primal drive, continue to play the game. Humor stems from life, which you are trying to create with words."

Satire is yet another comic response to one's view of humans or the world at large. As a comic mode, satire can be burlesque with the hope of correcting a given folly or abuse, or it can be a lens on the world, illuminating flaws, shortcomings and pernicious practices by way of the ridiculous, the grotesque or the hyperbolic. Filipacchi sees her work as serving the second purpose. "When I write satire, the purpose is to highlight the absurd or unsavory aspects of the world, of human nature and/or of our society." Her satire tends to be dark. For instance, in *Nude Men*, a 29-year-old man can't restrain himself from giving in to the sexual advances of an underage girl. In dealing with this perverse temptation, Filipac-chi calls upon *reductio ad absurdum*, satirizing temptation's power over people struggling to resist it.

## Key Humor Techniques

Whichever form you write, straight realism with humor, dark humor or satire, you have a stock of humor techniques to draw upon: understatement, overstatement, irony, paradox, juxtaposition — to name key ones. Incongruity is at the heart of humor, as Fountain notes. "Humor, as my wonderful professor at UNC-Chapel Hill, Louis Rubin, once said in class, is incongruity. Put two things together that don't usually go together, and see what happens. Tragedy? Comedy? Often both." Pendarvis appreciates the kind of humor that "comes from the incongruity between a character's dreams and his or her lack of ability to achieve them, or the depth of a character's emotions versus his or her unfortunate way of expressing them." Incongruity allows him to blend the tragic and the comic.

Another humor technique is using flawed or questionable logic. "One thing I seem to be fond of," says Filipacchi, "is manipulating logic in ways that seem logical but that produce a completely insane result." In *Love Creeps*, for instance, the protagonist, who has lost her desire for basically everything, stalks someone at random. She's operating under the absurd notion that "if she goes through the motions of desiring someone, it will result in the birth of real desire in her," says Filipacchi.

A third humor technique, one which Stuckey-French uses, relates to a character's voice — to the character's internal thought and reflection. To manage this technique, says Stuckey-French, you may have to bare your own soul. "You have to be willing, through your character, to reveal your own vulnerabilities, judgmental atti-tudes, petty thoughts, self-pity. To put these thoughts in the mind of a character, you're acknowledging that you've had the thought, and that can make you feel exposed. But everyone has similar thoughts. In fiction, they are funny." In *The Revenge of the Radioactive Lady*, for instance, on one occasion the reader is privy to the protagonist's concerns about her family's old house being so filled up that there's hardly room to breathe, and she ends on this unflattering thought: "And they'd been so eager to fill it up with kids! What the hell were they thinking?"

Humor can also be achieved stylistically, by the manner of the delivery. As Stuckey-French points out, this happens through clever word choice, pacing and time. "If you listen to the delivery of stand-up comics, you'll see how carefully they manage those things," she says. "Writers need to do the same, at least during revision." Note the pacing in this passage from *The Revenge of the Radioactive Lady*: "The whole being-in-limbo thing, the looking-to-get even thing, was getting old. She was growing weary of wanting to kill Wilson, of imagining herself killing him. She was itchy to actually do it."

Finally, technique-wise, there are certain old standbys, among them puns and wacky character names. But before you employ these two techniques, give them careful consideration. "Nah" to both, says Fountain, "not for the kind of work I'm trying to do. I'm trying to play it straight, if that makes any sense. Trying to tease out the humor from what's inside the situation, as opposed to tricking it up with word play or witty names." Fountain believes that overloading names with humor is a cheap shot. He does make some allowances, however. "It can be sort of funny in Dickens; in Wodehouse it's funny, but when you're reading him, you're buying into an entire absurd universe where the silly names make perfect sense." Pendarvis points out that in really bleak fiction, wacky names can "temper the bleakness of the comedy," as they do in *Catch-22* or in the film *Dr. Strangelove*. But this technique is a risk, he says. "You have to be one of the greats to get away with wacky names, I think, and it has to be in a certain kind of piece." According to Lipsyte, "I just stick to this rule: Cute is the enemy of funny."

## Successful Humor

If you want to handle humor successfully, be sure you read good models. "Read the sort of books you want to write," says Stuckey-French, "and pay attention to what makes them good." She also encourages reading widely: "Stretch yourself now and then by reading the sort of book you wouldn't ordinarily pick up. Find writers who give you permission to let loose. Writing well is a matter of setting free your own voice and your own observations about the world without censoring yourself." For Lipsyte, one reason to read a lot is to make sure you're not repeating well-trod territory. But beyond this, he recommends reading as part of a larger goal of immersing oneself fully in life: "My mind is a swirl of the books I've read, the people I've known, the movies I've seen, the good and terrible things I've lived through, a lifetime of small peeves and pleasures, stories people have told me, things I've overheard and a lot more."

If you read carefully, you will get a good sense for how the professionals handle humor well in fiction. But what about the creative process itself? Should you plan your strategies out in advance, or should you just let the humor happen?

You should do the latter, say several pros.

The process, says Lipsyte, is "not something that's strategized." Filipacchi adds, "Consciously trying to use a technique to produce humor is not likely to be very successful. It seems to me that humor is more likely to be successful when one follows one's instincts." Stuckey-French never plans ahead for humor, and Pendarvis says, "I never think about humor first. I'm always thinking about character. The humor, when it comes, is usually a byproduct of the character I'm writing about."

So get into your character. Get into your story, and let the humor spring forth on its own from these two basic contexts. "The humor needs to serve the story, needs to come out of the story, as opposed to being slapped on from the outside," says Fountain. For Stuckey-French, this means letting the humor come "through your character" and not attempting to put "humor into what you are writing." But do be careful, she cautions, about humorous treatment of characters. If your humor is largely at the expense of characters, your readers won't care what happens to them. It's best, she says, not to be "cruel to your characters, or callous and dismissive." Her advice is, "Keep a balance between the sentimental, warm moments and the dark. Life has both."

Writing effective humor requires a masterful handling of techniques and an understanding of how humor should function in a work of fiction. Perennial subjects of humor are the follies and foibles of ordinary humans struggling to make it in a difficult and sometimes harsh world. How you handle this, whether the humor is mild or acerbic, will naturally affect the tone of your work. What tone do you wish to achieve? Light, dark or, as Fountain puts it, "piebald"? What's your own sensibility, your take on the world, and what purpose or purposes will humor have in your fiction? Humor alone isn't enough. As with all things funny, you need more than just a punch line.

# Part VI
# Interviews of Writers

# Tim O'Brien

Tim O'Brien has published several novels, including *Going After Cacciato*, which won the National Book Award in 1979. He is most famous for his collection of linked stories, *The Things They Carried*. Other fictional works include *Northern Lights*, *The Nuclear Age*, *In the Lake of the Woods*, *Tomcat in Love*, and *July, July*. *In the Lake of the Woods* won the James Fenimore Cooper Prize for Best Historical Fiction in 1995. His first book was a nonfiction work, entitled *If I Die in a Combat Zone, Box Me Up and Ship Me Home*, which was named Outstanding book of 1973 by the *New York Times*. He's won two other prestigious prizes for his work. In August 2012, he received the Dayton Literary Peace Prize Foundation's Richard C. Holbrooke Distinguished Achievement Award, and in June 2013, he was awarded the $100,000 Pritzker Military Library Literature Award.

*photo by Greg Helgeson*

# The Things He Carries

Early in his career, with a published memoir and one novel already behind him, Tim O'Brien won the National Book Award for *Going After Cacciato*, a novel dealing with the Vietnam War, in which he served. The Vietnam backdrop seems fitting now, of course: All of O'Brien's work deals with the war, either as a setting used directly or as a force that later shapes the lives of its participants. And yet, while Vietnam is always present, he is writing about much more. As he points out in "How to Tell a True War Story," in *The Things They Carried*, war isn't just hell; it's about many other things, too, including "longing and love." For O'Brien the war is a starting point for any number of complex character possibilities. His work is a profound rendering of humans in their many dimensions — mixing the tragic, the comic and the poignant.

His memoir *If I Die in a Combat Zone* (1973) laid the groundwork for issues he later explored in fiction, including the mind-numbing rituals of battle and the nagging question of courage and cowardice. Like the memoir, his two novels that deal directly with the Vietnam War are penetrating studies of war's effects on the human psyche. *Going After Cacciato* (1978) toys with the premise of escaping the war, with the entire novel projecting this escape dramatically for the reader. What would it be like to leave the war and find one's way all the way to Paris, a place of freedom and gaiety? The imaginative possibilities become compellingly real — not only for the protagonist, Paul Berlin, but also for the reader.

O'Brien's second war novel, *The Things They Carried* (1990), was a Pulitzer Prize finalist — and Houghton Mifflin marked its 20th year in print with a new jacket (as well as O'Brien's revisions and corrections.) Here, his protagonist, struggling with his moral dilemma over the war, comes close to fleeing to Canada and decides he's a self-betraying coward for not doing so: Unwilling to risk disgrace and mockery, he sets aside his doubts about the war's moral legitimacy. The novel grimly recounts war and its effects. The language is vibrant, the characters colorful and haunting, the work experimental in its use of both fiction and nonfiction techniques.

Several of O'Brien's novels deal much less directly with Vietnam, yet the war experience continues to arise in various ways, and with one persistent theme: how the human imagination, capable of manifold transformations, deals with it, spins it, or provides emotional release from it. In his debut novel, *Northern Lights* (1975), a key character returns home maimed by the war. Is he a war hero? His experience in Vietnam matches up poorly with the conventional views of town leaders. The war may have been an "adventure," but it's not one he'll talk about. Seeking his own self-styled adventure, something to fuel his imagination, he recruits his brother (the protagonist) for an arduous winter's journey through the deep Minnesota wilderness, which nearly costs both of them their lives.

One of O'Brien's darkest works is *In the Lake of the Woods* (1994). At the height of the protagonist's campaign for the U.S. Senate, his hidden Vietnam past emerges: He played a part in the My Lai massacre. His career in politics is suddenly over. Since childhood, his tricks as a self-trained magician have enabled him to recast the world in his own terms — to make a new reality by pretending. But no tricks can dispel this ugly truth.

O'Brien switches to bizarre comedy in *Tomcat in Love* (1998). The protagonist, a macho male who continually seeks dominance over women, pretends he's an alpha war hero, having outwitted six Green Berets back in Vietnam. In this quirky first-person narrative, O'Brien challenges the reader with a compelling, richly comic and often unreliable narrator.

Two characters in *July, July* (2002), a tragicomic novel set at a 30-year college reunion, are greatly affected by the war. One has left for Canada and escaped the draft but suffers a great romantic love loss, which his memory works and reworks for years. The other, a college baseball player, goes to war and loses a leg, and finds that he has only his fond fantasies to rely on — namely a hoped-for future with his college sweetheart, however doomed to failure that prospect was.

On the whole, O'Brien's characters struggle to find hope in worlds made dark by both personal and societal forces. Their imaginations often inspire them to seize life for what it might possibly offer — an escape to Paris, an exotic trip to Africa or Rio or a sudden romantic tryst. His canvas is broad, covering the personal, the philosophical, the social and the political.

**How did winning the National Book Award early in your career affect you as a writer?**

Not much. Naturally I was delighted. But still, when you sit down to begin a new book, you don't think, "I won the National Book Award." The mind doesn't work that way. It focuses on a story that needs telling, on the exploration of character, on the difficulties of composing decent sentences. The award certainly gave a boost to my career, and it validated many years of hard labor, but in terms of the writing itself, I can't say it was either helpful or an obstacle. The only thing that can really help a writer is to keep summoning the nerve to confront the blank page every day.

**All of your novels deal in some way with the war. Do you start out with that intention, or does it just happen?**

A mixture of the two. Sometimes I start out with the intention of writing about Vietnam pretty directly. At other times I start somewhere else, with no thoughts at all about Vietnam, and then end up going there anyway. The story seems to guide me there. I'm sure that has to do with the life I led and how important Vietnam was to me as a kid. It was traumatic, and I still carry the memories and the ghosts and the horrors along with me, and I suppose my subconscious has pushed my stories in that direction. A good example of the latter is *July, July*. As I began that book, I didn't think I'd be dealing with the war, but I ended up writing about it anyway.

**Your characters do a lot of fantasizing, and in several of your works you emphasize the role of the imagina-**

**tion and pretending. This theme seems significant to you.**

That's an important part of my work. I'm a believer in the power of the imagination in ordinary human lives, and it's much more important than we often credit. If you're thinking about becoming a doctor, you don't just make a wholly rational, pro-and-con decision. You're going to imagine doctoring, helping people, the long hours of residency, the great pressures and rewards that play out in your daydreams. You're going to make some kind of determination based at least in part on what you imagine. Do I want to put my hands in gore all day? If the answer's no, you're probably not going to be a surgeon. In our daily lives, we make concrete choices in response to our daydreams and imaginings and flights of fancy. And that is, I think, key to why I'm a fiction writer. If that element were not present, I'd be doing nonfiction. Or I wouldn't be a writer at all.

**The imagination can be a beneficial or destructive force. The epigraph in *July, July* suggests the latter.**

"We had fed the heart on fantasies..."? Yes, the human imagination can certainly have a destructive aspect. For instance, if someone obsessively imagines making a big score in Vegas, and if that person finally empties out his savings account and gambles away every last nickel, that seems to me pretty destructive. In general, I think the human imagination has a compulsive or obsessive aspect to it, and the consequences of obsession can be negative in the extreme. Some of my writing, such as *In the Lake of the Woods*, tries to dramatize that negative aspect. But of course I also believe that imagination is what in large part separates us from the chipmunks. We can envision a future for ourselves. We can envision a better and more decent world. We can envision ourselves as better and more decent human beings. And now and then we can take a bold, glorious stride into that which we've imagined.

**The vast Minnesota wilderness appears in two of your novels. Is it a shaping force for your fiction?**

It's an emblem more than anything — an emblem of a spiritual "lost-ness" and of a spiritual "searchingness," combined. As a kid, I once got lost in the Minnesota wilderness. I spent a couple of miserable hours blundering around in the forest, an 8-year-old totally turned upside down. The experience hit me hard and stayed with me into adulthood. And throughout my fiction, I've called upon that experience as a way of addressing, or dramatizing, a certain spiritual disorientation and confusion people sometimes encounter. I certainly felt lost in Vietnam, and not just in a physical sense. Others might feel lost in a career that is going nowhere, or in a bad marriage, or in the loss of a beloved child. In my books, the whole notion of "lostness" ultimately takes on a psychological and spiritual dimension.

**Much of your work combines a gritty realism with bizarre, quirky characters — falling in the genre of dark humor. What does this suggest about your overall vision or world view, or does it?**

It does, I suppose. There's a real world out there that influences all of us, and I try to be realistic about that. But moving through that real world are human beings who have their eccentricities, fantasies, warped viewpoints and bizarre internal lives. So I suppose my fiction reflects that mixture of realism, on the one hand, and bizarre eccentricity, on the other.

For me, a good story embraces both the ordinary and the extraordinary. I'm not interested in simply holding up a mirror to the world. I'm not interested in reporting on actualities and calling the result fiction. To my taste, a good story is a mix of the so-called real world and a much more mysterious and elusive interior world we all live in.

**What are the challenges in using this dark comic mode?**

The main challenge, I suppose, is to sustain a balance between darkness and comedy. Comedy, of course, is at least partly in the eyes and ears and heads of the beholder, and there's always the risk that readers won't find certain material funny in the least. In two of my own books, *Tomcat* and *July, July*, a number of readers didn't find much to laugh at — or so I've been told — even if I, as the writer, thought a good many scenes were side-splittingly hilarious. Other readers did not find the books funny.

My guess is that I'll be remembered, if I'm remembered at all, for my so-called tragedies: *The Things They Carried, Going After Cacciato, If I Die in a Combat Zone* and *In the Lake of the Woods*. Personally, I consider *Tomcat in Love*, if not my best book, certainly up there among the best. Yet I realize that most "literary" folks will disagree. In the end, it's a matter of taste, I suppose. My sense of humor, which tends toward the outrageous, is plainly not for everyone.

**In *The Things They Carried*, a work of fiction, you blur the line between fiction and nonfiction. The protagonist is named Tim O'Brien, and the characters have the same names as people you dedicated the book to. Can you say why you did that?**

Two reasons. The first is I set out to write a book with the feel of utter and absolute reality, a work of fiction that would read like nonfiction and adhere to the conventions of a memoir: dedicating the book to the characters, using my name, drawing on my own life. This was a technical challenge. My goal was to compose a fiction with the texture, sound and authentic-seeming weight of nonfiction.

A certain playfulness was involved. It was as if I were a bored tennis player who one day invented a new set of rules and put up a new kind of net ....*These are the rules I'm going to follow*. As a writer, that technical aspect is important — at least to *this* writer it's important. My hope was that by imposing certain technical requirements on myself, I would end up as a consequence with an interesting, compelling and fresh way of telling a story.

Secondly, I can say that the book's form is intimately connected to how I, as a human being, tend to view the world unfolding itself around me. It's sometimes difficult to separate external "reality" from the internal processing of that reality. As an example, let's say you fall in love with somebody. Real things occur: courtship, a first kiss, marriage, a honeymoon and so on. But your *interpretation* of these real events is a dynamic of the mind. "Boy," you think, "that woman really loves me." And you find out six months, two years, 20 years later, that ah, she didn't. And yet the world you've lived in for those intervening months or years was an invented or imagined world.

I wanted to capture that feeling in *The Things They Carried*. I wanted to explore multiple planes of "reality" and multiple planes of "truth." Yes, there is a real war going, with real casualties and real horror, but at the same time those realities are being processed in a mix of memory and imagination. Which is how we shape experience.

The war might take on a heroic shape. Or it might be shaped with bitterness and irony and guilt. This shaping process ultimately subsumes "reality." Reality — or what we call reality — has traveled through the human mind and come out the other end as a blur. Which is why, late in the night, I'll sometimes find myself thinking back on Vietnam, asking questions such as, God, did I really *do* that?

**What about the use of footnotes, as in *Tomcat in Love* and *In the Lake of the Woods*? Why that technique?**

What I was just talking about. You live a life, and you footnote it. "I went to war" — footnote. "Reluctantly" — footnote. "I was drafted" — footnote. "I felt terrible about it, shouldn't have done it" — footnote. "But I'm not even sure about that. How do I know . . . what if I hadn't done it, it could be worse" — footnote. "If I lived in a world of absolute certainty . . . wouldn't . . .?" — footnote. Yet the world *is* complicated and ambiguous, and we footnote it.

You're lying in bed, and you recollect something out of the main text of your life — a blunder of etiquette, perhaps. And so you toss and turn, mulling it over, stewing in memory, full of embarrassment, and after a while you begin to footnote the blunder in various ways — a wee-hour running commentary on your own misdeed. I think all of us construct a story line for our own lives that consists in good part of such footnotes — qualifications, justifications, erasures, embellishments, adjudications.

**Do you have a standard writing routine?**

I get the kids off to school, and then I sit down at about 8:30 or so and write until they come home, which is around 4. I work on weekends, too, and on vacations — whenever and wherever I can find the time.

**How do you usually get started on a novel?**

It varies. Some novels begin with a scrap of language — for instance, "This is true," the first sentence of "How to Tell a True War Story." When I wrote that, I knew nothing at all about what would become the content of the story, or plot or character or theme, not a glimmer of a story line. I simply found myself tantalized by language itself, that flat declaration: "This is true." Instantly, I wondered *what* is true?

And, a few seconds later, I realized that the statement "This is true" had been made in the context of what I believed to be a work of fiction, which, of course, carries a bit of irony, since most of us don't conceive of fiction as "true." The very content of the story began to take shape as if by magic — how firm is so-called "truth," can truths evolve or reverse themselves over time, is truth a product of the mind, can one person's "truth" be another person's outrageous falsehood, can two "truths" be utterly contradictory and yet remain true?

Most importantly the question occurred to me: In what sense — if any — can fiction be regarded as "true"? Anyway, I then wrote another couple of lines: "I had a buddy in Vietnam. His name was Bob Kiley, but everybody called him Rat." Well, right away I was making stuff up; I had no buddy in Vietnam named Bob Kiley. The thematic focus and tensions of the story had crystallized without any conscious choice on my own part. Those three words — "This is true" — delivered a story to me.

**What else might generate an idea?**

Oftentimes, maybe half the time, a scrap of language will tempt me into a kind of playfulness, and that very playfulness will eventually lead me toward a kind of meaning, or toward a set of meanings I hadn't intended to explore, thereby opening up a whole new world of story.

Other times it's an image, a picture in my head, that won't go away, and eventually I'll try to translate the image into words. That's essentially how *In the Lake of the Woods* began, with a picture in my head of two people lying on a porch, a dense fog all around them, both people desperately unhappy. I had no idea who these people were, or why they were so incredibly sad, or what had brought them to that fogged-in porch. I knew nothing except that the image had been haunting me for a long while, maybe a year or two. It would occasionally pop to mind while I was washing dishes, or watching TV or reading a book. There was a certain mystery about it. Who were those two unhappy people? What was the source of their unhappiness? Would they find a path out of their troubles? So quite naturally, without any volition on my part, *In the Lake of the Woods* became a mystery of sorts.

Those two principles seem to lead me into a story: Either a piece of language tickles my storyteller's fancy or I'm seduced by a strong image that seems to cry out for dramatic exploration.

**How much revising is there in your writing process?**

Endless. I revise as I write. I might rework a sentence 10 times, 15 times or even, in occasional cases, a hundred times. And then, having finally locked the sentence down, I'll move on to the next sentence, and the same wrestling match will begin anew. Once a paragraph is completed, I may then go back and think, oh, my God, I don't even need that first sentence. So I delete it. But now I've got to revise the second sentence because it's become the first sentence, which requires a different tone or sound.

What I'm saying, I suppose, is that the sound of the prose matters to me. I aim for a certain chime to the prose, a certain music or melody. I'll often sacrifice the intended "meaning" of a sentence in order to achieve a more interesting sound. And therefore, in a very important sense, the sound of language is instrumental in the very content of a story or novel. Plot, characters, settings, physical descriptions — all these are at least as much the product of sound as they are conscious intent on my own part.

**Have you ever gotten really hung up on a novel? Any works you abandoned?**

Oh, God, I've abandoned lots of them. The magic of the unexpected didn't happen. I didn't surprise myself. The prose had a stale, moldy quality that couldn't be written away . . . . For me a book or a story can only succeed if it is driven by the unplanned and unexpected serendipities of storytelling.

**What do you tell beginning writers?**

Be stubborn. Be tenacious. Commit yourself to the inevitability of failure. Sentences are going to fail, chapters . . . whole books . . .

Secondly, I might also suggest that a writer pay close attention to his or her own life. Don't avoid your own passions and fears. There's a tendency, I think, to sublimate it all, or to become so oblique as to avoid entirely that which has hurt you or that which has jerked you awake at night. I know of no rule that commands a writer to be subtle at all costs. At times, I believe, it doesn't hurt to be blunt.

# Vaddey Ratner

Vaddey Ratner is a survivor of the Khmer Rouge regime in Cambodia. Her critically acclaimed bestselling debut novel, *In the Shadow of the Banyan*, was a Finalist for the PEN/Hemingway Award and has been translated into seventeen languages. She is a summa cum laude graduate of Cornell University, where she specialized in Southeast Asian history and literature. Her most recent novel is *Music of the Ghosts*, longlisted for the Aspen Words Literary Prize.

*photo by Kristina Sherk*

# In the Shadow of Terror

In 1975, when Vaddey Ratner was 5 years old, the Khmer Rouge took over in Cambodia. This was the communist regime that killed between one and two million Cambodians in ongoing purges. For the next four years, Ratner lived through extreme hardship and terror. Her debut novel, *In the Shadow of the Banyan,* is told from the point of view of Raami, a child facing the absolute tyranny of revolutionary fervor. First comes a massive evacuation of the city of Phnom Penh, its inhabitants relocated to the countryside to emphasize the primacy of the worker class over privilege and culture. Relocation soon becomes a means of breaking down bonds to place and establishing only one acceptable bond: absolute commitment to the revolutionary cause, the so-called "Organization."

As in *Nineteen Eighty-Four*, the expression of familial love and affection is not permitted. Though no one is secure from suspicion, Raami's family is especially vulnerable. As a prince, her father represents the old order, the feudal system, with its privilege, culture and education. Ironically, he, too, is disturbed by inequities in the feudal system and supports the revolutionary cause. As an act of valor, to save his family, he acknowledges his identity and soon disappears.

The extended family is broken up, and members are routinely executed. To escape further persecution, Raami's mother claims to be a former nanny. After losing her husband, she realizes they can no longer keep their former identities if they hope to survive. Starvation, lack of medical attention, and forced labor from sunup to sundown are standard. Only when Vietnam invades in 1979 are Raami and her mother able to escape to Thailand. The journey is arduous and dangerous. Ratner's haunting novel is a poignant story of suffering and loss and the triumph of the human spirit.

As for Ratner, she did not know English when she entered the U.S. in 1981. And yet she graduated valedictorian of her high school class and *summa cum laude* from Cornell University with a degree in

Southeast Asian history and literature. In writing *In the Shadow of the Banyan*, she drew from personal experience as well as considerable formal research.

**Your novel is based not only on your personal experience but also on your research on Cambodia. How did you conduct your research? Can you describe your process?**

All along, I knew my memory was incomplete. At Cornell, I focused on the history of Southeast Asia, particularly Cambodia, seeking an understanding of the historical, political and social situation at that time. During my studies and after, I also went traveling and lived in the region for nearly a decade. I wanted an accurate context for the story, but I didn't do research for the novel in the sense of reading and taking copious notes and then going off to write my fiction. I wanted my knowledge to settle and mature over time, knowing that specific facts and dates can always be quickly looked up.

**Fiction writers often find it hard to interweave materials of research into their works and still keep up the dramatic movement of the novel. How did you manage this? What obstacles, if any, did you need to overcome?**

In writing, I wanted the first-person narrative and my own understanding of the history and politics to blend seamlessly. It was the personal that drove me to understand the political. The personal losses and tragedies remained core. To this day when I think of my own survival, it is indivisibly linked to my father's disappearance, to the dissolution of my family and home.

My first full draft of the novel was almost 700 pages. Much of what I cut was the historical context, which I felt was not essential for most readers. While this material may have made certain details clearer, I felt it would have diluted the child's perspective and voice. It is Raami who carries the story forward. If I weakened her voice, her innocence and intuition, the dramatic effect would be severely reduced.

**You're really strong on setting. What are the most important steps to take to assure that setting is believable and integrated into the story?**

I could not have painted the setting as I did without going back to live in Cambodia for more than four years. It was important not only to capture in words but also to witness again how people relate to the landscape, to experience it alongside them. In fact, having *In the Shadow of the Banyan* described as a "historical novel" has taken some getting used to, because so much of the Cambodia then is still so apparent in the Cambodia now, in both its beauty and tragedy. When describing a setting that feels so immediate, so extant, I feel it's essential to be embraced by the landscape again, to immerse myself in that geography where there's no clear separation between past and present, where history is contiguous with today.

**Besides backdrop, what are some uses of setting in your novel? Mood seems to be definitely one.**

I feel I don't have the distance to deconstruct my own story in quite that way. What I was conscious of was not so much the technique but the goal — trying foremost to recreate the Cambodia that I remembered before the country became the "Killing Fields." To make it personal, to take it beyond the place I loved as a child and make it also a place my reader would love and care about, I needed to articulate it in the minutiae of a child's daily connection to the place, a connection cultivated with little preconceived notion or judgment of the surroundings.

**Your style has been called "lyrical." What does that mean to you? Are you a person committed to one style? If so, how do you describe that style?**

Again, style is not something I consciously think of when I write. When I sit down, my sole purpose is to tell a story that resonates. If something doesn't ring true with me, then I abandon it. I feel if I were to query my own style as I write, I simply wouldn't be able to write.

In terms of the language, I was conscious of making it as reflective of my native tongue as possible. What's more, Raami is the daughter of a poet, so she has a particular sensibility toward language. She sees the world through her father's words. I wanted not only to capture the rhythm of a very poetic tongue, Khmer, but also, through the narrative language of the novel, to intimate how the poetry of a people's everyday speech was silenced and transformed by the rhetoric of the revolution. I wanted to show that shift as the story progresses, but not in a way that would feel too conscious.

**Can you offer tips for other writers on improving style?**

When I start on a particular piece, I have certain challenges I want to confront, questions I want to answer, several things simultaneously to tackle and achieve. I'm conscious that I'm setting out to create. But once I'm fully in the story, I feel, I often transition from being the "creator" of the work to the vehicle for something larger than I'd intended. As the story takes on a life of its own, for example, the characters can become so real that I'm not only engaging in conversations with them but I have to listen to them. If I make a false move, they'll resist my rendering.

What I find most valuable is to avoid mimicking anyone or any style. For example, as much as I love layered, fragmented narrative and experimental writing, it was vital for me that this particular work — *In the Shadow of the Banyan* — be accessible to a wide audience.

So, I think, style is only as important as the goal. What is it that you hope to achieve with this piece of work? A writer needs to ask herself that. With *In the Shadow of the Banyan*, my goal was to honor the lives lost, the voices silenced, so language became very important to me. I wanted to memorialize beauty and courage, love and kindness, hope and humanity, with lyricism and poetry, with an intimation of something artful, to contrast with the mindless revolutionary jargon.

**Your characters seem very real. Walk us through a few steps of discovery you had with a character.**

They were real. To me, they will always be more than characters. But just because they are based on family members, people I once loved and still love, I never presumed the readers would necessarily automatically love them as well.

In creating characters that appear believable on the page as well as resonate with readers, I think in terms of more fundamental definitions of our humanness, the universality of our shared traits beyond culture and traditions, language and geography, politics and religion. What are a character's hopes and dreams, fears, regrets? What makes each stand out? Is it nobility in the face of degradation? Is it an inner fierceness in contrast to some perceived outer weakness?

Writing *In the Shadow of the Banyan*, I filtered all these questions through the perspective of a young girl, Raami, who's forced to grow up in extraordinary circumstances. Raami sees her father not only as someone of royal blood but of noble character, even if she doesn't have the language to articulate that. She finds in her mother a strength hidden behind her fragile feminine beauty. The story would be completely different if it were told from the perspective of Raami's father.

**Can you recommend some methods of characterization that might benefit beginning writers?**

Whether the characters are based on real people or completely imagined, you write and rewrite and rewrite until you stop thinking of them as characters but as people who inhabit a narrative landscape. And you trust them.

**Narrative point of view is especially interesting in this novel. How did you manage to filter the experiences of your child character through an adult lens? This isn't an easy thing to do.**

The ordeal so marked me that the child who endured it, whom I kept locked inside myself to protect her from the horror outside, still lives in me. I feel her. I can access her so fully, immediately, at will. What I have now is an adult language to articulate her hopes and fears, her confusion and acuity. In the novel, what Raami says in quotes, in dialogue, is true to her voice and vocabulary as a child. Outside the quotes, however, I allow the language of the child and the adult narrator to intersect, without clear delineation, so it is much more varied, layered.

Voice and perspective are very different. Raami's perspective only seems beyond her years because the narrative voice is so grown-up. Yet, a child of her age is capable of such observations and understanding, particularly in circumstances where her survival depends on it.

**What is your process for developing plot? Outline? Intuition? Discovery in the writing process itself?**

For this book, I had the overall narrative arc, knowing that I wanted to begin the story just before the revolution and end with the fall of the regime. In terms of the events that plot my story between these two poles, I had to work intuitively to select among countless scenes I could have included, keeping a pace that would move the story forward.

**How about theme? Is this something you consciously worked into your novel, or did you find that it just emerged more or less on its own?**

I came out of the Khmer Rouge experience mute. It was important to me, therefore, to say something about the power of language, when to use it and when not to. I also wanted to express something about stories and continuity — not only how they aid in our survival but how, for those who do not survive, their stories may be the only part of them that lives on. I wanted to speak to and honor the stories of those who died. For me, the question of theme or message is insep-arable from my own journey, my quest to understand my experience over so many years. Writing is part of that journey, and it's ongoing.

**Often writers are trying to answer a question with a novel. What is the problem you were trying to solve in this book?**

When facts fail us, when reality becomes too harsh to bear, when we have lost everything, what can we hang onto that allows us to move forward, to make sense of life, to invest it with meaning and purpose?

**You've spoken of having a second novel in mind. Has your debut novel led you toward this second one? If so, how?**

With *In the Shadow of the Banyan*, I wanted to honor those fallen lives. My next book is about the survivors: How do we contend with the shadow of genocide? It's a much bigger canvas in terms of time and geography, and it has the additional challenge that it does not so closely parallel my own life. Among other characters, I inhabit the mind and heart of an old man, a half-blind musician. It demands a very different approach.

# T.C. Boyle

T. C. Boyle has published sixteen novels and eleven short-story collections. His short stories have appeared in *The New Yorker*, *GQ*, *Esquire*, and *Playboy*. Of his novels, *World's End* (1987) won the PEN/Faulkner Award, and *Drop City* (2003) was a finalist for the National Book Award. He has won numerous awards and honors for his fiction, including, in 1999, the PEN/Malamud Award for Excellence in Short Fiction. *The Road to Wellville* was made into a movie in 1994, starring Anthony Hopkins, Matthew Broderick, Bridget Fonda, and John Cusack.

*photo by Jamieson Fry*

# Writing as a Way to Explore Things

A well-known satirist, T.C. Boyle has written wittily and incisively about famous monomaniacs who are often in pursuit of grandiose dreams, such as Frank Lloyd Wright, Alfred Kinsey, and John Harvey Kellogg, a doctor with strange beliefs who founded a famous sanitarium and health spa in Michigan and invented corn flakes with his brother (with whom he feuded the rest of his life). Boyle's love of history causes his novels to span 300 years, but he also addresses some key contemporary issues, including environmental threats, animal rights, and the global population explosion. In all, Boyle has published 13 novels and nine collections of stories.

His interest in history and penchant for the comic were evident from his first novel, *Water Music* (1981), which was set in the late 18th century. In this rollicking adventure tale, two men comprising an odd combo — a thief/whoremaster and a real-life Scottish explorer, Mungo Park — meet up in deepest Africa and together follow the Niger River to its source. (Park was the first European to lay eyes on the Niger.) The *Los Angeles Times* called it "a funny, bawdy, extremely entertaining novel of imaginative and stylistic fancy that announced to the world Boyle's tremendous gifts as a storyteller."

His considerable accomplishment as a writer aside, Boyle — who used to use the unwieldy middle name Coraghessan — is also known for his offbeat image, which can be a bit misleading. He has posed himself, in the words of writer Russ Spencer, "as a zany anti-establishment literary rock star — all steel wool hair, Van Dyke goatee, silver earrings, bad posture, black clothes, pointy shoes and razor sharp attitudinal wit. He's a former heroin-using Deadhead hippie freak who sang in rock bands and avoided the Vietnam draft."

But there are other sides to this Ph.D.-educated author, too. "I have this wild-man image and I am a little crazy," Boyle told the London *Guardian*. "But at the same time I'm a tenured professor, hardworking and diligent and a good family man. Karen and I have three grown children, and I must be the only American writer of my generation who has had only one wife."

A brief look at Boyle's takes on the three monomaniacs mentioned at the outset gives a pretty good idea of his literary flavor. As depicted in *The Road to Wellville* (1993), Kellogg's mania at his Battle Creek Sanitarium takes the form of draconian, bizarre measures to restore his patients' health. His rigorous regimen of dietary denial, enemas and sexual abstinence alone makes him a prime candidate for Boyle's satirical thrusts at this turn-of-the-century prophet of ideal health.

In this novel, Eleanor Lightbody, a third-timer at the clinic, brings her husband, Will, along with her in 1907 to deal with his drinking problem and bad stomach. Under the sharp scalpel of Boyle's wit, the "Battle Creek Method" soon proves to be not only exceedingly misguided but also life-threatening, and even the touted humanitarian motives of the "Chief," who exerts authoritarian control over his subjects, become suspect. Is Kellogg a total sham? Boyle's novel keeps us wondering.

In *The Inner Circle* (2004) Boyle deals with Kinsey, the nearly mythical sex researcher, whose life goal was 100,000 sexual histories of the "human animal." For Kinsey, sex is a normal "bodily function," not to be confused with love or marriage. Once in Kinsey's inner circle, both John Milk and his wife, Iris, get drawn ineluctably into the doctor's orbit of open sex, threatening their marriage. As Milk devotes much of his life to the sex guru, Boyle continually pushes the envelope, with darkly comic results. Milk, it seems, has increasing difficulty separating detached scientific study from "unprofessional" lust.

In *The Women* (2009), Wright, the world-renowned architect with a fierce loyalty to his profession, expects devotion on the part of his apprentices — or "acolytes," as they're called by Tadashi Sato, his student and the novel's narrator. The main focus in the novel is on the four women in Wright's life, women who, when he takes them on as mistresses, bring him joy yet complication: scandal in the press and the threat of law enforcement in a time of strict sexual morality. Overall, the stories of Wright's four women make for a compelling mix of action, romance, jealousy, pain and loss — a blend of the richly comic with the deeply tragic.

Of his more contemporary novels, Boyle used his environmental concerns as backdrops in two of them. *A Friend of the Earth* (2000) is a futuristic novel set in 2025-'26, when the problems of global population, deforestation, and global warming have taken their toll. Tyrone O'Shaughnessy Tierwater, the protagonist, recalls his years as an environmental activist, first as a member of a radical environmental group, then as a warrior on his own, bent on halting environmental destruction.

In Boyle's latest novel, *When the Killing's Done* (2011), environmentalists who set out to protect the Channel Islands off the coast of Santa Barbara, Calif., from invasive species encounter strong opposition from animal rightists. The novel pits a park biologist against an activist from a group called For the Protection of Animals — two characters unswervingly devoted to their causes. Both points of view become compelling and equally engaging as Boyle dramatizes the intensity of their commitment.

Boyle took up another hot-button topic — illegal immigration — in *The Tortilla Curtain* (1995). As a whole, Boyle's novels are informed by social, historical and political themes, though they certainly cannot be reduced to these. They are about living persons: their depths, complexities, needs and dreams. Boyle renders all this with intensity and emotion, and often with irony and acerbic wit.

**You've written a number of novels about famous historical figures — Mungo Park, Stanley McCormick (son of inventor and industrialist Cyrus McCormick), John Harvey Kellogg, Alfred Kinsey and, most recently, Frank Lloyd Wright. What attracted you to them?**

What attracts me to such figures, I suppose, is their wrongheadedness. With Mungo, who was a great hero and endured all sorts of privations and sufferings, it was perhaps a case of hubris that brought about his fate — but then, without hubris, where would we be? Can great things be accomplished without it? Or maybe chutzpah is a better word.

In the case of Stanley [in *Riven Rock*, 1998], his tragedy grew out of circumstances beyond his control — i.e., the schizophrenia that made him into, as the press of the day had it, "a sexual maniac."

Kellogg, Kinsey and Wright fascinate me in a slightly different way. Each was a great figure of the Progressive Era, each believing in the perfectibility of man and in his own gospel. Each was a guru, each an egomaniac. I like to wonder about the psychological cost to such men's followers. Give yourself up to me and my regime, each of these three would say, and I will make everything right.

**Your author acknowledgments show that you did considerable research for these novels. Did you face any challenges in handling these research materials?**

Not particularly. With Kellogg and Kinsey, it was a matter of reading extant biographical materials, then visiting Battle Creek, Mich., and Bloomington, Ind., respectively, not only to see where these men had lived and taught, but to plow through whatever materials were available in local libraries. A joy, really.

With Wright, because he is such a cult figure and so much has been written about him, it was a bit more difficult merely in selecting the material, and yet there were instructive — and yes, enjoyable — trips to Taliesin, Spring Green, and Madison [in Wisconsin], as well as to visit some of his extant houses elsewhere.

**Do you do most of your research before beginning a novel, or do you research as you write? How about *World's End*, which takes us back in history 300 years to the roots of two families in New Amsterdam?**

Ah, *World's End*. For that book, which is a kind of apologia for my unconscious youth in the Hudson Valley, I spent three months living near my boyhood town of Peekskill and rigorously researching history, ethnology and ecology as well as visiting historical sites. I had no idea what approach I would take — I simply absorbed material.

Generally, once I've settled on a subject, I plumb it until a scenario begins to reveal itself to me. I love history and love to present its oddities, to hold them up to the light for my own amusement and yours, too.

**Several of your novels take up environmental themes. What drew you to write about this issue?**

Looking back, I see that I have been concerned with environmental issues since the very beginning — my first book, a collection, was called *Descent of Man*, after Darwin. I like to consider our species in relation to the Earth that sustains us and to the other species with which we cohabit the planet. I love the natural world for its wonder and beauty, its apotheosis of the senses, and I mourn its degradation in our time.

I remember one of my early stories, "The Extinction Tales," from the aforementioned collection, in which I bemoaned the overpopulation of the globe, wringing my hands over the figure of 3.5 billion people upon the Earth. That was in the 1970s. As of this writing, we have just doubled that figure. How can we not be concerned? Terrified, really. For our species and for all the other rare and beautiful things going down in flames all around us.

**How do you decide how much background material to provide to give the reader a sense of these issues, without lessening the dramatic impact?**

I try to walk a fine line between delivering information and drama. Drama must always win out.

**Writing about topical, hot-button issues offers a challenge for the fiction writer — of not taking sides, of not editorializing. You clearly don't. How do you avoid doing this?**

Fiction, to my mind, is not advocacy. Fiction is art, is seduction, is joy and entertainment. I do not write fiction in order to make or score points, but rather to explore things — issues, positions, mysteries —

that intrigue or perplex me in some way. In order to do that, balance is required. A light touch. We don't want to be didactic.

**Your work tends to be satirical and darkly comic. How would you describe your vision of the human species?**

We see through a glass darkly. The existentialists had it right, at least in the beginning, before Sartre and Camus became politicized: Nothing matters in the face of individual extinction. We live in a preposterous dream. We are helpless, we are bereft, and the end is coming soon. (See my story "Chicxulub" for further comment.) P.S. I wish I had better news.

**Your analogies and similes are arresting, witty and funny. Do they just come to you, or do you have to work at them?**

Thank you. As I've said, creating art is to open up the unconscious and let things flow. You can't secrete a metaphor or bottle it in a jar.

***The Women* does interesting things with point of view and narrative technique. The introductions to each part are from a first-person narrator, one of Frank Lloyd Wright's students, with the parts themselves in third person. What do you feel you achieve with this narrative technique?**

What is achieved is up to the reader to judge. I will say, however, that the playful structure brought the book to life for me. I am indebted here to Vladimir Nabokov, among others. Of course, in having Tadashi narrate, I can comment on how we enter and read fictional worlds. The third-person sections and their often baffled footnotes allow for humor certainly, but they make the reader question the veracity of the text, which has been translated into English by Tadashi's American grandson-in-law. Wheels within wheels.

**Another example of creative point of view is in *A Friend of the Earth*, where the "present" time frame (2025-'26) is told in the**

**first person by Tyrone O'Shaughnessy Tierwater, while Ty's past is handled in the third person, with his thoughts in first person, in italics. Why did you decide to go with this method?**

Your comparison of the two books is apposite and hadn't really occurred to me, as I am seeking a way to make each narrative journey fresh. In the case of *A Friend of the Earth*, it seemed natural — in a book about global warming — to project into the future in order to assess, comically and sadly, its effects. And, as with the later book, *The Women*, the effect of the third-person sections, while not as overt, is to allow the reader to reflect on the fact that Ty, the protagonist, is writing them, and so his prejudices become apparent and the reader once again asks, what is real and what is invented?

**Your work is highly dramatic, and yet fully interior. How do you satisfy both fictional needs in your novels?**

I really don't know. There is a controlling voice in every narrative, and every narrative, no matter how intimate in its close third- or first-person point of view, admits that voice. And yet the trick is to make the reader forget the controlling voice and be seduced by the character's point of view. Which is why, as in the two examples above, it is sometimes intriguing — fun? — to burst the bubble and then puff it up all over again.

**Who would you say are your main literary influences?**

When I began writing in the early '70s, I was poorly educated in the traditional literature of the English language, but, in the way, let's say, of a rocker responding to the rock of his time, I gobbled up the writers then current, writers with a wicked sensibility, writers of lyrical talents and large vision: Robert Coover, Donald Barthelme, Gabriel García Márquez, Günter Grass, Thomas Pynchon and about 6,000 others.

**Of your own work, do you have a favorite novel?**

Because I am so often asked, I've elected *Water Music*, my first. I don't know if I've done anything quite like it since. Ditto *World's End*. It's interesting and not a little intimidating to look back on who you were when you wrote your early books and how you've changed since.

And, of course, that begs another question: How have I changed? Well, I'm happy to say that I retain most of my teeth and at least some of my hair, I've become enormously fat (I think I've gained maybe three pounds over my fighting weight), and I have crept inexorably closer to the grave. In terms of my work, I suppose I'm just a wee bit less of a wise guy and quite a bit more willing to take risks with the sort of narrative that doesn't come easily to me — e.g., excursions into non-ironic realism, as with the latest, *San Miguel*.

**You've published 13 novels, fairly long ones, as well as nine short-story collections. How do you manage such prolific output, along with teaching? What's your writing schedule like?**

Well, we've gone into extra innings now, and the score has changed. Let's make that 14 novels and nine and a half story collections. I've just delivered *San Miguel* and am working to complete the second volume of the collected stories, with a foreword by the author . . . .

The novel, incidentally, grew out of the research I did for my 13th novel, *When the Killing's Done*, set on the California Channel Islands, which I can see beyond my windows on a clear day. *San Miguel* is scheduled for fall 2012, and the second volume of the *Collected Stories* for the following fall.

How do I manage such a schedule? Obsession, pure and simple, and I would direct you for a fuller explanation to an essay on tcboyle.com called "This Monkey, My Back," in which I liken the thrill of artistic composition to a kind of drug rush. And high.

**Where do your writing subjects generally come from?**

For better or worse, I wind up filtering all experience through the medium of fiction. The result is that I can't properly respond to themes or subjects or events without plunging them into a deep fictional pond. Thus, happily for me, every breath we all collectively take builds toward my next story.

**Where did *Drop City* come from?**

*Drop City* grew out of the ecological impulse we discussed earlier. In this novel, set in the late 1960s, a group of back-to-the-earthers (read: hippies) uproots their commune and replants it in the very last frontier, Alaska. The question: Can we live sustainably, sensibly, outside the shadow cast by the ad-meisters and the spinning gerbil wheel of consumer society? The answer: No. There are far, far, far too many of us.

**Do you keep a journal?**

No. But I did for about a week, at the behest of my teacher at the Iowa Writers' Workshop, John Cheever, whose own journals are brilliant, moving and beautiful. I've always been afraid that the energy I have for my fiction would be dissipated if I were to channel some of it — any of it? — into keeping a journal. Alternatively, however, I have been writing a monthly blog on my website, running all the way back to the last century.

**How do you write? Do you begin writing, and just let it happen, or do you plan it out?**

I begin. If I am very, very lucky, something happens. But I am determined, each day of my life, to make it happen. Sometimes I succeed.

**How much do you revise, and how do you go about it?**

I am a fanatic. I revise constantly. When a manuscript is finished, it is finished. A final draft requires only the most minor changes.

**What advice do you have for beginning writers? What should they do if they want to get published?**

My standard advice is to come from a wealthy family. In addition, if they wish to be published, they should found a magazine which pays very high prices to famous authors and then squeeze their work in alongside the efforts of said authors. On the other hand, they could go my route: Work hard, never give up, and bombard every magazine extant with the greatest stories you can possibly conceive of. And a final prayer: Be lucky in your choice of partners.

# Elizabeth Strout

Elizabeth Strout is the author of six novels. Her short stories have been published in a number of magazines, including *The New Yorker* and *O: The Oprah Magazine*. She won the 2009 Pulitzer Prize for *Olive Kitteridge*. Her novel *Abide with Me* won the Book Sense pick, and *Amy and Isabelle* won the *Los Angeles Times* Art Seidenbaum Award for First Fiction and the *Chicago Tribune* Heartland Prize. She has been a finalist for the PEN/Faulkner Award and the Orange Prize in England.

# Strout's There

Spotting a former 7th-grade student parked near the marina, Olive Kitteridge, a retired school teacher, asks if he's going to invite her to sit with him. Without waiting for an answer, she opens the car door and settles in beside him. A large woman, she can barely fit in the cramped front seat. The young man, greatly depressed and suicidal, could do without her presence. But she gets him talking about his history since leaving Crosby, Maine, where this scene is set. She shares stories of her life, too — her son's depression, her father's suicide. Who is this woman who barges in on the life of her former student?

For one, Olive Kitteridge is small-town Maine — its people, their histories, their everyday doings. But she is more than a type: She is an outspoken, sometimes abrasive woman who barely tolerates her retired pharmacist husband; a woman who, during her son's wedding reception, clandestinely sabotages and steals selected personal articles belonging to her despised daughter-in-law; a woman who breaks down in tears when she encounters a young anorexic girl on the brink of starvation. She is also the central figure in Elizabeth Strout's eponymous Pulitzer Prize-winning novel-in-stories, one of four novels set in and explorative of small-town Maine.

As with other Strout protagonists, Olive Kitteredge is also a lens for the many trials and tribulations of ordinary folks in her small town — and, on a more universal level, a perspective on the human condition itself. Strout's work is never the idyllic, the pastoral — although it may be set there. Hers is traditional literary realism, sometimes with a satirical bite, as in her second novel, *Abide with Me*, in which the parochialism, gossip and pressure of small-town people might call to mind the pedestrian nature of the townsfolk of Sinclair Lewis's *Main Street*. Yet Strout is a writer of generous compassion for her many and varied characters. She pulls us intimately into their lives — and by extension, into our own.

Strout consistently does so through the use of the omniscient point of view, not such an easy task as many fiction writers can testify. Since her debut novel, *Amy and Isabelle*, she has used this authorial point of view not only to create sweeping, memorable portraits of three Maine towns — Crosby, West Annett and Shirley Falls — but also to capture the feelings of the characters who inhabit these places. They live hard lives in these towns, with long winters and restrained warmth. They're frustrated in their search for happiness and toggle from one kind of tragedy to another. Yet if Strout has a strong sense for the nature of suffering, she also provides abundant comic relief — often subtly humorous, at times laugh-out-loud funny. "It's just life," Strout says, "and life is funny."

Strout's fiction deals deeply with the personal but also moves on to the social — to class issues, primarily. In her most recent novel, *The Burgess Boys*, she navigates the religious and political as well. Here, Somalis who have found a place of refuge in Shirley Falls are clearly at odds with the town's long history of homogeneity. Then a young citizen places a frozen pig's head in the local Somali mosque. This event soon escalates, involving the legal system, politicians, the locals — and the Burgess brothers, born and bred in Shirley Falls and filled with the fight of patriotism for their town.

The following is an edited version of my phone conversation with Elizabeth Strout.

**You've been praised for your ability to "humanize characters." How do you accomplish this? What steps did you take, for instance, to create such a complex character as Olive Kitteridge?**

It's the ability to imagine very deeply. It's kind of like drilling down. I've gotten under the topsoil. Now I've got to go under the next layer, under the next layer, and so on. A lot of it's unconscious, but as I try to think of it consciously, it is that sense of continually going down, down, down. I think it's one reason it takes me so long to write. I just need to find out more and more and more as I go.

**How do you determine the tensions and conflicts your characters struggle with? Do you plan these in advance, or do they come to you as you write?**

I mostly do not plan anything in advance. I'm not a planner. I'm not very organized, so I tend to work in scenes, and they're not necessarily in order at all. What I will try to do when I sit down to work, particularly in the first stages of a book, is to write what it is that I'm seeing or feeling most urgently at that moment. And then hope that it will find its way into the overall tapestry — if it doesn't, it just ends up on the floor.

**You make use of the omniscient point of view in your novels, sometimes with fairly extensive authorial commentary. And yet we get quite close to your characters. How do you manage such a difficult balancing act?**

It's something I've spent my whole writing life trying to get a handle on. I think of it kind of like a spotlight that is moving around the planet, and it swoops down and takes a very close look at one person and then kind of moves off into the landscape and then finds another person to concentrate on. You can't switch point of view too abruptly. The reader doesn't want to feel pulled out of the experience of reading. It works as long as readers can feel like they're still tucked into that voice that's telling them a story. I think it really comes down to narrative voice. If you've got the narrative voice strong enough, you can do that kind of swooping out of the intimacy of one person's mind and then into the intimacy of another person's mind.

**Your settings are quite vivid. How do you manage to create such detailed settings? Can you take us through your process with an example, say, from *The Burgess Boys*?**

I keep asking: What do I see? If Bob Burgess is going to walk down Seventh Avenue on Park Slope, what does he pass? What does that look like? I'm very much of an over-writer, which is why I revise constantly and throw away *so* much. I throw away tons and tons and tons of stuff, and so I will write all this, and then I'll think: Which details do I really need to give a sense of what that's actually like for him?

**Your work deals a lot with small-town Maine. What draws you to write about this area, and what steps do you take in your work to avoid depending too much on fact and not enough on the resources of the imagination?**

I lived in Maine for the first 23 years of my life. I've lived in New York City for 30 years. I didn't really set out to write about Maine, but living here, I found that that landscape kept calling me, so a lot of that is memory because I come from generations of Maine people and it's very deeply engrained in my DNA. It's deeply familiar territory to me. For *The Burgess Boys*, I did take trips; I needed to see more specifically. The only thing I've ever used directly from life is the pig's head incident in *The Burgess Boys*, and even then, though that was factually real, I conflated that with other incidents that had happened in that town. For instance, there was not a rally around the pig's head incident, but a rally around something else that the mayor had done earlier. I used that pig's head incident because it was very compelling, and it was just sitting right there in front of me. The real perpetrator actually shot himself before the trial and was older than Zachary, so I fictionalized Zachary and made him somebody younger and less knowing. I didn't feel confined by facts because I was just using them as I needed them.

*The Burgess Boys* **deals with an important social and political theme. You take up larger themes, beyond the personal, in your other works as well. Can you speak to this?**

If you're really writing about life, they're going to be there. And I think that once you see that, once you see what you've written, you can either bring them out a little bit more or dampen them down according to what you're trying to do. All the way back to *Amy and Isabelle*, it always surprised me that people didn't see that as a book about class because it *is*. Isabelle's working in an office room of a shoe mill, and she thinks she's superior; she thinks she should be a teacher. She thinks she should be among the professionals, but she's stuck with these working-class people, and for a long time, she is quite snobbish about that. But in *Abide with Me*, these are *not* working-class wives. These women have money, not much, but enough to stay home. So I think if you're writing truthfully to your subject matter, these things will emerge. If I'm writing about kids who try to run away from Maine to go to New York and have a better life, then that stuff is going to show up because it's *there*.

**The Burgess Boys is somewhat experimental in narrative technique. It begins with a fictional prologue, written in first person, then moves into third person, in the novel proper, as a tale constructed by the first-person narrator of the prologue. Why did you choose this narrative technique, and what is accomplished by it?**

It's funny that I did that since I've never written a prologue before. I'd been working on *The Burgess Boys* for a number of years, probably about four or five, before I wrote that prologue, and one day I thought, well, why don't you fiddle around with a prologue? I was doing it as a kind of exercise, and even if I had it, I thought I might very well not use it. But then as the whole book took shape, I thought I'm *going* to use it. It's funny because it kind of goes against certain things I believe in as a writer. For instance, I don't like to change from first person to third person. But there was something about it that is truthful. Wherever we come from, we sit around mothers or old friends, and we go: "I wonder what happened to that woman?" Or: "What happened to those girls?" That kind of storytelling is just so intriguing to me. You really do wonder, and you don't know. And yet you realize as you grow older that they've gone on with their lives just as you have, and that's intriguing. Here's somebody that's just going to tell you the story. It's not a frame story because when I finished the last paragraph, I didn't want an epilogue; I didn't want the tone to change.

**On the whole, your work tends to be "quiet," and yet it's full of tension. How do you manage to achieve this tonal quietness in the midst of so much conflict?**

Again, this goes back to the narrative voice — this sense of telling a story. Kids still like to be read to — I hope they do — and that sense that I'm all comfortable and cozy and safe, so tell me a story — as long as the narrative voice is making me *feel* safe, and it has to be sort of a quiet, calm voice —well, then, bad or traumatic things can happen, but the reader will feel like *I'm still in good hands* because the narrator is not going to pull any tricks on me, or the narrator is not going to try to show off. It's all going to be OK because that's what the sound of the voice tells me.

**One thing that makes your fiction literary is your insightful use of the language — for instance, in *Abide with Me*, where one of your characters feels like "the inside of his chest were being scraped by a serrated grapefruit spoon." Care to comment on how you come up with such a spirited and apt expression?**

My mother must have wanted grapefruit spoons. I remember that from a young age. I haven't seen one in forever, but that image of scraping, it's probably just a feeling I had at some point, or again, just that sense of imagining — imagining, imagining, imagining. What does this *feel* like? Just finding a way to render it that's original — not relying on cliché, or conventional text, but what can I find that is truthfully what that feels like? A grapefruit spoon came to mind. A hundred and fifty things will dawn on me, so what I have to do is go back and keep the one that seems the best.

**What advice do you have for beginning and early-stage writers?**

I know the frustration which never goes away. You want so much to sit down and get it right. You have to learn to tolerate that frustration. You have to be patient and just keep writing. You're only going to learn it by doing it and by reading. You read and you write, and you read and you write. That's the hard part for beginning writers: having to accept that it may be a very long process. Also, you have to be willing to expose yourself — to put your true emotions in your work, or it will be flat. It really won't be something people want to read or find any comfort in reading because it won't be conveying to them some aspect of the human condition that they've experienced but don't know they've experienced until they read it — and then they'll say, "Oh, I've felt *that*."

# Christine Sneed

Christine Sneed has published two novels, *Little Known Facts* and *Paris, He Said*, along with two story collections, *Portraits of a Few People I've Made Cry* and *The Virginity of Famous Men*. Her short story "Quality of Life" appeared in *The Best American Short Stories 2008*, and her story "The First Wife" appeared in *The O. Henry Prize Stories 2012*. She teaches for the MFA programs at Northwestern University and Regis University.

*photo by Adam Tinkham*

# Le Mot Juste

"A strong protagonist," says Christine Sneed, "does much of the heavy-lifting in a work of fiction. The plot itself might not be very compelling or original, but if you have characters that seem to live and breathe on the page, they will more likely than not keep a reader invested."

Sneed's protagonists keep readers invested because they are layered with such depth that we come to know them like real people. We know what dominates their thoughts: what they want out of life, what they might have to settle for. Her two novels are rife with complicated conflicts, sometimes of her characters' own making, and yet they don't willingly borrow trouble. They make choices, like all of us, and some choices are like stepping into a river. There are undertows. The pleasure in reading a Christine Sneed novel is seeing how her protagonists struggle to stay afloat as well as they can — and to do more than that, if they can.

Sneed also fuels reader interest with intriguing story settings. For her first novel, *Little Known Facts*, it's Hollywood, though it would be more accurate to say the Hollywood movie industry itself. The novel centers on Renn Ivins, a rich, world-class actor, but an abject failure in the family department: a womanizer with two unsuccessful marriages and two mostly estranged children. His behavior can border on the bizarre, especially when he clashes with his son Will over eligible women. To get beyond his father's gravitational force, Will moves to Paris and gets busy writing a film script entitled *Little Known Facts* about his dysfunctional family. On the whole, Sneed's characters struggle to situate themselves outside of, or within, this Hollywood mogul's solar system.

Her current novel, *Paris, He Said*, is set mostly in the City of Lights. Jayne Marks, a fledgling artist, isn't succeeding in the New York art world. She meets gallery owner, Laurent Moller, a wealthy Parisian who invites her to live with him in Paris, where he promises to support her career. For Jayne, Laurent's offer is a ticket out of a life going nowhere fast, and she might be falling in love with him. In lesser hands, this novel could end up a tawdry romance, but Sneed's premise becomes an opportunity for novelistic probing. Capturing the deep interiority of her characters, Sneed portrays the ordinary push and pull of human relationship, the uneasy dynamic of expectation and result, and the unwieldy prospect of human happiness.

Sneed's command is particularly evident in the trajectory of her characters, her careful delineation of their self-knowledge. Character development is a gradual accretion of felt experience, the sensitive distillation of experiences and the realization of a new, possible equilibrium, however tenuous. But nothing is wrapped up in a tidy package.

Literary fiction, Sneed says, "ideally mirrors, with precision and insight, the world and our experiences as thinking and feeling social creatures. This mirroring is also, however, one of the aspects that can frustrate readers who are looking for answers, for closure. The world, at least in my experience of it, doesn't consistently offer the answers we are hoping to have when something ends — a relationship, a job, or, in this case, a story."

In the end, Sneed's gripping narrative voice is the hallmark of her fiction. As a stylist, she crafts detailed, lucid prose that holds her protagonists up to the light, exposing the myriad interstices of their complex beings. In addition, her acute sense of the right word —the *mot juste* — helps draw readers into the characters she so marvelously creates.

**How does setting generally come to you in the process of writing a story or novel? Why did you choose Paris as a setting for your new novel? What did it help you accomplish?**

I generally have a pretty good idea of where a story or a novel will be set before I start writing a new work of fiction. In the case of *Paris, He Said,* I knew before I'd written the first word that I wanted Paris to be the setting where most of the novel's events took place. I was a French major in college and spent the obligatory junior year abroad;

writing *Paris, He Said* allowed me to examine my sometimes-complex feelings for the French and their culture. Many Americans have such a strong attachment to France, and Paris in particular, and again, I hoped to understand my own feelings for this country and city a little better, as well as explore Paris's hold over the American imagination. It is the celebrated aspects of Paris's beauty — its art, architecture, fashion, food, parks, grand boulevards — that seduced me into setting my novel there.

**The setting in this novel is vividly portrayed. Can you walk us through your process of creating it? Did you study maps, take pictures, do very much research?**

I have visited Paris probably a dozen times since the year I studied in Strasbourg. When I was writing *Paris, He Said,* I traveled twice to the city from my home in Evanston, Illinois, for several days to make sure that I correctly portrayed the details I chose for the novel, and I did study maps and travel guides such as Lonely Planet's Paris guide. I also took pictures and scribbled many pages of notes as I walked through the city, especially the 18th arrondissement, which is where Laurent Moller's apartment is; I located it on rue du Général Foy, a few blocks southwest of the Gare Saint-Lazare train station, near a beautiful little park called the Square Marcel Pagnol. I looked at photos of Paris as I was writing some of the more descriptive passages, too. This helped me recall the feelings of awe that I felt when seeing these streets and landmarks in person.

**How were you able to gather enough information about Hollywood to able to write *Little Known Facts*? What made you want to write about the movie industry?**

Like many other people, I've always been curious about Hollywood and the film industry. When writing *Little Known Facts*, I drew on my impressions from the visits I'd made to L.A. over the last 12 years or so, and I have family members who work in the industry. Hearing some of their stories about the difficulties of making a living as an actor or producer or screenwriter — and about what might happen if you do make it — inspired me to write about the effects, as I imagined them, that fame has on the famous and their intimates.

**You often make use of expository prose and narrative summary. This is a risk in fiction writing, and yet you achieve dramatic power. How do you manage to do this?**

Well, I do sweat these parts of the story quite a bit; I do a lot of editing. A couple of years ago I saw George Saunders speak in Chicago around the time of the release of *Tenth of December*, and he said something that I continue to think about often, that is, how he tries for a line-by-line energy in each of his stories. I realized that this is also something I aspire to. If you're using interesting enough language, and you're doing your best to immerse your characters fully in a fictional world — one that seems immediate and sincere and authentic — these expository passages will ideally snap to life, but it takes time, for sure, along with a sometimes ruthless editorial eye. There really is a lot of revision involved. One thing that I try to do in my work is show how much I love the world, and to write with precision about it. I name the type of tree, for example, and describe its leaves. I want to be able to see it clearly, and I hope my readers will too.

**Spirited dialogue is crucial to page-turning work. How do you write dialogue? What are some tips you can give beginning writers?**

One thing I've come to realize is that the dialogue in good films has helped me learn to write better dialogue in fiction. And paying close attention to people who are talking who don't know you're listening — occasional eavesdropping on the bus or the subway, or in line at the library or at the movie theater — is very instructive. I like to listen to other people in an unguarded moment

You notice how some people change the subject without ceremony; non sequiturs are an excellent tool in dialogue writing because people's thoughts are often discursive, and reflecting this in dialogue can create an authentic ring to an exchange between two characters. It's also a good idea to dispense with the routine parts of conversation, such as: "Hi, how are you?" and "I'm fine, and you?" Pauses also are sometimes a good choice. The playwright Harold Pinter made effective use of them. Silence can be very expressive.

**How do you get started on a novel? How much do you manage the process, and what are your writing goals as you proceed?**

I usually begin with a character, and I often have a title, though in the case of *Paris, He Said* and *Little Known Facts*, ironically, I didn't. The titles came later, but with the short stories I've written, the titles have almost always come first. While I'm writing, I often jot down ideas in a little notebook I keep on my desk — plot points, bits of dialogue, notes on structure. I also do try to write a certain number of words every day. One writer friend goes by line count. Whatever it is that helps you get words down on the page, that's what you should do. But I think it's good to have a goal in mind when you sit down at your desk.

**Is there a moment in the writing process when you know: *I've got it*?**

I don't think I ever feel confident that I do. But with luck, I reach a point where I realize the characters seem to be people who could exist, and that if I met them on the street, I'd recognize them.

**When did this happen with Jayne and Laurent?**

I didn't really have a confident sense of who Laurent and Jayne were until I started the second draft of *Paris, He Said*. Once I started rewriting, however, I realized that I did know who they were. The process of getting to know a character is similar to how it is in real life: You spend time with someone and gradually you begin to understand who this person is, and possibly, some of what resides in his or her private heart.

**Laurent's story isn't as central as Jayne's, but he's clearly an important character. What did he need to accomplish for your novel to work?**

With Laurent, I knew from the beginning that he was cosmopolitan and a devoted, but not an amoral, pleasure-seeker. I wanted to try to understand how someone like him operated and saw the world, and I was thinking about powerful, wealthy men such as entrepreneurs like Steve Jobs, perhaps, and film stars or other celebrated artists who have access to the most beautiful women and men in the world. What kind of person do you become when you have so many opportunities to experience pleasure? Does it make you a happier person than someone who doesn't have access to glamorous people and experiences? This was at the core of my attempts to understand and create a character like Laurent Moller. He had to be someone who could make a reasonable argument for his behavior because this is a novel, at heart, in which I have to make sense of how people like Laurent, a man of many privileges, choose to live their lives.

**In both of your novels, you shift from third to first person. Why did you make these shifts, and what were you trying to achieve?**

First-person point of view allows a kind of intimacy that is harder to access with third-person, but there's also the danger that a first-person narrator will alienate the reader, and so the distance or detachment almost instantly at hand with third-person is valuable if you're striving for more objectivity in the story. I found switching point of view invaluable while writing *Paris, He Said* in that it permitted me to approach Jayne's and Laurent's interior lives from different angles. I could have them speak in their own voices and also have a third-person narrator portray them with more of a sense of detachment, if not complete objectivity.

In my first novel, *Little Known Facts*, I used first-person with a few of the characters that I wanted to lend especial poignancy to — Renn himself and his two ex-wives, for example. There's something more plaintive in their sections, perhaps, than in the others. They are making appeals to readers — to like them, to trust them — that I didn't think would have as much power in third-person.

**In *Paris, He Said*, why did you choose sections for your two point-of-view characters instead of alternating perspectives?**

I originally wrote this novel solely from Jayne Marks's point of view, in close third-person, but as I was working on the second draft, I kept thinking about Laurent having his say, and I knew that I very much wanted to dedicate at least one section to him, but I didn't want to switch from one character's point of view to the other within the same section. It would have compromised my attempts to create a fully-realized emotional and intellectual life for each of them, independent of the other. Having my main male character explain some of his behavior, to defend himself, in a sense, in his own extended section, was one way I tried to transform him into a more complex and possibly more sympathetic character.

**What can beginning writers learn about point of view? What's your advice, based on your own writing?**

Frequently when a story isn't coming together, point of view is one of the first elements a writer should examine: Should this be in first-person instead of third? It can be instructive, for sure, to change from one to the other. Narrative voice is also very much connected to point of view. For me, overall, I'd say that point of view is instinctive. I hear the voice in a certain way and know that it has to be first or third. I write more in third-person than in first; I like the detachment of third. It seems, perhaps ironically, more freeing than first, which is very much governed by the personality you're creating with the "I" that guides the story.

**How much revision do you do?**

I do a lot of revision. It's especially crucial with a novel manuscript. I rewrote about 90-95 percent of *Paris, He Said* from the first draft to the second. I basically started over; I opened a new Word document, copied in a few pages from the first draft and more or less trudged forward as if I were writing a new novel. Then I wrote five more drafts. My editor and I worked on seven drafts all told before she signed off on it and it went to the copy editor. She and I both scrutinized each sentence closely. I suppose that I am usually trying for a kind of prose that reads like poetry, a quality John Updike once said that he aspired to too. He wanted a reader to be able to choose any one page out of his novels and be able to read it as if it were a poem. Overall, the revision of this novel was absolutely exhausting. My first novel, *Little Known Facts*, however, came out almost intact; this was a rare experience, though, for me. It might be my first published novel, but it's not the first one I've written.

**Do you have a regular writing schedule? A regular writing place?**

I don't have a regular schedule, but when I'm working on a novel manuscript, I generally try to write every day, and get about a thousand words down if possible. I do have a preferred place for writing though. It's the desk in my kitchen/study area. It's near some west-facing windows, and it gets a lot of bright afternoon light. It's the one place in the world where I feel relatively focused and sane.

**Any tips for beginning writers on getting novels completed and published?**

You have to be very persistent about putting your backside in the chair every day and facing rejection and continuing to work despite the disappointments and frustrations. You also have to be able to differentiate between criticism you can use and the kind that you can't. In workshops I usually find that one or two people will read work in the way the author hopes to be read, and they will give feedback that speaks to one's own preoccupations as a writer. The other feedback, the writer has to be able to filter out. I also think it's important to finish a full first draft before you show it to someone because it's very easy to get derailed when you're in the middle of a long project if you show someone new pages and he or she says, "I don't think this character/this plot thread/this structure works."

**What's your final advice to beginning writers?**

Saying no when you'd much rather say yes to an invitation to see a movie, or to go shopping, or to go away for the weekend — this is one the biggest challenges of being a writer. You have to find a balance; do say yes, for sure, sometimes, but also get disciplined about saying no.

# Sandra Cisneros

Sandra Cisneros is a poet, short story writer, novelist, essayist, whose work explores the lives of the working-class. Her numerous awards include NEA fellowships in both poetry and fiction, the Texas Medal of the Arts, a MacArthur Fellowship, several honorary doctorates and book awards nationally and internationally, including Chicago's Fifth Star Award, the PEN Center USA Literary Award and the National Medal of the Arts, awarded to her by President Obama in 2016. *The House on Mango Street* has sold over six million copies, has been translated into over twenty languages, and is required reading in elementary, high school, and universities across the nation. Her other books include *My Wicked Wicked Ways*, *Woman Hollering Creek*, *Caramelo*, *Loose Woman*, *Have You Seen Marie?*, and most recently *A House of My Own: Stories from My Life*. *Puro Amor*, a dual language story written and illustrated by Sandra, will be published in October 2018. Founder of awards and foundations that serve writers, she is the organizer of Los MacArturos, Latino MacArthur fellows who are community activists. A dual citizen of the United States and Mexico, Sandra Cisneros earns her living by her pen.

*photo ©Keith Dannemiller*

# Close to the Bull's Eye

Consider this lineup of characters:

Cathy, "queen of cats," her house overrun with felines.

Marin, "waiting for a car to stop, a star to fall, someone to change her life."

Alicia, pulling out all the stops to get a university degree, despite her father's objections.

Earl, a jukebox repairman, with several boxes of 45 records and a series of women friends coming and going.

Esperanza, the protagonist, who wants a house of her own, not her daddy's, just *hers*, hers in every respect.

These characters and others draw us into the sometimes raw, sometimes lyrical world of *The House on Mango Street*, Sandra Cisneros' 1984 debut novel. Through a series of vignettes, Cisneros creates a portrait of a mixed-race area in Chicago. In the course of the novel, Esperanza matures, gaining a sense of selfhood as well as a sense of community. An old woman with psychic powers confronts her: "When you leave, you must remember to come back for the others. A circle, understand? You will always be Esperanza. You will always be Mango Street. You can't erase what you know. You can't forget who you are." Esperanza comes to recognize the wisdom of this advice.

The novel, which has become a classic, has sold close to six million copies. But one could misunderstand the nature of this success, says Cisneros. "Everyone thinks that my first book was an overnight success, but I would tell people, 'That was a *long* night.' Because people don't realize you write the thing over a decade, and then it takes a decade for it to get its recognition."

If the road to writing a novel is long, the path itself, for Cisneros, isn't obvious; it's one of continual discovery. "I think all writing is a question and we're walking towards the answer. You don't know the question until you get the answer, and you don't get the answer till you get to the end." With Cisneros's fiction, readers too must enter

246

into this mystery of discovery, into her complex prose replete with similes, metaphors, and analogies — which often make for sheer poetry. Note, for instance, the poetic quality of this passage from her second novel, *Caramelo*.

> Doubt begins like a thin crack in a porcelain plate. Very fine, like a strand of hair, almost not there. Wedged in between the pages of the sports section, in the satin puckered side-pocket of his valise, next to a crumpled bag of pumpkin seeds, a sepia-colored photo pasted on thick cardboard crudely cut down the center. The smiling Narciso seated leaning toward the cut-out half.

Consider the simile "like a strand of hair," the rhyming phrase that follows, the concrete language, the rhythm, and the suggestive "cut-out half." Her fiction is often infused with passages exhibiting this fine compression and a lyrical quality that make readers take a moment to appreciate the beauty and reflect on the meaning. Much of Cisneros' work draws on her personal life, but what memory calls up is always transformed or transmuted into art by the power of her creative imagination.

Cisneros may be a poetic fiction writer, but she approaches the two genres of poetry and fiction with different aims in mind. "You write poetry when you can't see, when you want to write about a molecule of time. You write a story when you have something on your mind that you want people to listen to. I grew up with a lot of people talking at the same time, and we never listened. So when you could say something that people would listen to, that was a story to me."

In addition to her two novels, Cisneros has written a collection of short stories, *Woman Hollering Creek*, and several volumes of poetry. Her second nonfiction book, *A House of My Own: Stories from My Life*, is due in October 2015.

I phoned Sandra Cisneros at her home in Mexico. The following is an edited version of our conversation.

**You make use of personal experience in your fiction. Can you comment on the role of memory?**

I tell my younger writers not to write about the things that you remember, but the things that you wish you could forget. Those are just huge in your heart. And that way you can get right to the seed of a story. That's usually where I begin. Some memory I wish I could forget. All you have to do is write from some very true place in your heart. You cut to the chase when you write about things you feel frightened to think about, the things that haunt you. I think that's important for writers to remember: Write from some true place.

**Your characters are complex. How do you go about creating them? In *Caramelo*, for instance, how did you arrive at that most memorable of characters, the Awful Grandmother?**

I remember reading *The Floating World* by Cynthia Kadohata. This novel has an awful grandmother, one who does not live up to the stereotypes of grandmothers that we think about in books. She is just the opposite. I got inspired by that book, and it made me start thinking about my own relatives, about works by women writers of my culture, and how I was just saturated by all these nice grandmas, and I thought, "That's not the grandma I know!" I had an awful grandmother myself. I thought she'd be more fun for readers to read about than someone who's nice. When I'm creating characters, I try to think about the usual, the typical, the stereotypical, and how can I shatter that? That's usually how I get going.

**Your work explores ethnic identity, gender and class. How do you manage these themes so they emerge in the storytelling and are not imposed from without?**

I don't think about these things when I'm writing. I really try to shut off the thinking part of my brain. If you want to think, write an academic paper. Don't think about such things until you edit. And then you can add, embellish, and the next thing you know, if you're very honest, all of the other stuff comes with it if it didn't come before. That's the other side of the telescope when we write. We don't have to worry about such matters as we're writing.

**Being a fiction writer calls for a certain vision. What is that for you?**

I think that writers are observers and not out of choice. We're like unsuccessful social beings; we're stuck on the margins. I think women especially get marginalized from things that happen in their family or their culture. And I think the more marginal we are as human beings, the better observers we are. Being stuck as a girl made me invisible. It's what you want to be as a writer. You want to be a spy, and I think that being a girl in my family and in my culture allowed me invisibility. There I could watch, not because I wanted to, but that's where I was stuck. And also I wasn't a successful human being socially in school, and that also allowed me a kind of invisibility, which was painful at the time, but very good training for being a writer.

**Marginalization, especially of women, is certainly an important theme in your work.**

I think we have special vision as writers according to whatever wounds we've suffered. We have special vision to see people who are also suffering those same wounds. I've paid attention to people who were marginal. I've paid attention to people who were ignored, or people who weren't popular, because I knew what that felt like. I think being an only daughter with so many boys around allowed me a special vision of looking and seeing and maybe understanding men in a way that I might not have otherwise had I been an only child. I'm pretty much into women's stories, but I really don't think about gender when I'm writing. I just write from what's coming from my heart. I think we write about the same things our whole life. I'm still writing about marginalization issues, and I feel that in every book, I'm getting closer to the bull's eye, because the older you get, the farther away you are from particular events, so the clearer you can see yourself.

**Your work deals with the lives of Mexican Americans caught between two cultures. Can you comment on the conflicts both men and women face in your fiction and how they resolve these conflicts?**

I'm not a critic of my own writing. I don't think of myself as someone who can answer that question. I only know that I write from very deep emotions, and I never know what I think until after I write it.

**As a Chicana writer, do you seek to help create a Chicana identity for your Chicana readers?**

Early on I did, but not anymore. Now I don't think about creating a Chicana identity; I think about writing from a place that's just mine. What do I know that no other writer knows? I write from that place. And to that extent my work is very much grounded in my culture because that's who I am. I have to write about what I know. I try to write in such a way that someone coming from as far away as Japan could read my work and understand it. I want it to be understood by someone who knows nothing about it.

**And yet your work is often bilingual. Isn't there a risk there?**

I write very honestly what I hear a character saying. And when I can't translate what they're saying, I play the Spanish. I do try to be very careful about using Spanish so that people coming from a different culture could read my work without knowing a syllable of Spanish; they could understand what I'm saying through the context. I try always to translate, as much as possible, the syntax and the word choice. I really try not to gratuitously use that language. I use it when there's no other choice.

**Your prose style is vivid and engaging. It's been called "poetic."**

I like poetry because it's so succinct. *Carmelo* is full of so many little details, but I hope every line's poetic. When I'm writing fiction, I try to make the lines as beautiful as poetry. My friend is a fiction writer, and he always says, "You need to do bigger strokes. You're painting like a miniaturist." And that's true. I do linger and pay attention to little details. But I don't try to write poetry; it just comes out. If I were talking to you about anything, similes would come out because it's the way I see the world. When I think of the writers that I like the best, writers like Marguerite Duras, Harriet Doerr and Jean Rhys, I hope to write as lyrically as they do.

**So you don't compartmentalize poetry and fiction. There's a real carryover between the two for you. Any recommendations for beginning fiction writers?**

I think it's good training for fiction writers to write poetry and vice versa; I think it's important for us to write in different genres. Doing so keeps us flexible, and it gives us powerful ways of describing the world. I always ask my students who are poets to write fiction and fiction writers to write poetry. Writing poetry forces you to pay attention to the unit of the syllable. As fiction writers we're used to thinking about plot; but we should think also of the syllable. That's why I take so long to write fiction because if I change the order of the words in the sentence, then I have to change the whole paragraph because I'm listening very attentively to the arrangement of the syllables.

**Your work is very strong on scene. How do you create scenes? What's your process? Anything beginning writers can take away?**

One thing I do is save what I call "buttons." By buttons, I mean little scenes, little dialogues, things that I've written notes on, things that I remember, or things that I heard on the street. I have a little file of buttons, and I try to write a button a day. Just a scene. I don't write from the beginning. Even if I don't know what I'm writing, I just write a scene. It could be a scene that I wish I could forget or a scene of dialogue that is so strong that I want it included in the book, but I may not know where it's going to go yet. I'll look and see what I feel excited about, what brings me a lot of fun to write about. That's what I write about that day. I don't work in linear order, just whatever is exciting and fun. I also think of writing as doing these little squares, these little embroidered pieces, and then you put them all together.

**In terms of sheer volume and range, your novel *Caramelo* breaks away from *The House on Mango Street*, which is a collection of vignettes. But you're mostly known for your first work. Care to comment?**

I think *Caramelo* is a much better book. I wish more people would appreciate it. I took 10 years to write it, and the tenth year proofing it. It was like I began with wrestling the angel of death. In *The House on Mango Street*, there's a kind of extended family of neighbors. At that time, I really couldn't handle the reality of all my relatives and my big family. How could I deal with all those people? It's like writing a Russian novel. So when I was younger, I just made the family smaller, but when I got to be 40, I realized I really hadn't written about things that I'd lived through, and so in *Caramelo*, I started with the intent of writing about my family and the way they really are. *Caramelo* is much more autobiographical than *House*. It's my favorite. It was such a difficult book to write, so of course we always like the one that almost killed us, right?

**How did you go about creating historical persons and contexts in *Caramelo*? What was your research process?**

I didn't know a lot about my relatives, and so I would make up what I didn't know, and for a novelist writing about real people, it's better if you don't. A lot of times what I would do is cut out a picture in a magazine. I have lots of photography and a lot of books on photography. I would either cut out a picture or look in one of my books for a photograph. I have a number of books on Mexico, so I would look for historical photos of the time I was writing about. By looking at photographs of someone who looked like my relative but wasn't my relative, somebody who looked like my father, somebody who looked like my grandmother, a house that might have been where they could have lived — that helped me because the truth shackles you to reality. You can't use your imagination. I would also turn on music from the period I was writing about to get in the mood, to get the flavor of a different time.

**_A House of My Own_ is a departure for you, isn't it? The nonfiction genre. Tell us about it and what the writing was like?**

The book is collected essays from 30 years of my life. A lot of these essays were published in little, hard-to-find journals, or out-of-print ones, not the mainstream places. I wanted to collect them mainly because I thought they'd be lost otherwise, and then I added some new ones and tweaked the old ones. And then I had to arrange them and put them all together and edit. It took a lot of work. I was working on them in 2008, and then I put it down, and I said, "I'm not picking this up again until I have an editor!" It was just too difficult for me. I'm not used to writing about myself; I usually write fiction or poetry. I guess I've felt a little bit intimidated in writing the stories in this book because most nonfiction books I think of as being more cerebral, but these are more personal stories.

**Do you have any tips for early stage writers?**

I think it's really important for younger writers to have a community, a kind of spiritual family. Writing is so solitary, and it takes us to deep emotional places. It should. If it's not taking you to such places, you're not working hard enough. Fellow writers can sustain you for the long process of creation, for the long haul.

# Viet Thanh Nguyen

Viet Thanh Nguyen is Associate Professor of English and of American Studies and ethnicity at the University of Southern California. He has authored the 2016 Pulitzer Prize winning novel, *The Sympathizer*, which won several other prizes, including the Dayton Literary Peace Prize, the Andrew Carnegie Medal for Excellence in Fiction, the Edgar Award for Best First Novel, the Center for Fiction First Novel Prize, and the Asian/Pacific American Award for Literature. It was a finalist for the 2016 PEN/Faulkner Award for Fiction. He is also author of *The Refugees*, a short story collection. Besides his fiction, he has authored two non-fiction books, including *Nothing Ever Dies: Vietnam and the Memory of War* (Harvard University Press) and *Race and Resistance: Literature and Politics in Asian America* (Oxford University Press).

*photo by BeBe Jacobs*

# From Both Sides

Viet Thanh Nguyen recently won the Pulitzer Prize for his debut novel, *The Sympathizer*. Fiction writer, nonfiction author, scholar, and professor at the University of Southern California, Nguyen was only 4 years old when the Vietnam War ended, and yet he has given voice to a generation of Vietnamese people caught up in the war. His body of work constitutes an alternate version to the American story of the war "over there," however critical the various books and movies on that conflict have been. Nguyen's story is not only that of the 3 million Vietnamese lives lost in that war and the hundreds of thousands of Vietnamese boat people who were lost at sea, but also the lives of surviving refugees in their American diaspora.

*The Sympathizer* is told from the point of view of a young Vietnamese captain who is ostensibly on the side of the South but is actually a communist sympathizer — a "man of two minds," as the Pulitzer Prize committee put it. When Saigon falls, he and other refugees find a safe haven in America. Dense with prose, the novel is thick with interiority, fleshing out the unnamed narrator's complex stance on the war and his attendant guilt when he's required to kill two suspected communist sympathizers in America. The war, we discover, is not over for him or his fellow refugees. The Vietnamese General, whom the narrator served under in South Vietnam, remains his superior in the United States and hopes still to continue the war back home by gathering a voluntary army. Meanwhile, we watch the anti-communist political turmoil that remains a constant among Americans who are unhappy with the way the war turned out, most notably in Nguyen's unforgettable blustering American Congressman.

In his nonfiction book *Nothing Ever Dies*, Nguyen spares no punches in letting readers know that the Vietnam War, like other wars the United States has fought, is part of a history of U.S. imperialism. The Vietnam War didn't go well. The American soldiers buried in Arlington National Cemetery and memorialized on the Memorial

Wall constitute an attempt to give meaning to the deaths of American soldiers. Yet memory is a politicized construct, Nguyen says. In America, there is no wall to remember the Vietnamese. If one were built, it would be nine miles long. In Vietnam, those who opposed the winning side are left to decay unmemorialized and forgotten.

Hollywood especially receives Nguyen's penetrating criticism. As he states in "Our Vietnam War Never Ended," which serves as an afterward to his novel, Hollywood war films seemed to be all one-sided, and that side wasn't the Vietnamese: "I watched *Apocalypse Now* and saw American sailors massacre a sampan full of civilians and Martin Sheen shoot a wounded woman in cold blood. I watched *Platoon* and heard the audience cheering and clapping when the Americans killed Vietnamese soldiers. These scenes, although fictional, left me shaking with rage. I knew that in the American imagination I was the Other, the Gook, the foreigner, no matter how perfect my English, how American my behavior. In my mostly white high school, the handful of Asian students clustered together in one corner for lunch and even called ourselves the Asian Invasion and the Yellow Peril."

Just like in his nonfiction, Nguyen's fiction is hard-hitting and spares no punches. At times, *The Sympathizer* is raw with black humor: The narrator's political assassinations are both savage and over-the-top, reminiscent of black comedy in Tim O'Brien's work. Nguyen's novel is also satirical. The blustering Congressman calls to mind Ben Fountain's Texans sold on Iraq in his recent novel *Billy Lynn's Long Halftime Walk*. But Nguyen's voice is distinctive, and clearly a new American voice. And it must be said that *The Sympathizer* can't be categorized simply as a war novel. It's much more universal than that. On a larger scale, it's a novel full of humanity, laying bare a dark side easier to ignore than contemplate.

**What drew you to write a novel about the Vietnam War and its aftermath?**

Although hundreds of novels had been written about the Vietnam War in several languages, none had done what I wanted to do. That was to write a novel that addressed the viewpoints of all sides, and to be critical of all sides. The war was a tragedy and a horror that everybody who fought in it was responsible for, and while some previous books had recognized that, they focused only on the experience of one side. Inevitably this produced some limitations in perspective and in understanding the war, its participants, and its observers. My goal was to encourage a re-examination of all the viewpoints of war through centering an approach from Vietnamese perspectives, which have been overwhelmed by American stories in the postwar period.

**You've said elsewhere that you did some research for *The Sympathizer*. Did you conduct your research before or during the writing of the novel? Which method do you think works best with historical novels (or does that depend)?**

Much of the research was already done because I had read books and seen films about the war all my life. I also drew on my life experience growing up in a Vietnamese American community. Even so, I still needed to do additional research for the novel, in particular for the fall of Saigon and the making of *Apocalypse Now*. Since the fall of Saigon is the opening sequence, I researched that before I began writing, and read every book and some articles that had been written about it. I found many useful anecdotes and vivid details, and I was able to compose a timeline of the fall — or the liberation, depending on one's point of view — down to the minutes of the last days. That timeline was critical for the pacing of the sequence. As for *Apocalypse Now*, I researched that while I was writing the novel, in anticipation of that sequence, and again read all the books about the movie and Francis Ford Coppola. In addition, I did a considerable amount of online research to fill in many finer details of the novel — street names and maps, logistics of military organizations and bureaucracies, the plot to take back Vietnam, CIA torture techniques, and the like. I think doing enough historical research to stimulate one's writing is necessary, but writers shouldn't wait to write until they think they've researched everything. In that case, you'll never write anything at all. Do enough to start, and save the rest as necessary while you write.

**How long did it take you to write this novel, and what was your overall process?**

A little over two years. The context, however, is that I suffered for well over a decade writing a short story collection before the novel. That was a miserable experience, but it apparently taught me a great deal about literary craft. It was like the wax-on, wax-off training sequence in *The Karate Kid*, which Daniel (Ralph Macchio's character) hated but which paid off in his sudden ability to defend himself. Coming to the novel was like ceasing to do chores and getting to do the fun stuff. I was lucky that I had two years off from teaching due to a fellowship and sabbaticals, and I wrote four hours a day every day of the week, in the mornings and early afternoons. Then I'd go to the gym and run on a treadmill for an hour, which was a very important part of the process. I was inspired by Haruki Murakami, although he runs marathons outdoors. I like air conditioning. After 15 minutes or so, the runner's high would kick in and all kinds of ideas would start emerging in my mind about the next day's writing. That's how I plotted the novel, because I only had a two-page synopsis when I began. I had the broad strokes, but the details came from the running and the momentum of writing. I wrote a chapter a month, which included a first draft and a revision. By the end of the second year, I had a full draft that had already been revised once. I did one more revision in a few months, and that was what was sold. It was 170,000 words. Working with my editor, I cut it down to 145,000 words in a matter of weeks. That involved trimming back language and cutting a few scenes, but keeping the structure intact.

**What motivated you to write your nonfiction book *Nothing Ever Dies*?**

I'm a scholar. I had spent a decade researching *Nothing Ever Dies* while I was also writing short stories. All that research about the

Vietnam War — and all the thinking about theories of representation and ethical memory that I processed during that time — fed into the novel. The novel's explicitly political and philosophical, and that came from my academic work. Some readers don't like that, but to me, most contemporary American fiction seems to lack any kind of serious politics or serious ideas. The novel likewise influenced the writing of *Nothing Ever Dies*, injecting it with fictional strategies of rhythm, emotion, and narrative. Fiction and nonfiction accomplish very different things, but they can overlap. I wanted my fiction to seem nonfictional, and my nonfiction to seem fictional. At the same time, in fiction I could say things I couldn't get away with in nonfiction without footnotes. And in nonfiction, I could make things explicit that I couldn't say in fiction because of the viewpoint of my protagonist.

**How do you view *The Sympathizer* in the tradition of war novels, not only in American literature but other literature as well?**

When most people think "war novel," they think of soldiers' stories. *The Sympathizer* has those. But it also has the stories of civilians. Implicitly, the novel insists that a true war story has to take into account not just combat and soldiers, but civilians, the home front, and the military-industrial complex. For me, war is more than guns and shooting. That's the spectacle that distracts us from how pervasive war is throughout a society and how it makes all of us complicit through things like paying taxes and watching horrifying images on TV without doing anything to stop them from happening. I was inspired by unconventional war novels like *Slaughterhouse Five* and Céline's *Journey to the End of the Night*, which begins in World War I and then goes all over the place. And António Lobo Antunes' *The Land at the End of the World*, about Portugal's Angolan War and how it never ended for its protagonist. Wars don't end just because politicians say they do — that's another key point of *The Sympathizer*.

**How did you decide on your protagonist and his political leanings?**

Making him a spy, and choosing the spy novel as a defining genre for my book, came immediately to me. I wanted to tell a serious story and an entertaining story, and spy novels have a long tradition of being able to do both through authors like Joseph Conrad, Graham Greene, and John Le Carré, to name just three. To make my narrator a mixed-race person of French and Vietnamese heritage was also logical, because part of the seriousness of the novel was about the conflict of race, culture, nation, and difference that involved Vietnam, France, the United States, and all of the East versus West stereotyping that has saturated European and American thinking about Asia. So my character as a spy was going to be involved in many major political events, and as a Eurasian was going to be constantly dwelling on his duality, which would stand in for a universal sense of duality. Part of that duality extended to his politics, which were, on the one hand, a commitment to communism, and on the other hand, an infatuation with American culture and capitalism. He would be very capable of criticizing American culture and capitalism, but he would love them, too, and that capacity would influence his views on the failures of communism. I wanted this novel to be very political but not dogmatic, and making my narrator ambivalent in this way helps to prevent that slide into dogmatism.

**What are some major literary influences on your fiction? Can you comment on specific evidence of influences, if any?**

From American literature: Melville and Faulkner's interrogation of flawed American character and ambition, especially around racial sin; Joseph Heller's satire and humor; dashes of Hawthorne's allegorical sensibility and Poe's haunting; Emerson's philosophical gaze on the American self; the whole tradition of African-American literature and its vital sense of anger and sorrow and its deep critique of the American horror, especially as found in Toni Morrison and Ralph Ellison, whose *Invisible Man* I am deeply engaged with and against in *The Sympathizer*. From European and Latin American literature: Gabriel García Márquez's use of history and national culture as his palette; Dostoevsky, who influenced Ellison, and whose focus on insanity, interiority, and interrogation, and on crime and guilt, in books like *Notes from the Underground, The Brothers Karamazov,* and *Crime and Punishment* were fundamental to me; Céline and his willingness to reject realism, sending his protagonist from the trenches of World War I to Africa to Detroit and back to France in the span of a hundred pages, which inspired me to think I could cover vast territory as well; Günther Grass's *The Tin Drum* did similar work for me and made me want to come up with a protagonist who could be at the center of war and history, too; Baudelaire's images, which I read to fire up my own imagination as I reworked every single sentence in search of an image; W.G. Sebald, whose melancholic meditations on the inescapable tragedy of the past are very important to me, as is his digressive, sprawling style; and finally Lobo Antunes and his dense, imagistic prose, which served as the catalyst for my own. I read a few pages of his novel every day, and when I started to get hot, I began to write.

**Your novel is certainly heavy with prose, and yet quite scenic. Why did you go with a relatively experimental method of no punctuation of dialogue?**

I like high modernism and low genre. I'm bored by middlebrow literary realism, which seems to be the dominant mode of contemporary American fiction. I don't care about quotation marks and directing the reader and making things easy for the reader. I don't want my fiction to be an example of the MFA style of "show, don't tell," of giving the reader a window onto reality, of lending a sense of transparency to the prose. Stylistically, I wanted something dense, image-heavy, and digressive, because I like those things. But I think they also serve purposes in relation to my narrator and my subject. He's writing under interrogation, and he's defiant. His interrogator wants straightforward, simple writing, and our spy won't do that. He's trapped in his own head, his own memories, and the style expresses that sense of being trapped, in this case in words and images. At the same time, I also wanted the novel to be constantly moving forward, and that's why I use the generic conventions of [a] spy novel, hardboiled detective story, political thriller, immigrant saga, historical fiction, black comedy. The dense words are moved forward by the plot, or so I hope. The density of the words, meanwhile, serve as a screen over the actions of the plot, a filter that the reader notices and through which he or she must see.

**Setting is very important in this novel. Can you tell us how you went about creating setting?**

I wanted settings to be clear but not overly described. Not Dickensian. Not concerned with very fine details you might find in realistic fiction, like long descriptions of scenery, or furniture, or food, and so on. I think the description of settings tends to be cinematic, because I use details sparingly, and focus not only on material or geographical things, but also on people and moods. One example is the General's liquor store and the gathering of exiled southern Vietnamese veterans. I spend little amounts of time on the neighborhood; on some of the store's contents; on the clothing and comportment and mindset of the veterans; and then move towards the General and his wife, Madame; and onwards to the reporter interviewing them, Sonny; and then finally to Sonny and our narrator meeting. The camera, in other words, gradually moves in from outside to inside, from wide angle to close up. Each part of this move isn't oversaturated with details, but the accumulation of a few details for each move adds up to describing the entire setting and atmosphere.

**What tips do you have for beginning fiction writers? What do's and don'ts would you suggest?**

Plan for the long haul. If you're extremely talented and lucky, you'll be famous in a few years. Most of us, including me, are neither that talented nor lucky. It took me 20 years of writing before I could write *The Sympathizer*. I got to that point by writing a lot, reading a lot, and enduring a lot. The practice of writing is a kind of self-instruction that no number of writing workshops can teach you. You have to learn how to do it yourself. The writing makes you a writer, it builds your discipline, enhances your talent, and draws forth the reserves of your character. Reading deeply in your preferred genre or style is very important, because there you learn the tradition you want to belong to or go against. Reading deeply in one category also reveals a basic truth — most of any one thing is bad. Knowing what's bad and what's been done before allows you to be good and original. Read widely to learn from people far afield from you, in genre, style, concern, culture, national origin. Become tough through exposure to the opinions of others, through which you will eventually learn your own genuine opinion of your writing. Rejection is hard to deal with, but so is the persistent sense that no one cares about what you're doing. Learning your own opinion of your writing is saying that you have to learn what you want to write and who you are as a writer. In the end, writing because you care about writing, and writing to be true to yourself, are the only things that matter. And that is how you survive the long haul to becoming a writer, not because of the lures of publication, fame, or profit.

# Alice Hoffman

Alice Hoffman's debut novel, *Property Of*, was published by Farrar Straus and Giroux when Hoffman was 21 years old. She has published 30 works of fiction, including literary, children's, and YA. Her novel *Here on Earth* was an Oprah Book Club pick. She wrote the screenplay for *Independence Day* (1983). *Practical Magic* was made into a movie starring Sandra Bullock and Nicole Kidman (1998). *The Dovekeepers* was adapted for TV in a 2015 miniseries.

*photo by Deborah Feingold*

# Story Magic

In the interviews I had with Alice Hoffman, in late June and early July, the author of 30 fictional books told me, "I always feel that fiction is the truth and nonfiction is a lie."

I'm tempted to link this comment to Nathaniel Hawthorne's famous quote on romances — that the truth they reveal is "the truth of the human heart." Hoffman can be compared to Hawthorne, as her work is informed by magic, mystery, and suspense — where dark secrets are slowly, but inevitably, brought to the light of day, and, like Hawthorne, it isn't the "light of common day." Perhaps, like Hawthorne's romances, Hoffman's novels are best read at twilight. But for all their comparisons, Hoffman's work is indisputably more realistic than Hawthorne's, however much mystical forces inform it — where Hawthorne conjures magic, Hoffman dwells in magical realism.

Hoffman is probably best known for *Practical Magic*, which was made into a movie in 1998 that starred Sandra Bullock and Nicole Kidman. But her work in fiction is vast, publishing in literary, children's, and young adult markets. A number of her books are historical, delineating complex family sagas. She is a careful researcher, bringing historical people, places, and events to life — and with an impressive range of periods and places: *The Dovekeepers* is set 2000 years ago, in Roman times; *The Marriage of Opposites*, 19th-century St. Thomas and Paris; *The Museum of Extraordinary Things*, an early 20th-century Coney Island freak show. Her newest novel, *The Rules of Magic*, is a contemporary novel with roots back to Salem, Massachusetts, in the 1600s, a harrowing period in which many so-called witches were wrongfully accused by Judge John Hathorne, grandfather of Nathaniel Hawthorne, who suffered ancestral guilt over his relative's ignoble role in these trials. The protagonists of Hoffman's novel are indeed witches, but they're the good kind, with definite rules to follow — the first being "do no harm," or, in Latin, *Primum non nocere*. But in Hoffman's work as a whole, spirit worlds can bring about evil just as often as good.

Hoffman's prose style draws the reader in with her power to capture, with great force, the many sensuous details her characters experience, so that her protagonists come alive in a richly developed setting. One cannot help but savor the language. Hoffman may be best read when one is not in a hurry to move on — and yet her characters and conflicts do move us forward, so we are delighted to see her story proceeding, her plot gathering momentum like a storm. She is, after all, a master of intrigue, and we want to know which secret will be revealed next.

From a cursory look at her canon, one might get the idea that she's focused on the novel form, but a significant portion of her work is made up of the short form as well, a form she truly appreciates. "I'm a big fan of linked short stories," she says. "I have three books of linked short stories: *Local Girls*, *Blackbird House*, and *The Red Garden*. These books are the most fun I've ever had writing."

Hoffman also believes in the power and importance of writing for younger audiences. Of her YA books, Hoffman says, "What you read at the age of 12 and 13 and 14 stays with you in a very intense, deep way — that is the literature that makes you the person that you are and the writer that you are."

Writing is a complex process for Hoffman. Turning out 30 works of fiction over a long career certainly calls for a process, but it doesn't come in one definite, prescribed approach: "My thinking about a novel always includes writing. I always write my way in. Sometimes 10 years can pass before I go back to it, and sometimes it's the next thing I write."

**Magic, mystery, and secrets are clearly important in your fiction. Can you say why? Does magic serve a plot function? Do you purposely pursue subjects that involve these elements, or do they just come to you?**

I don't purposely pursue magic — it's just part of the prose that I write. I grew up reading fairy tales and myths. For me, magic has always been a part of literature as a reader and as a writer. Magic doesn't have so much to do with plot as it does with voice. For instance, you can tell a story in a realistic way, and if you're Hemingway, it's great, and it works. For me, magic is about the way the story is told rather than the story itself. It's not a hocus-pocus influence in the plot. It's more the tone of the story, the way the story tries to draw you in and create a fictional world. I'd like to add that I think the most important thing for beginning writers is to find their own voice.

**Can you say which fairy tales you read as a child and what you drew from them for your fiction?**

For me, it's not specific fairy tales but the whole tradition of fairy tales. I'm also really interested in women telling stories. Those stories, whether they're myths or fairy tales, belong to the great tradition of women telling stories to their children and grandchildren. So that whole tradition of how stories are told is really interesting to me as a woman and a writer. I always loved the way that fairy tales are told in a realistic voice, a kind of blending of the real and the fantastic.

**A number of your novels are historical novels. What kinds of things do you research?**

That's really hard to say because when I do research, I'm researching every aspect, and it often depends on the book. For instance, when I did research for *The Dovekeepers*, there was very little, pretty much nothing, as far as research about women in the time period I was writing about, so what I did was write about nomadic people in the Middle East today. After all, the way you take care of the horses or donkeys or whatever is the same now as back then. When I was writing about Rachel in *The Marriage of Opposites*, I looked at a lot of books of photographs. I did a lot of research on bats and birds. I want to try to create the world. In a historical novel, you're creating a world for your characters to inhabit. It was really nice to receive a letter from someone who grew up on St. Thomas, who said they felt like they were re-entering their childhood when they read the book — that is exactly what I would want.

**What is your research process like? Do you do all your research before writing? Or do you write as you research?**

I do quite a bit of research before I start a project, then stop for a while because I have to take a step away from history and write a novel. When I'm done with a first draft, I go back again and do a great deal more research. So I think I do kind of a layered research; I keep going back and doing more and more, but I'm still focused on the fact that I'm writing a novel, not a history.

Research can be never-ending. Especially with *The Dovekeepers*, I realized that. That book took me five years to research and write. There was a point when I realized that I could research it for the rest of my life. I was never going to know everything about the time period. There was a point when I just decided to start writing.

**How much of the research you do gets used in a novel, how much not used?**

I don't know. I mean, definitely I know more than I put in the book to help create the characters. I don't use the specific information. It's probably true that 20 or 30 percent of what I research never has anything to do with the book itself, but it has to do with creating the world.

**In your current novel, *The Rules of Magic*, how much research did you do in terms of the history of witchcraft and magic lore?**

I've always been interested in witchcraft, and I've done research my whole life. I did a bit more for *The Rules of Magic* because I was writing specifically about a particular judge, Judge Hathorne, at the witchcraft trials in Salem. I read whatever I could find about him, and I found him a really interesting character. As to magic, for me it's always a pleasure to study magic and to find out more and more. Everything in the book about magic lore was something that I researched. For instance, the use of medicinal plants and herbs. Still, while the research is interesting, it's not what's important. Really, the most important thing is writing the novel and creating the characters. That's the big difference between an historical novel and a history. What I'm mostly interested in is the novel part of it. All the research that I do is in service to that.

**Your characters are sympathetic, interesting, and compelling. Do you discover your characters as you write, or do you pretty much know them beforehand? What about surprises?**

I think it's really important to know your characters. I think it's really good to make a lot of lists and tell everything about your characters: what books they read, what they're wearing, what their relationships are like. Write down everything about them. Then you have to kind of write your way into them. My characters grow as I write them and become more themselves as they reveal their innermost spirit. That's the way it should feel when you're writing a novel: the characters are alive, making their own choices, and you're just following them. When that happens, they almost always surprise us. This certainly was true in *The Rules of Magic*. Moreover, as the writer, I want to be surprised; I want to be drawn in. The reason that I read a novel is the same reason that I write a novel.

**How do you decide on narrative point of view? What advice do you have for beginning writers on handling omniscient POV, which you sometimes use?**

I don't really decide on the narrative point of view —the book comes with a point of view. For instance, I don't tell myself this is going to be a first-person book or this is going to be third-person narration. I write a little bit in first person or a little bit in third person. I kind of play around with it, and then something just clicks and feels right. I think it's always great to experiment with different points of view. For beginning writers, it's really interesting to write fiction from varying points of view to see how that changes the mood and characters.

As to omniscient point of view, I think it's much easier to write in first person, and I think it's also more fun to write in first person, but sometimes you just can't tell the whole story from the first-person POV. It's fine if you're writing *The Catcher in the Rye*, but in other cases, it can be limiting.

### In drafting a novel, how do you begin? Can you describe your process of getting into your story?

I begin by writing various notes, by creating the characters, usually by making lists so that I know everything about them and the material that I'm not going to use. I do a lot of research about place and the physical and natural environment of the setting. And then I make an outline. That outline changes in writing, but it gives me a place to begin. A novel comes into being because you write it. You can do all the planning things, the outlines, and I believe in all that, but basically a book comes from writing your way into it.

### What about plot and theme? What about using symbols to create meaning?

I think plot is really important — it's the thing that makes you want to turn the page. I don't believe in theme. I believe in story but not theme. It can be destructive if you begin with a theme because you're deciding what the story is about before you even write it. Theme applies to reading fiction, not writing it. A lot of people have a great idea, and then they don't know why they can't write their book.

Writers don't decide what symbols mean. Symbols arise from the text. And then when you use them, you say, "Oh, that's what it says. That's what I was thinking." Because I always feel that with writing, there is an outside story and an inside story. The outside story is what you plot and what you think the book is. As soon as you're writing it, you discover there's also an inside story, and it may be one that you never really thought about, and you don't really understand it till you write it.

**Beginnings and endings of novels are tough to write. Any recommendations for early-stage writers on creating compelling openings and avoiding tidy endings?**

Beginnings can change, so you just have to start and take a leap of faith. A lot of times you end up cutting the beginning. You can always go back and rewrite it. That certainly happened in *The Rules of Magic*. I started out with a lot more going in the beginning, and I ended up cutting half of it. It's about hooking the reader on the first page. If you don't draw someone in, they probably won't read further. In your beginning, you need to start with something major or at least set the tone and the language so that the reader wants to turn the page. I think that's the most important thing. It has to have intensity. It could be drama, it could be language, it could be many different things, but it must have intensity.

As to endings, I begin a book with the ending so that I know where I'm going even though I don't particularly know the whole journey. Sometimes that changes, and sometimes it remains the same. The thing about endings is you have to feel that it's over. You could write about these people forever, but there comes a point when you feel like the circle is closed. You've told the story. It feels right to you.

**How much revision do you do? How do you go about revising? How does the final draft compare to the first draft?**

I'm a big believer in revision. You have to rewrite the entire manuscript rather than do it in bits and pieces. Often my first draft and last draft are completely different. Sometimes characters disappear and new characters appear. I make huge changes. Half the characters in the first draft of *The Rules of Magic* didn't make it to the final book. In the first draft, I didn't know what I was writing about. I had to discover this, and then I had to go back and rewrite it. The novel changed radically. I think as a writer you have to be unafraid to cut your own material and to get rid of prose you love if it doesn't serve the novel.

**You've published a stack of novels. Do you ever work on more than one novel at a time? Perhaps two? Do you see any downsides to this approach?**

I only work on one novel at a time, but I have notes about other novels, sometimes outlines, sometimes chapters. They're like planes on the runway waiting to take off, but they're not ready yet. As far as working on two novels at a time? Everybody works differently. But for me, I don't think I could actually work on two novels on an intense level. I think it would really be easy to lose focus. It's hard enough to focus on one novel — it's a lot of work. I personally think working on two would kind of dilute whatever you are putting into the novel. I think it would be difficult.

**What's a typical work day and work week like for you? What about a particular place to write?**

I don't really have a typical workday or typical work week. I do set goals, usually in terms of pages and how many pages a week or day I will do. Sometimes I fail, but at least it gives me a goal. I do think it's important to write every day. I don't always do it, but when I'm in the thick of writing, I do it. If you're writing every day, it becomes a habit. It's a practice, almost. The more you do it, the better you are at it. As to where I write, I don't want a view. I don't want to be someplace beautiful — I want to look at a blank wall. I'm interested in creating something, imagining something.

**Who are your favorite authors? Which authors have had the greatest influence on your writing and in what ways?**

I think the greatest living novelist is Toni Morrison. I've been influenced by her beautiful work. I don't think it's influence so much as inspiration. I think that's what happens when you find a great writer, and I think she's a great writer. It's inspirational more than anything else. It makes you want to write something beautiful and great yourself. That's what happens when you fall in love with a great writer.

I've also been influenced by the work of writers that I read when I was young, especially Emily Brontë, Grace Paley, and the very wonderful Ray Bradbury. For me, it's really different with Bradbury. When you read somebody at age 12 or 13, you can be influenced in a psychological way. And that's what happened to me with Ray Bradbury. His work influenced me as a person.

**What tips do you have for early-stage writers in terms of getting their work published?**

I think the more that you send your work out, the more chance you have to have it published. My advice is to read literary magazines to discover the ones that you like and the ones that you feel would be a good fit for you, and then send out your stories. I think it's really important to read the magazine before you submit to it, even though the first magazine I ever submitted to I didn't read.

I'm a big believer in joining groups. Writing classes, graduate programs, writers' workshops. I think it's good to be with other writers and to have a reason to write. I'm on the board of Boston's GrubStreet. They have classes and workshops at every level, including this great thing called Novel Incubator, where you basically write a novel for the class, working with a mentor. It's important being with other writers and having a deadline and being forced to write.

Another thing is to go to conferences. There are many conferences all over where there are agents and editors, and sometimes you can show them your work. There are summer programs as well. These are good places to meet people.

I think the most important thing is to think about the fact that writers write. And that you can't put it off until everything is perfect because nothing ever is perfect.

# Adam Johnson

Adam Johnson is a Professor of English with emphasis in creative writing at Stanford University. Winner of a Whiting Award and Fellowships from the Guggenheim Foundation, the National Endowment for the Arts and the American Academy in Berlin, he is the author of several books, including *Fortune Smiles*, which won the 2015 National Book Award, and the novel *The Orphan Master's Son*, which was awarded the 2013 Pulitzer Prize. His fiction has appeared in *Esquire, GQ, Playboy, Harper's Magazine, Granta, Tin House* and *The Best American Short Stories*. His work has been translated into more than thirty languages.

*photo by David Gonzales*

# How I Write

Adam Johnson is an associate professor of creative writing at Stanford University. His novel *The Orphan Master's Son* won the 2013 Pulitzer Prize in Fiction. The Pulitzer committee described *Orphan* as "an exquisitely crafted novel that carries the reader on an adventuresome journey into the depths of totalitarian North Korea and into the most intimate spaces of the human heart." The novel was also a National Book Critics Circle Award Finalist and named one of the best books of 2012 by *The Washington Post, The Wall Street Journal* and *The Los Angeles Times.* Johnson is the author of two previous works of fiction: a short story collection, *Emporium* (2003), named Debut of the Year; and a first novel, *Parasites Like Us*, that won a silver medal for fiction at the 2004 California Book Awards. Johnson's work has appeared in *Esquire, The Paris Review* and *Harper's Magazine.*

**Why:** If I've ever had an epiphany, it came in a creative writing workshop. My whole life I'd been told that I had all these perceived flaws. I was a daydreamer, a rubbernecker, an exaggerator, a liar — all those things. But in a story, everything I'd been dinged about my whole life added up to something other people appreciated. I saw that a writer could be a real person but also do something that speaks to other people.

**Research:** When I was younger, you had to go to a library. If that didn't work, you had to go to a bigger library, and if that didn't work, you had to go to an archive. But now you can write a book about North Korea, the most secretive place on earth, from a computer. You can email experts listed on university websites. You can even Google Earth, and there are a lot of aid workers taking down the stories of people, doing the fieldwork for you because they see it's important. That's the beautiful thing about research these days.

**Process:** I go to the library for six or eight hours and I write, and then I go home to my wife. On my laptop, I usually have two documents open. One is the narrative I'm working on, and one is usually a blank page that I can make mistakes on, play around with and throw those words away. At the end of the day maybe I'll have a paragraph, maybe I'll have a page of work, and then I'll move it over to the story I'm actually writing.

**Dark humor:** A story's turbulence needs humor for the reader to release tension. When I read aloud in public, I can feel a tension building in the audience. There's difficult material, and they want to let go of it somehow. Give them one chance to laugh, even in a small way.

**Writing challenges:** It's all a struggle. When you write a short story, you think, "Oh, I know how to write a short story now," but the next story *isn't* easier because you just learned to write *that* story. Each narrative you tell has to discover itself completely anew. And a lot of novelists wouldn't be surprised that once you write one novel, the second one is actually even tougher, even though you might think it will be easier.

**Advice for new writers:** I've always valued labor over talent. My students who are the most talented I think grow the least because they lean on their natural ability rather than developing their skills. Writers do need a full complement of writerly talent, but it's the ones who put in the hard work who really grow for the better.

# Sue Monk Kidd

Sue Monk Kidd has authored three novels, *The Secret Life of Bees* (2002), *The Mermaid Chair* (2005), and *The Invention of Wings* (2014). *The Secret Life of Bees* was adapted as a movie in 2008, starring Dakota Fanning and Queen Latifah.

*photo by Alex Stafford*

# How I Write

Sue Monk Kidd is the author of three novels. Her debut novel *The Secret Life of Bees*, published in 2002, garnered attention from both critics and the reading public. Made into a movie in 2008, the novel is set in South Carolina in 1964, at the height of racial tensions over the new Civil Rights legislation. Her most recent novel, *The Invention of Wings*, an Oprah Book Club 2.0 selection, is set in 19th-century South Carolina and focuses on the life of sisters Sarah and Angelina Grimke, who rejected their wealthy family's ownership of slaves and devoted themselves to the burgeoning abolitionist cause. "They were, arguably, the most radical females to ever come out of the antebellum South. I fell in love with their story," Kidd has said. She is a deeply interior writer, capturing the thoughts, feelings and apprehensions of her characters in a fullness that makes them very real to readers. Her characters search to discover their true paths and hope for better in the midst of societal ills and cruelties.

**Fiction:** An idea comes to me from the inside out, and I will play with it. If I play with it awhile and it really starts to sprout a story, then I know it's a novel that I can really write. But it also comes through my personal history. I grew up in the South, pre-Civil Rights, pre-feminist America. I guess subjects for our work are probably a little bit of a mystery [as to] where they come from, but I do think they make a portal through our own personal history.

**Process:** I'm pretty dogged and methodical and slow. I let an idea incubate for a while — as I said, I play with it — but when I start writing, I keep banker's hours. I work every day for long hours, immersed in the whole thing, really working with my craft in a disciplined way but allowing for spontaneous, mysterious inspiration to come.

**Craft:** My novels usually start with two questions: "Who is my character?" "What does my character want?" The whole story will flow out of the answers I'm able to bring to those two questions. With *Secret Life of Bees*, I had this image in my head. It started with this image of a girl lying in bed, and bees were coming out of the cracks of the wall in her bedroom and flying around the room. An unusual image, but my imagination seized on that, and I just played with it for a long time, and it really started to create a story. Who is this girl? What does she want?

**Research:** I did about six months of research before I started writing *The Invention of Wings*. I sought out a lot of primary sources, biographies. I read everything I could. I went to historic sites and places. In writing a historical novel, detail is everything. You want to create this authentic world where readers can feel like they can see it, feel it, hear it. I enjoyed the research, but I had to finally force myself to quit researching and write.

**Revision:** I rewrite as I go. It's a slower process, but somehow that works best for me. I allow myself to rewrite and rewrite and rewrite a chapter, and then I have a certain moment when I realize that yes, now, it's exactly like I want it to be, and I can go on.

**Advice:** I think so much of writing is about the courage to express ourselves, to be true to our own voice, to find *our* vision, *our* voice, and put it out there. Also, allow yourself to write badly in the beginning. That's good tried and true advice. And then let it evolve as you rewrite.

# About the Author

Jack Smith has published four novels: *Miss Manners for War Criminals* (2017), *Being* (2016), *Icon* (2014), and *Hog to Hog*, which won the 2007 George Garrett Fiction Prize and was published by Texas Review Press in 2008. He has published stories in a number of literary magazines, including *Southern Review, North American Review, Texas Review, Xconnect, In Posse Review,* and *Night Train.* His reviews have appeared widely in such publications as *Ploughshares, Georgia Review, American Book Review, Prairie Schooner, Mid-American Review, Pleiades, Missouri Review, Xconnect,* and *Environment* magazine. He has published a few dozen articles in both *Novel & Short Story Writer's Market* and *The Writer* magazine. His creative writing book, *Write and Revise for Publication: A 6-Month Plan for Crafting an Exceptional Novel and Other Works of Fiction*, was published in 2013 by Writer's Digest Books. His coauthored nonfiction environmental book entitled *Killing Me Softly* was published by Monthly Review Press in 2002. Besides his writing,

Smith was fiction editor of *The Green Hills Literary Lantern*, an online literary magazine published by Truman State University, for 25 years. He presently teaches for Writers.com.

# Acknowledgments

"Avoiding Clichés: Recognizing Them & Getting Beyond Them," *Novel & Short Story Writer's Market,* 2012 edition.

"Beating out the Stiff Competition in Fiction Writing," *Novel & Short Story Writer's Market,* 2013 edition.

"Close to the Bull's Eye," [interview of Sandra Cisneros], *The Writer,* August 2015.

"Deriving Theme from Character and Plot," *Novel & Short Story Writer's Market*, 2018 edition.

"Developing Your Prose Style: Form Following Function," *Novel & Short Story Writer's Market*, 2012 edition.

"Exploring Exposition & Summary," in slightly different form in *Novel & Short Story Writer's Market*, 2017 edition.

"Foreshadowing & Echoing," *Novel & Short Story Writer's Market*, 2018 edition.

"From Both Sides," [interview of Viet Thanh Nguyen], *The Writer,* February 2017.

"He Said, She Said: Writing Strong Dialogue," in slightly different form in *Novel & Short Story Writer's Market*, 2016 edition.

"How I Write," [interview of Adam Johnson], *The Writer,* July 2013.

"How I Write," [interview of Sue Monk Kidd], *The Writer,* June 2015.
"If You Build It," *The Writer,* June 2016.

"In Good Humor," *The Writer*, August 2014.

"In the Shadow of Terror," [interview of Vaddey Ratner], *The Writer*, June 2013.

"Jumpin' Jack Flash," *The Writer*, May 2017.

"Keeping a Journal: What's It Worth?" *Novel & Short Story Writer's Market*, 2012 edition.

"Know Your Antagonist," *Novel & Short Story Writer's Market*, 2013 edition.

"Le Mot Juste," [interview of Christine Sneed], *The Writer*, December 2015.

"Not Just Second Class: Writing Secondary Characters in Fiction," in slightly different form in *Novel & Short Story Writer's Market*, 2016 edition.

"Putting Words to Work," *The Writer*, February 2018.

"Returning to the Elements," in slightly different form in *The Writer*, February 2015.

"Rise of the Novella," *The Writer*, March 2017.

"Second Degree: The Second-Person POV," *The Writer*, August 2016.

"Setting the Tone: How to Handle Voice in Your Fiction," in slightly different form in *The Writer*, January 2018.

"Start to Stop," *The Writer*, November 2014.

"Story Magic," [interview of Alice Hoffman], *The Writer*, October 2017.

"Story Study: Conducting Research in Fiction," *The Writer*, October 2016.

"Strout's There," [interview of Elizabeth Strout], *The Writer*, August 2013.

"The Things He Carries," [interview of Tim O'Brien,] *The Writer*, July 2010.

"Tips on Handling the Omniscient Point of View in Fiction: Is 'playing god' the right POV for your story?", *The Writer*, January 2017.

"Writing Authentic Dialogue," *Novel & Short Story Writer's Market*, 2012 edition.

"Writing as a Way to Explore Things," [interview of T.C. Boyle], *The Writer*, June 2012.

"Writing Historical Novels," *The Writer*, May 2014.

www.ingramcontent.com/pod-product-compliance
Lightning Source LLC
Chambersburg PA
CBHW050715180626
46814CB00002B/445